OCR
RECOGNISING ACHIEVEMENT

HODDER
EDUCATION

Official Publisher Partnership

D0192129

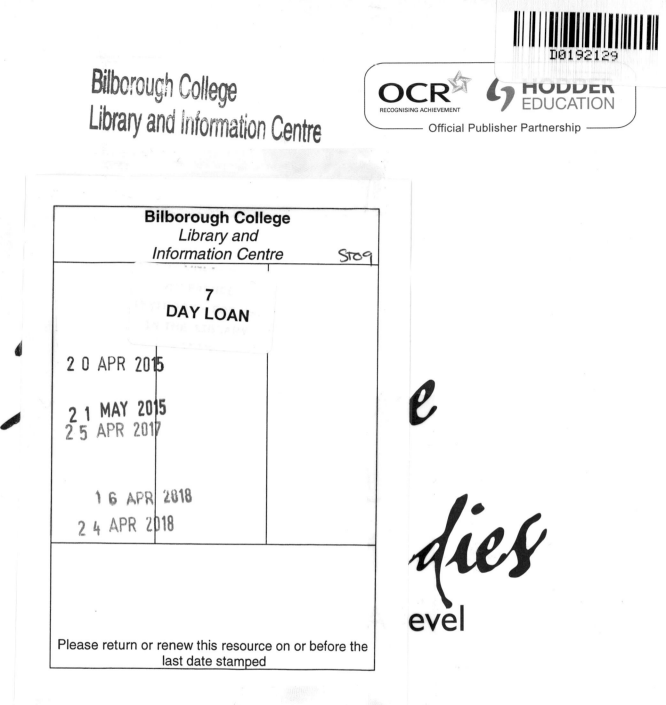

dies

evel

nm

with Gail Deal and Mark Lewinski

Additional contributions by Alistair Conquer
and Hannah Goodinson

HODDER
EDUCATION
PART OF HACHETTE LIVRE UK

Hachette Livre UK's policy is to use papers that are natural, renewable and recyclable products and made from wood grown in sustainable forests. The logging and manufacturing processes are expected to conform to the environmental regulations of the country of origin.

Orders: please contact Bookpoint Ltd, 130 Milton Park, Abingdon, Oxon OX14 4SB. Telephone: (44) 01235 827720. Fax: (44) 01235 400454. Lines are open 9.00–5.00, Monday to Saturday, with a 24-hour message answering service. Visit our website at www.hoddereducation.co.uk

First published in 2008 by
Hodder Education,
Part of Hachette Livre UK
338 Euston Road
London NW1 3BH

Impression number	5	4	3	2	1	
Year	2013	2012	2011	2010	2009	2008

Cover photo © Stockbyte/Getty Images

Typeset in Palatino and Helvetica Neue
Editorial and production by Topics – The Creative Partnership Ltd, Exeter
Printed in Italy

A catalogue record for this title is available from the British Library

ISBN: 978 0340 967 539

Contents

Terms in blue in the text are defined in the Glossary.

About the authors

John Pymm

is Dean of the School of Sport, Performing Arts and Leisure at the University of Wolverhampton. He is Chief Examiner for A-level Performance Studies and has considerable experience of syllabus development and assessment, both in the UK and internationally.

Gail Deal

is Head of Performing Arts and Music at Esher College. She is a senior examiner on the written and practical elements of the A-level Performance Studies course.

Mark Lewinski

is Head of Drama at Impington Village College and International Sixth Form, Cambridge. Examination and moderation work has included English, Media Studies, Expressive Arts and all units of the A-level Performance Studies course.

Preface

Performance Studies is a fairly new subject on the A-level curriculum, but one that has grown enormously since the first syllabus was introduced in 1989 by the University of Cambridge Local Examinations Syndicate. At that stage, fewer than 100 candidates entered for the first examination, which was called A-level Performing Arts. The subject has gone through a number of changes in the almost 20 years since then, but a number of essential elements have stayed the same; during that time the subject has continued to be offered exclusively by Oxford, Cambridge and RSA Examinations (OCR).

It has been customary in British schools, colleges and universities to study the art forms of dance, drama and music as though they were completely separate subjects with almost nothing in common with one another. Some caricatures sum up the situation in 1990: it was rare for dance students to have any interest in the music to which they danced; drama students generally took little notice of the important role of song in drama; music students often cared little for developing the performance memory required in dance and drama and hid behind music stands as if playing for a graded music examination. Yet in other cultures around the world, there was little or no separation between the art forms. In the arts of Africa and South-East Asia (among others), there was a vitality that was born of the arts working together. The development of the earliest syllabuses in Performing Arts sought to introduce such an approach to the study of dance, drama and music in the United Kingdom.

That has been a highly rewarding experience for those engaged in it. Time and again, teachers of Performance Studies have spoken of how their own experience of the arts has been transformed by working with their colleagues in other art forms. The impact of so many teachers being inspired by the possibilities of working across the art forms has led to an explosion in numbers of candidates entering for A-level Performance Studies (as it has been known since Curriculum 2000).

It has not been without its critics, however. Some exponents of individual art forms have denied the synergies between the art forms that can be exploited through Performance Studies. Others have seen the subject as a threat to the very continuance of individual disciplines. Neither view gives a true picture. Performance Studies offers an approach to the study of dance, drama and music that affirms all three as valid and vital art forms in their own right. It seeks not to replace, but to broaden; to introduce students (at a point in their academic development when they are perhaps most receptive to new ideas) to a way of working that draws on existing skills and develops them further in a new context.

Not all candidates who enter for Performance Studies will be equally skilled in all three art forms, and neither, in all honesty, will the professionals who teach them. In embarking on A-level Performance Studies, students will develop skills in all three art forms, will study a broad range of practitioners, will perform to a range of audiences, and will be equipped to work effectively in a group where the decisions taken affect the outcome for all the participants. These are rigorous and demanding tasks, and should be undertaken only by those who want to share the risks as well as the rewards of studying a young subject which has transformed the whole approach to the arts in Britain over a 20-year period.

In June 2005, one examiner wrote in his report on the work he had seen:

> *'I did not meet one single candidate who had not enjoyed the work and I would guess that few students drop out. Performance Studies really changes students' lives. They mature during (and because of) the process and for some, even if they do not proceed to performance courses at University, this is an experience that they will remember all their lives.'*

As the Performance Studies specification moves into its fifth version, now with four units of assessment rather than six, it is a tribute to the vision of a generation of teachers, students and examiners that the subject is established and embedded in the mainstream of British post-16 education. This book is offered to the next generation of Performance Studies students in the hope and belief that they will catch the vision of what can be achieved when dance, drama and music work together.

In a book of this type there are obviously many people to thank and I would like to highlight the work of my fellow authors, Gail Deal and Mark Lewinski, for their professionalism and good humour in working with me to produce copy so efficiently. My thanks also go to Alistair Conquer for providing additional contributions on performance in the Far East. For the production of the comprehensive glossary, I am indebted to Hannah Goodinson. Much of the content of the book has only been possible as a result of the conversations and debates I have had over several years with my fellow examiners for A-level Performance Studies; their enthusiastic support in making this subject a success is beyond measure. In particular, I would like to pay tribute to the outstanding contribution that Louise Powell has made through her magnificent work as Subject Officer for Performance Studies at OCR since 1999. Finally, I would like to offer my sincere thanks to Martin Davies at Hodder Education and my colleagues at the University of Wolverhampton for their support and encouragement in seeing this book through to completion.

John Pymm
University of Wolverhampton
Easter 2008

UNIT 1
Creating Performance

In this first unit of Performance Studies you will cover a lot of ground: learning new technical terms, developing your performance skills in workshops, devising short pieces in dance, drama and music, and working in groups to devise a longer piece to be performed in your local community. You may be new to working in all three art forms, but the reason for studying Performance Studies is to enable you to identify the similarities and differences between the art forms, and to work in a collaborative way across them.

The practical activities you will take part in are

● Skills workshops
● Devising and performing original short pieces in each of dance, drama and music
● Devising and performing a longer original piece that combines all three art forms, and is performed in a community venue.

The assessment will be based on

● A written commentary on the pieces you have devised (3000 words)
● Your performance ability in the 'community' piece.

Workshops

The first part of this unit concentrates on workshops that will help to develop your performance skills and will also help you to learn technical terms by exploring them practically. In each of the three art forms – dance, drama and music – there are five essential technical terms that you will need to master in practical workshops led by your teacher. The practical work you do will be different depending on what your tutors have taught you. You could use the following exercises to refresh your memory of the practical work, and to attempt some further practical exercises.

→ # Dance key terms

In dance, the five essential technical terms you need to master are

- **motif**
- **action**
- **relationships**
- **dynamics**
- **space**.

Motif

A motif in dance is a simple movement or gesture that is easily recognisable, and is often used to help illustrate an aspect of a story. For example, in Matthew Bourne's *Swan Lake*, the pressing together of the palms of the hands with elbows bent, arms enveloping the head and fingertips pointing forward is a simple movement used to show the beak of a swan. When creating a motif, it is a good idea to relate it to the story or stimulus and the ideas that spring to mind first of all.

■ Workshop on motif

Use the image of a frog catching a fly as a stimulus. Discuss initial ideas relating to the stimulus then invent one simple motif to show the frog's movement. This could be the frog's tongue flicking out to catch the fly. The tongue itself could perform this action.

This motif can now be manipulated in several ways: another part of the body could perform the action, e.g. the arm, in order to make the movement bigger and clearer. Take your fingertips to your lips with the elbow held close to the chest. Extend your hand until the arm is straight. Direct this action towards an imaginary fly.

At the same time, the level of the motif could be altered by jumping upwards with both legs drawn up under the body and the knees bent and turned out. In addition the fingers of the hand not being used as a tongue could be splayed to show the hand of the frog. Next a turn could be added by performing the same action with the jump turning in the air. A string of movements could be developed starting with the tongue flicking out followed by the arm impersonating the action of the flicking tongue.

The motif could be repeated two or three times in succession to show that the frog is not successful in catching the fly. It could be repeated at various stages in the dance until at last the frog is successful. The fly could be performed by a different dancer who reacts each time by trying to escape.

Action

There are six actions in dance: travelling, turning, elevation, falling, stasis and gesture. It is important that you know about each of these actions.

Travelling can include, amongst other things, walking, running, hopping, skipping, rolling and darting. It is the action that takes a dancer from one point on the stage to another.

Turning includes rotating on one foot or two, or on other body parts, e.g. the bottom, on which one can spin. Break-dancers manage amazing turns on their backs. In ballet the turns are given special names such as pirouette and can be performed inwards or outwards. Turns can be performed on the spot or travelling on a line or a curve.

Elevation means that the dancer is lifted upwards to a higher level. The dancer can be lifted by another dancer in a variety of ways (e.g. by one hand or two). The dancer can also jump to achieve elevation: from two feet to two feet; from one foot to the same foot (hop); from one foot to the other (leap), or from one foot to two feet. These jumps may be made to turn through 90, 180, 270, 360 or more degrees. Sometimes only a 45 degree rotation in the jump is needed.

Falling can be from different levels and at different speeds. It is best to practise falling with a mat for safety, and with a partner. Weight-taking exercises can increase confidence as one dancer falls back into another's arms. The body of the dancer falling can be turned and taken to the floor as in the cathedral scene in Lea Anderson's *Flesh and Blood*. In aerial and trapeze work the fall is from a greater height, adding more visual impact and the idea of danger.

Stasis, or stillness, is about lack of action – no movement at all; a related word is 'static'.

Gesture can be simple (e.g. a wave of the hand or a rude hand gesture), or just a shrug of the shoulders; a small gesture can communicate a powerful meaning in spite of being small.

■ Workshop on action

Using the stimulus of a Chinese dragon, work in groups of four. Imagine how the Chinese dragon moves and what kind of pathway it weaves. The group should experiment first with a travelling pattern which makes an S shape on the floor, then add on two more S shapes. The direction should be from stage left to stage right. The group should use a stepping pattern with small steps at double speed. This is performed with no contact between dancers until they are confident, then each dancer can hold the waist of the dancer in front. The odd-numbered dancers should do four steps on tiptoe while the even-numbered dancers bend their knees lower to perform their four steps. Then the pairs of dancers swap in order to give an undulating movement of the dragon's back. The pathway can snake around the stage using the diagonals.

Next the group of four dancers break into two pairs and perform a short martial-arts sequence incorporating kung fu kicks and hitch kicks, turning if possible. The arms can be used to perform slicing actions towards the opponent. The legs can perform large sweeping, circular movements. One dancer should advance while the other retreats. Eventually one dancer falls to the floor and the fight is over.

Like Chinese acrobats, the dancers should perform a series of gymnastic cartwheels and back bends if possible. The dancers stand on each other's backs and roll over each other using back-to-back cartwheels. Jumps and turns can be included in this section.

To show stasis, four or more dancers should come together to create a tableau signifying the Chinese dragon's body, using different levels. To conclude, the dancers should move out of the tableau and line up to take a bow using the gesture of hands pressed together in prayer accompanied by a bow to the audience.

Relationships

A performer can be on stage alone (solo) or perform in a duet, trio, quartet, or other size ensemble, or the whole company can be on stage as an ensemble. These relationships can be used in many ways to create visual images on stage. Dancers can perform in canon, in unison and on different levels to each other. The level of contact between dancers can range from none at all to extreme physical contact. The relationships between the dancers depend on the style of the piece and the characters the dancers are interpreting.

■ Workshop on relationships

Split up a group of twelve dancers in as many ways as possible and experiment with how they can be positioned on stage facing front – a line of twelve, two rows of six, three rows of four and then two dancers downstage and ten dancers upstage, a circle of eleven dancers around one dancer in the middle. Once you have a formation, try altering various aspects such as the facing or the level. Use the nine areas of the stage and try bunching dancers together to form huddles. Then ask them to move across the stage slowly facing front and then back. There are more variations the more dancers you have. For inspiration watch some films by Busby Berkeley, the master of geometric choreography.

In a group of five, work on a simple sequence of just four movements to eight counts. Perform this in unison. Now each dancer in turn should add on a movement and the other three execute it until there are eight movements. Work on this in unison. Perform it in double time and then at half the speed. You can use this method to create a large movement section of a dance. Experiment with canon, where one dancer performs a movement then the next dancer performs the same movement, and so on until all the dancers have performed it.

Dynamics

The dynamic of a movement refers to its quality. This might be sudden or sustained, bound or free, sharp or smooth. According to Rudolf Laban, there are four features of dynamics: time, weight, space and flow. Imagine moving your arm in a circular motion from holding it low next to your torso through to the front and up above your head. The dynamic of this movement can be altered in time by performing it slowly or quickly; the weight of the arm can be made heavy or light; the movement through space can be direct and straight or serpentine, and the flow of the movement can be continuous or jerky.

■ Workshop on dynamics

Experiment with altering the quality or dynamic of a leg movement. Stand on one leg and take the other off the ground so that the knee comes up to your chest. Try performing this slowly and then quickly. From the position with the knee held high, jab the heel into the ground, then point the toes. Stamp the foot on the ground and then try to clean the floor with the sole. Dip the toes as if in water.

Try other dynamics by experimenting with hand movements – wringing out the washing; waving goodbye; waving a finger at someone to tell them off; shaking hands firmly; gripping a pole; carrying an object (e.g. a heavy suitcase or a light sandwich or a cup of coffee). You will need to experiment with force, strength and energy when executing each movement. There should be a strong relationship between the dynamic of the movement and the stimulus or subject matter of your dance piece.

Space

The performance area should be considered as a three-dimensional space. It has length, width and height.

The two-dimensional plane of the stage floor has nine distinct areas: the part nearest the audience is downstage, the part furthest away from the audience is upstage and in between these two is centre stage. The directions on stage are from the performer's point of view and are given as upstage left, upstage centre, upstage right, centre stage left, centre stage, centre stage right, downstage left, downstage centre and downstage right.

Performers have a choice of pathways and may consider travelling in lines, curves and circles to begin with. They should mark out a variety of pathways, experimenting with moving in different directions such as forwards, backwards, sideways and in circles and on diagonals.

Next performers should consider the height of the stage and how this affects jumps and lifts. Other levels can be achieved by lying on the floor or kneeling.

The nine stage areas

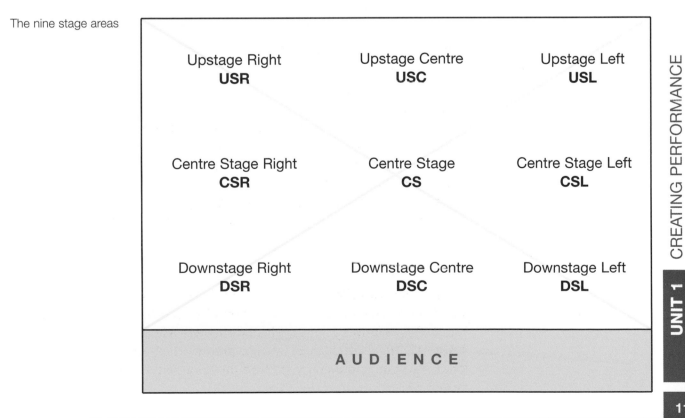

Upstage Right **USR**	Upstage Centre **USC**	Upstage Left **USL**
Centre Stage Right **CSR**	Centre Stage **CS**	Centre Stage Left **CSL**
Downstage Right **DSR**	Downstage Centre **DSC**	Downstage Left **DSL**

A U D I E N C E

■ Workshop on space

Working in pairs, dancers stand facing each other centre stage and start a travelling sequence by walking away from each other. They can experiment with circles increasing then decreasing in size. While walking, they introduce simple arm movements, which move through space in curves and circles. The arm movements are made bigger and smaller. The two dancers come back together and one dancer stands with feet in a wide second position while the other dancer goes through their legs.

Try a layered tableau by positioning one dancer (A) centre stage on all fours. Two dancers join dancer A and position themselves on all fours on either side of A. Another dancer lies underneath their bodies, stretched out on the floor and at right angles to their torsos. A fifth dancer stands on the back of dancer A. Two more dancers join and look for spaces between the other dancers' limbs and bodies where they might extend or place a limb.

Try simple lifts or standing on furniture such as tables and chairs to reach a higher level. However, be mindful of health and safety issues.

Remember to choose pathways and directions that reflect the stimulus.

→ Drama key terms

In drama, the five essential technical terms you need to master are

- **dialogue**
- **characterisation**
- **physicality**
- **proxemics**
- **tension**.

Dialogue

Dialogue is the term used for the communication that exists between characters in a play. The term usually refers to scripted words.

Dialogue can be formal, e.g. an interview, or informal, e.g. two friends discussing a film. An audience's reaction to dialogue can be influenced by a performer's accent or dialect.

The number of performers involved within the dialogue can also influence the audience. A monologue is a form of dialogue, normally used for dramatic effect, which is performed by one character only (with other characters present). A single character's dialogue performed when alone on stage is called a soliloquy and is often used for reflective purposes. However, the non-verbal communication between the characters and the subtext (the meaning behind the words spoken) are often equally important, and can 'say' more than the words the characters speak.

For dialogue to communicate effectively to an audience, and for the meaning to be fully understood, performers must bring together their visual and verbal actions. Much human interaction takes place with few or no words. The workshop that follows uses a simple situation in which a complex non-verbal dialogue can easily be improvised.

■ Workshop on dialogue

This exercise can also be used as an example for discussion of characterisation, physicality and tension.

Tip: The longer student B does not ask, the greater the tension.

Students work in pairs. Student A is already waiting at a bus stop as student B approaches. Student B should show some recognition of student A but no dialogue is communicated. To add dramatic effect, student B should refrain from asking the obvious question, 'Do I know you?' (or similar), for as long as possible.

Student A should always deny knowing student B when asked and should decide before the performance if it is because (a) they do not want to admit knowing them or (b) they genuinely do not know student A. The reason for the denial should only be revealed at the end of the performance.

The improvisation is played to the point where one of the following has happened.

- Student B attempts but fails to convince student A that they know each other.
- Student B convinces student A by force of evidence that they really do know each other.
- Student B never plucks up the courage to ask outright and gives up.

Note

The bus should **not** arrive just in time to prevent one of the three scenarios above. Discuss why this is dramatically undesirable.

Characterisation

Characterisation is the way in which the qualities of a stage persona can be communicated through stage action. It requires the coherent structuring of a role to communicate personality, motivation, attitudes and mood. The use of facial and vocal expression, gesture, movement and posture also needs to be considered. Status – the importance/self-importance of a character – is also a vital ingredient of the way a situation can be played.

It is possible to act in a way that creates immediacy in the characterisation (i.e. a character may appear to exist only in the present). However, a background or history to the role will usually help performer and audience to understand the character and create depth and dimension. Performers can generate dramatic tension through the interaction of contrasting characters in dialogue with one another and the potential conflict of wills.

■ Workshop on characterisation

In this exercise you will be interpreting a very short and fairly neutral section of existing dialogue from a real play involving no more than four characters (10–12 lines maximum). The exercise can be repeated several times using the same script as varying different aspects of characterisation can create a variety of situations and outcomes.

Characterisation workshop using an extract from Pinter's *The Birthday Party*

Tip: The given circumstances are an essential formula for any performer in any situation to play the role: Who am I? Where am I? What do I want?

The name of the play, the situation and its playwright should not be given to students, but it should be stressed that this is real script. The extract will be chosen by your teacher.

Read the script in pairs/groups and decide who the characters might be: where they are, when and what is going on; jobs and occupations; personalities; what they are trying to do. All of these are wide open, from tramps to royalty, from children to the aged, from life-and-death situations to the completely trivial – virtually nothing is off limits.

Play the situation to show the characters and situation as strongly as possible.

There are three stages in working with the extract.

Immediacy: Play just the lines given, using status, voice and physicality to communicate as much as is possible about what is going on.

Development: Improvise a short script that develops the characters to a clear conclusion.

Backstory: Create the dialogue leading up to the given text to show why the characters are behaving in this way.

Physicality

Physicality is about the use of the body to communicate character and/or meaning. It includes both body language and the physical manner used by the performer to show the intention of the character. It can range from casual and naturalistic to precise and highly choreographed physical movement. Body language, gestures, energy and facial and physical manner are all aspects of physicality.

■ Workshop on physicality

This exercise should be carefully and precisely rehearsed, and without an audience until ready.

Initially the stage should be empty and well lit. It is also essential that the performer can see the audience. There should be wings or screens both sides to allow the performer to appear and exit without breaking role. Every action on the stage will have an impact and therefore must have a specific and chosen purpose. There is nothing 'normal' or 'ordinary'.

Individuals walk across the stage in a manner that shows the audience a chosen emotion towards that audience (which must be secret until shown). Words must not be used; non-verbal utterances (sounds which show feelings) can be used, but should assist the action not be vital to it. On stage, the performer must engage and hold eye contact with at least one member of the audience until it is clear that the performer completely dominates the space. Any less than this and the power of the action will be lost.

Each student in the group shows their walk in turn. At the end, each member of the audience should identify the emotion that was communicated and what made them feel it. The performer should not confirm or disagree with what is said. If there is a mix of responses, this means that mixed messages were given. Replay the exercise if there is potential to improve.

Place a chair centre stage. Each student should prepare a scene in which they come on to the stage, show a specific feeling to the maximum towards that chair, then leave, to maximum effect. Again, eye contact with the audience is essential.

Tension

'Tension' refers to building the action on stage to lead the audience to believe that something sudden and critical will happen, and that when it does, the situation will have changed into a new one. The characters on stage may be aware or unaware that change is impending: the audience hold their breath to see how the characters react to the shock or surprise of the snap change in the situation.

Tension is a temporary state, which can have only limited duration and demands sensitivity in timing. If it is too short, or too long, the anticipation effect is weakened.

■ Workshop on tension

This exercise is related to the physicality workshop above, but involves the interaction between two characters who pass across the stage. As before, the stage is well- but not over-lit. It may be better to use the diagonal of a large space rather than a small proscenium arch; there is nothing 'normal' or 'ordinary'. As the characters draw closer and pass, the audience will read and interpret every aspect of what they see.

Two students pass by one another. Each has an extremely strong emotion towards the other. This will become apparent as they become aware of one another's presence. The audience should be placed so that they can see the faces of both performers until they have passed. They observe how tension builds, identify the moment at which it breaks, and how.

Polished presentation: In pairs, create and rehearse an action where two individuals walk across the space and pass without touching or speaking. Both should show what they feel about one another as strongly as possible.

Spontaneous challenge: When students are playing for the first time, they may tend to show attitude before starting the walk. Once they are confident in their ability to show a feeling of their own choosing, the emotion they show will become known to their opponent not in their still pose but only once they begin to walk towards one another. The audience may judge who 'won' by several criteria:

● Who kept the tension longest without breaking it?
● Who showed the most powerful emotion?
● Who won the psychological battle?
● Who do the audience sympathise with most?

Proxemics

'Proxemics' refers to the spatial relationship between characters and/or objects in a performance. The term was first introduced by the anthropologist Edward T. Hall in 1959. Any object on stage – including a performer – should be placed there for a purpose that the audience can clearly understand. Random placing of characters or objects creates irrelevant images likely to confuse the audience. Proxemics shift constantly with the movement on stage and skilful performers become aware of how they are creating new meanings as their positions change.

Proxemics create a visual effect. Proxemics are integral to any action on stage, so can be difficult to investigate separately from physicality and characterisation, because all three elements depend on the spatial relationships between characters and objects.

■ Workshop on proxemics

For this exercise, use as large a space as possible, so that pairs or small groups can work in isolation from each other.

Begin by discussing as a whole group the effects created by three possible positions of two ordinary chairs in an otherwise empty space. For example, close, facing could indicate confrontation, dialogue or interview; close, facing away could indicate disagreement; 2 metres apart, one facing towards, the other away could indicate yearning by one for the other, who does not care or does not realise, or that one wants to make up after a disagreement but the other does not.

In pairs or small groups, create and rehearse a sequence of five positions of two chairs so that the audience may interpret a simple 'story' through these positions. The performers should place the chairs, then move out of the space, leaving the chairs for a few seconds. They should then re-enter the space and set the new position, and so on. At the end of the exercise, the audience describe the stories they 'saw', after which the performers reveal their intentions. The discussions that arise should identify whether the proxemic sequence communicated effectively and to what extent.

Tip: Positioning of the audience will influence their perception of the proxemics. If there is access to stage blocks, experiment with placing your audience at different heights and distances in relation to the performance.

→ Music key terms

In music, the five essential technical terms you need to master are

- rhythm
- melody
- harmony
- timbre
- texture.

Rhythm

Rhythm is often described as the most important aspect of music. The term 'rhythm' refers to the relative length of each note and it is often possible to recognise a piece of music from its rhythm, even without the melody. Rhythm is often provided by percussion instruments: the drummer in a rock band, the percussionist in an orchestra. Without rhythm, music would lack a backbone, and there would be no sense of direction or purpose. Rhythm helps us to identify the shape of a melody, and gives a direction to the music.

Rhythms can be regular or syncopated. A regular rhythm is like a heartbeat – steady and secure – sometimes described as a pulse for that reason. Syncopated rhythms are not regular: they work against the beat. Most popular music and jazz relies on syncopated rhythms.

■ Workshop on rhythm

Work in pairs, numbered 1 and 2. Player 1 either claps or plays on a drum a steady regular pulse. You can decide on the tempo (speed) of this pulse by using a metronome. Whatever number the metronome is set to, that is the number of beats per minute. Player 2 allows player 1 to establish the pulse in a regular and steady manner, and then joins in with a syncopated rhythm that works against the pulse. This should be improvised for as long as possible, up to about 3 minutes, in order to create interesting patterns. See if player 2 can remember any of the syncopated patterns – it is important to try to use a rhythm more than once in a piece. The more that ideas can be repeated and adapted, the more likely a piece of music is to be memorable. Rhythms that change constantly are not memorable.

Once each pair has become confident in the use of regular and syncopated rhythms, combine two pairs so that two students are clapping or playing the regular pulse, and the other two take turns to improvise a syncopated rhythm over the top.

Melody

Everyone loves a good tune, and melody is the aspect of music most likely to stick in your memory. It is very difficult to describe what makes a good or memorable tune, but the ability to hum or sing parts or all of it is almost certainly one of the factors. It is hard to make up an original melody – after all, there are only eight notes in a major or minor scale, and there is a limit to the number of combinations of these notes. As we have discussed already, however, the notes of a melody are shaped by the rhythm that brings them together.

Some songwriters have shown a natural gift for writing melody, and this is true whether they are classical or popular songwriters. For example, the melodies of Franz Schubert, George Gershwin, the Beatles and Abba have little in common, but each in their way are memorable, well shaped and carefully crafted.

■ Workshop on melody

Melodies are often quite short, and are made up of groups of just a few notes, referred to as motifs. As in dance, a motif might be something very short, but be used to build up much longer ideas. One of the most important starting points with a melody is to keep it short. It can be very challenging to produce a long melody so this exercise is based around a motif of four notes.

In small groups, select a short motif in which everyone sings the same four long notes. The first thing to ensure is that everyone has the same notes and is in tune with the rest of the group. Get used to breathing in time and trying to balance the sound with the other people in the group. When this has been achieved, sing the motif through several times without a break. Then think of a second sequence of four notes and repeat the process. If the first four notes are called motif A and the second four notes are called motif B, you will have two halves of a phrase. Try singing in groups motif A – motif B – motif A, so that you have a 12-note melody. You can then change the lengths of some of the notes, to make the melody more interesting. This will produce the basis for a longer melody.

When you have mastered this, you can work on longer melodies. Take a short line from a poem and try making up a simple melody for it. Once you have done this, let the whole group try to sing the line. You can then take another line and do the same thing, making sure that the style of the second line matches the style of the first line. Once you have a melody for four lines, you have the makings of a song melody.

Harmony

When two or more instruments play together, or two or more singers sing together, harmony can be created if the two parts have different music. Most people think of harmony as putting chords to a tune, and this is a good starting point for understanding how it works. In a hymn tune, for example, the four voices (soprano, alto, tenor and bass) often sing in harmony with each other, and produce a pleasing effect as the harmonies support the melody. Not all harmony has a pleasing effect, however. Sometimes a composer may wish to produce a harsh or dissonant effect by putting together chords that clash. It is important to remember, therefore, that harmony may be consonant or dissonant, depending on the effect the composer wishes to achieve.

■ Workshop on harmony

This exercise involves working with simple chords to understand how triads work. In groups of three, hum the note C, then E, then G. Next each member of the group hums a different note to produce a triad of C major: C, E and G ('triad' refers to the use of three notes in the chord). Once this has been practised, try singing a different triad. Each person moves up one note and the triad becomes the notes D, F and A. This is a triad of D minor. Trying singing the first triad, then the second one, then the first again – count four beats on each triad. This is the beginning of a chord sequence.

When this sequence C major – D minor – C major can be hummed confidently, bring in a fourth member of the group who will improvise a short melody over the top of the chord sequence. Listen carefully to whether the harmony supports the melody or whether it clashes with it. Experiment with both.

Now work on different triads. The triad of G major has the notes G, B and D, the triad of F major has the notes F, A and C. Work in groups to put together a chord sequence that uses these chords and the ones you have already worked on.

Timbre

'Timbre' refers to the type of musical sound produced by a particular singer or musical instrument. For example, the trumpet has a brilliant and piercing timbre, whilst the oboe could be said to sound sad or plaintive. A soprano voice may be able to cut through a performance so that it holds a powerful and high melody; an alto voice may be ideal for singing solo ballads or jazz. Every instrument has a different timbre, and accomplished performers can achieve a range of different timbres from their instrument.

It is probably easiest to think of timbre as 'colour'. Composing music is not just about making up rhythm, melody and harmony. The same piece will sound radically different depending on which instruments or voices perform it. A pop song arranged for string quartet or brass band will sound very different to when it is performed by a rock group.

■ Workshop on timbre

For this exercise you will need access to a number of electronic keyboards. On most keyboards, there is an enormous variety of different sounds – or timbres – available. Try to remember the short melody that you made up in groups in the melody workshop (see page 18) and play it on the keyboard. If the group cannot remember the previous melody, that does not matter so long as a new melody can be made up. The purpose of the exercise is to enable you to compare what the same melody sounds like played by different instruments.

First, try a piano sound. You will find that the sound is percussive, and dies away quite quickly. If you have a melody composed of long notes, they will probably die away before you want them to. Now compare the effect of using a violin or strings sound. There is much less attack at the start of the note, but the sound is capable of being sustained far longer. On many keyboards it is possible to combine sounds – if you put piano and strings together you can achieve two quite different timbres that complement each other well.

Go through the different families of instruments – strings, brass, woodwind, percussion – and experiment with playing a similar melody on different instruments. You can create a character for your melody by playing it faster or slower, by changing the rhythm, or by changing the timbre. As you work though the different sounds, make notes on the effects of changing the timbre. If the keyboard has a recording facility, try recording some chords (as in the harmony workshop, page 18), then play a melody over this when you play back.

The chords will need to be sustained: decide what sound best suits the character of the melody.

Texture

The texture of music refers to the number and type of different instruments or voices sounding at any one time. Just as a painter uses a range of colours to create contrast, a composer may try to bring together the different 'colours' of instrumental and vocal sounds. If a piece uses only one sort of instrumental timbre, the resulting texture will be quite different from a piece that uses a variety of timbres. Imagine a song performed by a quartet of tubas, or an ensemble of piccolos! Most music has a variety of different timbres, and the texture is the effect of these combinations. It is possible to create contrast in music by changing the texture. In a song, for example, an instrumental section could work as a good contrast to the sung sections. In an orchestral piece, a short solo section for violin or flute might create a very different texture to the tutti sections where all the instruments play. In a choral piece, soloists may have a section accompanied by the chorus, and other points where they sing alone. Contrasts in texture may be achieved in many ways, and some music deliberately has no contrasts in texture, in order to achieve a particular effect.

■ Workshop on texture

For this exercise you will need a variety of percussion instruments, one or more keyboards, and one or more singers.

First, a pulse needs to be established, probably by using some bongo drums or similar. Then a number of people play a syncopated rhythm using a variety of other contrasting percussion instruments. Try entering these one at a time. Then try combining them. The effect of combining them could work well, or they could conflict with each other. By listening sensitively to the other members of the group, try to decide when it is best to enter with your rhythm. Also decide when it is best to stop. Do not assume that once you have started to play, you have to continue for the rest of the piece! Be sensitive to other people, and listen to the effect on the texture.

Second, devise a slow piece using the same principle. Start by playing sustained chords on the keyboard. A voice then starts to sing a slow melody. This could be a line from a poem set to music. Decide which percussion instrument is best to bring in to accompany this, and build up the texture. One performer should act as the director for the piece, indicating to the others when they should come in and when they should stop.

Third, work as a vocal ensemble in a similar way to the harmony exercise (see page 18). Build up a choral texture using a set of chords, but in addition, try to introduce either a percussion instrument, or an accompaniment on the keyboard.

Whichever of these textures you decide works best, make notes as to why the balance and contrast work with that particular arrangement.

→ The performance process

Now that you have finished the skills workshops, you will be required to devise three short pieces, one each in dance, drama and music. These need last for only 3 minutes, which does not sound long, but it takes at least an hour of preparation time to devise enough material to last for 1 minute. More important, there is a process of devising original performance work that is structured and systematic. If you were thinking of just putting a few ideas together and then showing this to someone, think again! You will also have to devise a much longer piece, lasting 30 minutes, with a community focus, and this will build on the same performance process as the three short pieces. (For more on the community piece, please see page 26.)

The performance process consists of three phases:

1 Improvising
2 Rehearsing
3 Performing.

Each of these has a major importance in achieving a successful performance of your original work.

Improvising is the stage where ideas are tried out. This is the most creative part of the process, since there can be no 'rights' or 'wrongs'. It is much more a case of everyone putting forward their own ideas, and experimenting with them practically. However, there needs to be an agreed time frame for this. It is very easy to continue to experiment and not come to any decisions about the structure of the piece. By the end of the improvising section of the process, there needs to a version of that piece that can then be rehearsed.

Rehearsing is not about creating new material, but about rehearsing what has been created in order to ensure that it can be performed fluently, confidently and engagingly to an audience. This involves the discipline of performing the piece over and over again, looking critically at it, ensuring the pacing and timing work, making sure that your intentions are clear to the audience. It may be that some aspects of the piece do not work and that refinements are necessary. That is an important part of the rehearsal process, but it should grow from the needs of the piece, rather than as a result of members of the group continuing to generate new ideas.

Performing is the point at which a finished piece is performed to an audience. Audiences respond well to clearly structured, confident performances and this is what your piece should aspire to. Even a short piece has to communicate to its audience and it is important that everything is polished, well rehearsed and has something to say. An audience will be more impressed by an effective 2 minute performance than by a rough-and-ready piece several times that length!

CREATING PERFORMANCE

UNIT 1

→ Devising the dance piece

There are various stages to devising a short group dance and there are different ways to approach this task. Here are some examples that may be used as springboards for creating a 3 minute dance piece for up to six dancers.

■ Improvising

Responding to a stimulus

A stimulus for dance could be visual, aural (something that can be heard) or thematic/abstract. For example, a painting, cartoon, photograph, sculpture or a short extract from a film could be used as a visual stimulus. Whatever it consists of, however, the group must spend a few minutes looking at it, and if it is a film clip, you should watch it several times. A short piece of music or a sound effect (e.g. the rumbling of an earthquake) could be used as an aural stimulus. A thematic or abstract stimulus could be something like 'The seasons'. Here we shall take as an example the stimulus of a swan to illustrate the process you should follow to create your dance piece.

Each dancer should jot down their initial reaction to the stimulus. This can take a variety of forms: a list of words, continuous prose, drawings or recording on to an iPod (some mobile phones also have this function). It does not matter how these initial reactions are noted as long as they can be revisited and discussed within the group. You could even video the initial discussion about the stimulus.

From the initial ideas or reactions, produce a mind map. If the group gets stuck finding things to say about the stimulus, then ask questions. For example, how does a swan move on land and on water? How does a swan sleep? What kind of nature does a swan have? How is this shown through movement of the wings? Further research can be carried out at this stage by looking on the internet for images (e.g. film clips of *Swan Lake*, both the traditional and modern versions).

Developing the dance

From the initial mind map the group can select ideas around which to improvise. Ideas that have performance potential should be selected and those ideas which quickly lead the group to a dead end rejected.

You should make sure that the five elements of dance – motif, action, relationships, dynamics and space – are fully considered in devising the dance. For example, a motif could be selected to represent the neck of the swan, and an action for the beating of the wings. Tableaux could be created to signify the various shapes connected to swans. Some of these might be symmetrical (representing the V shape made by a bevy of swans in flight) and others could be asymmetrical (showing a mother swan with her cygnets following her). At this stage you could start to map out pathways for the dance – to represent the swan travelling in water and on land. The stage could be divided into river and river bank.

In a group of six there are many opportunities for using different relationships between the dancers, from ensemble to solo. Usually dancers count in eights when making movement and this is a useful way of creating movement.

Dynamics can be used to vary the way the movements are performed and to add texture to the piece. You should bear in mind the nine areas of the stage and the levels, in order to use the entire space imaginatively. For example, the low level could be used to reflect the shapes swans make when swimming along the water's surface.

As the dance is to be 3 minutes in duration, there could be three sections. To structure the dance, three tableaux could be used to start these sections. You should consider having a climax and some highlights to make the structure more interesting.

Once the piece has been made, choose instrumental music to accompany it and choose at least three lighting changes (one for each section, perhaps) to create mood and atmosphere. You could look for appropriate images to project to create a setting. Check that you have included compositional devices such as unison, canon and motif development. Check that all six actions have been included and that they relate strongly to the stimulus. Revisit the mind map.

■ Rehearsing

The piece should be rehearsed several times and recorded on DVD so that you can watch it in performance and look for areas where it can be improved. For example, dancers should work on performance skills such as timing, focus, facial expression, musicality, projection and muscular strength.

Once the group is happy with the movement content, costume and make-up should be addressed. A dress rehearsal must take place before the final performance to make sure that the costumes are appropriate and workable. Extreme make-up can be used to show, for example, the white face of a swan and the colours of the beak. Any projections must be tried out with the lighting and sound in a technical rehearsal with the technician before the final dress rehearsal. The latter should be treated as the first proper performance of the piece.

The group needs to consider how dancers will enter and exit the stage and how you will organise your bow. The bow is staged in order to say thank you to the audience for watching. The audience clap to show their appreciation. If the entrance, bow and exit are not rehearsed, the piece will look messy and unprofessional.

■ Performing

The final performance should take place in front of an invited audience and offer some programme notes. The performance should also be recorded on DVD. Afterwards, the group should watch the recording and evaluate the piece and their individual contributions to it. It is a good idea to record the ensuing discussion and evaluation, as this will form the basis of the written commentary (for more on this, please see page 31). The group may wish to talk to members of the audience to assess their reaction to the piece and the performances.

→ Devising the drama piece

■ Improvising

Playing with dramatic ideas at the start of the process is essential to the effectiveness of the entire piece. Begin by 'firing up' your mind. Irrespective of what sort of stimulus is chosen for the piece, there will be a very high imaginative response from your brain from the moment you see it, but this will last only a couple of minutes at most. During this time, all ideas, especially the most tangential, should be recorded. You need to recognise that 90% will otherwise be lost, and cannot be replicated at a second go.

Do this first stage individually, with pen and paper. There must be no discussion as this dampens the sparking of ideas. After 2–3 minutes, join with the others in your group and compare ideas you have in common. Explore the most extreme ideas: amongst these may be the most exciting and original. As with the other art forms, dismiss nothing at this stage. There are no 'bad' ideas – only what might suit later rather than now. Agree on several ideas that you can try, and file the papers in an 'ideas box' that you can revisit when more inspiration is needed. Think of this as being the lifeline when that it-doesn't-work moment occurs!

The talking stage is seductive and enjoyable, but you must put a time limit on sit-down discussion. After this is finished, there must be no chairs or sitting: once you have several ideas to try, get up and do. Proxemic images are often the first and most manageable action. Create a freeze image to show a moment or aspect of the idea if dialogue and movement are uncertain. Construct two more: one should come 10 seconds before, the other, 10 seconds later. Find a way of connecting all three with structured movement, stylised, like a 'video clip'. That will give you 20 seconds of focused action and three tableaux. Add sound as required, and review.

Develop the action using time structures. This offers many possibilities as you build outwards, forwards, back in time, or through a parallel sequence. A storyline may work best in nonlinear order (e.g. starting mid-story, tracking back to the start, then jumping to the conclusion may be more intriguing than beginning–middle–end). Find the obstacle, the dramatic conflict, which has to be managed. Are the characters working together against it, or is there conflict between them? Which do you want it to be? Create differing perspectives – characters who see the same event in different ways create depth.

It is highly effective if you can take the audience somewhere other than the obvious. Never give an audience what they think they will get! Once you have decided where your piece is heading, try either to get there in a way the audience does not expect or to end somewhere different. Once that ending has been established, review the whole piece to identify whether the structure leads towards it in the most effective manner. You may wish to stylise the drama. There is almost always a more interesting way of showing what can be shown than a group of naturalistic characters speaking. At worst, this will simply look like a scene from a soap opera.

■ Rehearsing

The same points about rehearsing the piece over and over again apply just as much to drama as to dance and music. In the case of drama, however, there may also need to be an editing process where you decide as a group how much the drama needs to be spelled out. The natural tendency is to want to tell all the aspects of a story and this can be quite wearisome for an audience. In rehearsal, issues of pacing and contrast should be at the forefront. But some of these issues can be dealt with by simply cutting some material. If the pacing seems too slow, almost certainly something needs to be cut. If the pacing seems breathless, try lengthening an episode to slow it down.

The vital outcome of the rehearsal stage is that everyone knows their lines, everyone has a clear understanding of the status of their role at all times, and that the impact of the ensemble as a whole is what the group intend. 'Clean' the piece at least twice. Find at least four new things to put in and reshape with total rigorousness anything that does not sit comfortably, until it fits with the rest of the structure.

■ Performing

As with the dance piece, it is vital that the performance is fluent, precise, well polished and makes an impact. This has more to do with effective rehearsal of the piece than with the quality of the initial ideas. A successful piece of drama – even one that lasts only 3 minutes – needs pace and precision. Whatever you create, make sure it is snappy, loud and sharp: no performance that has anything less than maximum energy and exactness will be worth watching. In particular, ensure that the transitions between scenes or episodes have minimum movement from point A to point B. Make sure that you record the performance (on DVD), and make honest notes on the quality of what you see and its effectiveness.

→ Devising the music piece

■ Improvising

There are many different musical styles and the first thing to decide in the improvising phase of the work is what style of music you intend to create. It may be that, having looked at the elements of music in the workshops, you want to compose a short song. On the other hand, a soundscape or film track using different timbres on the keyboard or synthesiser may be more appropriate. You could decide to produce a purely vocal piece, or one that involves percussion instruments. Whichever option you choose, it is important that the five elements of music that you have explored in the workshops on pages 17–20 are fully integrated into the final piece.

That being the case, the improvising process should work through how the piece will use melody, rhythm and harmony, what instrumental and/or vocal timbres will be used, and how it will be structured to use varying textures. At this stage, keep the ideas simple: short chord sequences, simple melodic motifs, repeating rhythms. It is easier to expand these to create longer ideas rather than continuing to create more and more ideas.

The aim of the improvising stage should be to produce a working structure for the piece. A simple way of doing this, irrespective of the style of the music, is to go for a simple three-part structure, generally referred to as ABA (ternary form). The content of the first and third sections would be very similar in this structure, and this makes it easier to come up with a contrasting middle section. This contrast could be through (for example) a change of melody, a change of texture or a change of harmony.

■ Rehearsing

The music piece you have created might be relatively short, but it is essential that every detail of it is well rehearsed. The timing between the parts must be completely synchronised; the tuning of the voices needs to be spot on; the pacing of the piece needs to be appropriate; changes in tempo, entering of different parts, all need to be co-ordinated, rehearsed and sequenced. It is a very good idea to record each rehearsal so that each member of the group can listen to it at home between rehearsals. If it is possible to create a podcast, each person will be able to hear a digital recording of the piece. In addition, the group will need to think about the broader dimensions of the piece: what the performance will look like, the spatial relationship of the performers to one another, the confidence of their posture and their sensitivity to one another.

■ Performing

Even in a short performance, there should be a professional standard of presentation. The instruments and equipment should be set up in advance of the performance, and a sound check undertaken to ensure that the balance of the performance is sensitive. The rest of the space should be uncluttered and have plenty of room for the performance to take place. Do not perform in a music classroom: the performance image of the piece should be comparable with the standard you would expect in dance and drama. Make a DVD recording of the final performance, and use this as the basis of the evaluation of the success of the performance in terms of your intention in creating it.

The Community Piece

This piece is much longer than the short pieces in dance, drama and music. Each member of the group has to have at least 5 minutes' exposure during the piece, so it can last up to 30 minutes in performance if you have six students in your group. The minimum group size is two students, and their piece would last for 10 minutes. In this piece you will be assessed on your performance ability.

Most important, this piece aims to combine all three art forms, and you should ensure that each member of the group is able to demonstrate their ability in dance, drama and music through the piece. This means that as the piece is devised, an equal weighting must be given to all three art forms. Do not devise a piece of drama and then try to slot dance and music in later as this will look odd and give the audience the impression you have tried to devise a musical. The obvious exception to this is if you intend to devise a musical!

What the A-level specification says

This piece considers links between the elements studied in the other three pieces.

Working in groups of between two and six, candidates devise and perform a piece in a specific performance style that relates to a community-based stimulus. The piece may be performed at a venue elsewhere in the community, although primary schools and residential homes are specifically excluded, as is Theatre in Education (TIE) as an approach.

The piece must combine elements of all three art forms and be based on a situation specific to a local community. The focus of this piece is on the intention of the piece, the way it explores its theme, the venue where it is performed and the audience for whom it is performed.

In the written commentary, candidates should state the intention of the piece and evaluate to what extent the piece in performance has fulfilled this intent. The work of relevant practitioners should inform the devising and candidates need to discuss this understanding.

Work on the community piece should also follow the performance process of improvising, rehearsing, performing.

→ The performance process

This piece should build on the work you did for the three short pieces. It uses the same process of improvising–rehearsing–performing (see page 21) except that each phase will now last for considerably longer. It is likely that you will have around six weeks to complete this community piece. Your tutors will take care of the arrangements for the performance venue, for deciding the style of the piece and for producing a timeline of how the process will operate. There will be no time for indecision: your group will have to make every session count so that the piece is well conceived and the public performance is a credit to you.

The improvising phase for this piece will be considerably longer than for the short pieces. The ideas need to be strong and the piece well crafted. It is tempting to start by thinking about the content of the piece, but the proper starting point is the style you intend to perform in. Your tutors will decide this and there are a number of possibilities. Styles such as *commedia dell'arte*, pantomime, mystery play, pageant, community play, street theatre, music hall, vaudeville and folk traditions are all suitable, and there are many more that would also allow you to put together a strong piece in a clear and consistent style. It is best if the piece keeps to a single style. If it contains a number of different styles, it may seem inconsistent, or it may confuse the audience who watch it.

The content of the piece will obviously be very important, and must reflect an aspect of your local community, or a topic relevant to it. Whatever topic is chosen, however, the piece needs to be crafted in a performance style that you have been taught.

Rehearsing will need to be rigorous and sustained, with a thorough rehearsal schedule including costume and technical. Expect your tutors to intervene and direct at points, although they will also be looking for you to work together as a group to become independent learners who can take direction. You need to allow at least two weeks for rehearsal of the piece.

Performing will be a much more significant occasion than for the short pieces. Your tutors will arrange for you to perform in a community venue if at all possible, and you should invite an audience who are likely to be sympathetic to what you are trying to achieve in your piece. If the performance is outdoors, however, you may have little choice as to who stands and watches and who passes by.

→ Case study

This case study is based on a piece devised by five students who had studied the conventions of Greek theatre in response to a local museum's exhibit of Greco-Roman pottery (much of it depicting Greek myths). This inspired a piece based on the story of Pandora's Box. In the Greek myth of Pandora's Box, Zeus creates a beautiful woman called Pandora and sends her to earth to marry Epimethius. Zeus gives Pandora a locked box that he commands her never to open; the key he gives to Epimethius. Overcome by curiosity, however, Pandora steals the key from Epimethius and opens the box. Rather than beautiful, good things, however, the box contains troubles and woes, more than she could have imagined, and once the box is open, it is impossible to close it again. The last thing to emerge from the box is Hope to enable people to keep going in spite of all the other, bad things.

■ Improvising

The style of the piece made use of several conventions of Greek theatre: a chorus, mask work, the unities of place, time and action, the integration of the arts. The piece itself addressed the issue of eating disorders among teenagers, since the performance was aimed at a community venue and there was likely to be a predominantly young audience. Despite the style being distant from the contemporary world, the subject matter was not, and the group felt that the chosen style would enable their audience to see a present-day issue from a different perspective. The performance images were created to heighten the tension of the present-day Pandora, who obsessively opened the 'box' of image and makeover, and developed an eating disorder in seeking perfection of image.

The group decided that they would interweave elements of the original Greek myth with the modern setting, and this provided an interesting fracturing of the timeline. In the early stages, the group focused on creating strong images, and also on integrating movement and music into the scenes. From the outset, the use of choral speech and movement was central to the devising process, and much of the action grew from the tableaux created at the start of the process. Costume was also decided early on as a means of identifying with the style, and a way of distancing the audience from the issue.

The performance venue

The performance was held in the museum itself, making full use of the many and varied public spaces. These included a balcony, near the main entrance, a room with subdued lighting, an open central area and a courtyard to the rear of the museum. The main performance space (the courtyard) was much larger than the group required as there were only five of them. The challenge for the group was whether they could narrow down the focus of the piece and work on the proxemics in such a way as to create power from the closeness of the performers. Ultimately, the decision was taken to move the performance to the inside of the building since they could make full use of the different levels..

The use of instruments can help to create an interesting image, as well as providing music for the piece.

Links between the art forms

One of the most attractive features of the style and the subject matter was the potential that they held for the art forms to work together. In particular, one of the members of the group played the harp, and this fitted in very well with the style of the piece. Another member played the violin and these two instruments together could be used to provide musical interludes between some of the episodes.

The improvising process was complete after four weeks of intensive devising. During that period the group achieved the following:

- Detailed performance research on conventions of Greek theatre, supported by theory sessions from their tutors
- Clear ideas about how they might use these conventions in their own performance
- An approach that explored the use of movement, music, mask and chorus, as well as the creation of some exalted dialogue and some present-day dialogue
- A structure that contrasted the original story with the contemporary issue, using a number of episodes to communicate this through image, movement and dialogue.

■ Rehearsing

The group had allowed two weeks for rehearsal. This phase of the work was a pleasurable experience for them as they had been so thorough in devising their ideas. The piece lasted for just under 25 minutes and allowed each performer a broadly equal amount of exposure. However, the pacing was slow and the transitions were often dependent on lengthy blackouts, lasting almost a minute in some cases. For the harp and violin players, there was also the problem of positioning themselves on the stage and moving to their instruments so that there was a natural progression into playing them. They considered recording the music to enable them to have more physical freedom in the performance, but this was rejected as they believed the performance image created by them playing the harp and the violin (in costume) outweighed the difficulty of managing the transition.

During the rehearsal period, the group worked on aspects performance as follows.

- Pacing, tempo and dynamics of the performance: they managed to shave 3 minutes off the playing time of the piece, simply by rehearsing to the point where everyone knew the piece as second nature.

- The transitions became much more slick, so that the movement to different parts of the set were completely natural, and there was no problem in integrating movement and music.

- The projection of the dialogue and the choral speaking: this was not good, and needed a much greater sense of elevation, so that the audience were at once engaged by the elevated style of the piece.

- One or two scenes were slightly long and tried to spell out the story in huge detail: the group worked on the principle that 'less is more' and made the piece more powerful by cutting the length of some of the episodes.

- The original myth was not obvious by the end of the piece: the group decided to consider a return to the story at the end to give closure to it.

■ Performing

The final piece lasted for 25 minutes. There were strong performance skills in all three art forms and the piece was clearly derived from Greek-theatre conventions. The audience were asked to comment on the performance at the end, in order for the students to find out whether their intentions had been achieved. The audience were told in the programme notes that the piece had two aims:

- to explore some conventions of Greek theatre, told through the story of Pandora's Box

- to explore the theme of eating disorders as a parallel to the Pandora story – the link being the opening of the beautiful box only to find misery rather than fulfilment.

The members of the group were assessed on their performance of the piece and scored very well. There are two parts to the assessment: the devising of the piece (for which the whole group scored very similar, and very high, marks) and the quality of the performance skills (for which they were also credited highly).

There was general agreement that the piece was successful in this and that the scenes were of an appropriate length. Some people thought that the relative length of sections dealing with the original story was not great enough, and that the present-day story tended to dominate, especially at the end. However, others thought that since the group had intended to point towards a modern-day parallel, this was acceptable, and proved that they had been successful in this. Other feedback the group received was

- the style was clearly appropriate to Greek theatre, especially in its use of the three art forms

- not all of the performers were equally able in all three art forms, although all had tried to incorporate dance, drama and music

Central image from *Pandora's Box*, showing the proxemics of the scene.

- the storyline was appropriate to the audience, which was composed largely of teenagers and parents
- the piece was engaging, and held the audience's interest as there was plenty of contrast and variety in the structure.

The Written Commentary

In addition to the assessment of the community piece in this unit, you must also produce a written commentary. This should discuss all four practical pieces and be around 3000 words in total.

You will have to use examples from each of the pieces equally and demonstrate your ability to use technical language appropriately.

→ How to structure the written commentary

The commentary as a whole should be structured in two sections. Section 1 should discuss the three short pieces and Section 2 should discuss the community piece.

■ Section 1 – Discussion of the three short pieces in individual art forms

This section should follow the structure of the performance process: improvising, rehearsing, performing.

Improvising

This should take examples from the three short pieces to show

- the way in which the elements of dance, drama and music have been used to create performance
- how you have created and refined your performance ideas
- any creative links between the three art forms that have emerged during the work
- links between the structure and purpose of the devised pieces.

Rehearsing

This should take examples from the three short pieces to show

- how you rehearsed the performance work
- any issues of pacing, timing, balance, transitions, structure
- creative refinements made to pieces in the light of rehearsal.

Performing

This should take examples from the three short pieces to show

- the intention of each piece and whether you achieved it
- the performance context for each piece
- performance issues that arose and how they were dealt with
- the reaction of the audience, during and after the performance.

■ Section 2 – Creating the community performance piece

This section should cover the following areas:

- the style and intention of the community piece
- the performance venue for the community piece
- links between the three art forms in the community piece.

This section should also contain an evaluation of the success of the process and performance in terms of your performance intention, and a discussion of how the art forms were integrated.

UNIT 2
Performance Contexts 1

→ Why study a practitioner?

In this unit, the focus is on studying a piece of dance, drama or music in detail. The reason for doing this is to draw out the most important approaches used, trends followed and influences on the practitioner who devised the piece. There are three lists in the A-level specification, and in the examination you will have to answer questions on the work of two practitioners, each from a separate list. You are not allowed to take copies of the pieces into the examination, so be prepared to learn them by heart! In the case of dance and music, this could involve learning short examples in notation to quote in the examination

→ What's in a work?

For the majority of practitioners, looking at one of their best known pieces gives a good insight into their style. Whilst you have complete freedom to choose any work by that practitioner, it is important to select something that reveals his or her characteristic fingerprints. These include

- The way that structure and form are used
- How the elements of the performing arts work in the piece
- Stylistic influences that can be seen in the work
- The cultural, social and historical context
- Performance techniques required to perform the piece.

The practitioners set for this paper are

Section A
- Matthew Bourne
- Shobana Jeyasingh
- Lloyd Newson

Section B
- Caryl Churchill
- Athol Fugard
- John Godber

Section C
- John Adams
- The Beatles (at least **four** contrasting songs should be studied)
- George Gershwin (at least **four** contrasting songs should be studied).

Dance Practitioners

Matthew Bourne (born 1960)

Matthew Bourne has made dance accessible to a wider audience by taking existing musical scores of well known ballets and updating them to make them relevant for a modern audience. His work is performed around the world to an ever-growing fan base and his is the only dance company in Britain touring commercially without needing funding support. He is well known for his reworking of *Swan Lake* (1995), which became the longest-running ballet in London's West End and also on Broadway. The swans are played by male dancers in iconic feathered costumes with trademark dark eye make-up and stripe as in the photograph below.

Matthew Bourne's *Swan Lake*

→ Background and context

Matthew Bourne was born in Walthamstow, London in 1960. At the age of 22 he started his dance training at the Laban Centre, where he gained a BA (Hons) in Dance/Theatre. He spent a year performing in Transitions, Laban's dance company, and then went on to form Adventures in Motion Pictures (AMP) in 1987, followed by New Adventures in 2002. Bourne has been the subject of several documentaries including *The South Bank Show* (1997) and the Channel 4 documentary *Bourne to Dance*. He also presented Channel 4's *Dance 4* series.

Bourne's work is fun and entertaining. His love of American musicals is obvious in his use of lavish sets, imaginative lighting, carefully designed costumes and clever choreography. He has been influenced by a wide range of choreographers including Sir Frederick Ashton, Isadora Duncan and Busby Berkeley. It is no surprise that Bourne's recent work involves choreography for musical productions such as *Showboat* (1991), *Oliver* (1994), *South Pacific* (2001), *My Fair Lady* (2001) and *Mary Poppins* (2004).

He also created *Play Without Words* for the Royal National Theatre's Transformations Season in 2002. This was based on Harold Pinter's *The Servant* and was a breakaway from the reworking of classical ballets. Bourne has won many awards for his work including an Olivier Award for Best Theatre Choreographer for *Mary Poppins* and an OBE in 2001 for Services to Dance.

→ Bourne's use of music

One of Bourne's characteristic approaches is to take an existing ballet and rework it whilst using the original musical score. He has done this with several well known ballets, sometimes changing the title of the original ballet completely as with Taglioni's 1932 ballet *La Sylphide*, which he renamed *Highland Fling* (1994). He later used the same approach with Bizet's 1875 opera *Carmen*, which he changed to *The Car Man* (2000). In the case of one of his best known pieces, *Swan Lake*, he retained the original title for his own 1995 production, just as he did two years later with Prokofiev's 1945 score of *Cinderella*.

Bourne acknowledges his lack of formal training in music and studies the music through repeated listening to it. He uses the time signature, tempo and phrasing to create the dances and uses dancer's counts.

→ Setting in time and space

Not only does Bourne often change the title of the original ballet, he also changes the setting. He reworked Massine's *La Boutique Fantastique* (1919) into *Boutique* (1995) and set it in a shop in Carnaby Street, London in the 1960s. In *Cinderella* (1997), Bourne chose the unexpected time period of the Blitz in London, which is poignant since Prokofiev wrote his musical score during the Second World War. Similarly, the Jive and the Lindy Hop dances were inserted into *Cinderella* as they were well known social dances of the 1940s.

'I would never start from scratch. By the time I get to rehearsal, I would know the music inside out. I would have the story written out scene by scene. Details of the characters would be written out and I would have a lot of research material planned out ...films I would want the dancers to see, places for them to go, etc. The movement is the last thing that happens. I need dancers to get a feel for what we are doing. The dance is the last thing that happens.'
Matthew Bourne

→ Bourne's working process

Bourne's approach is to give an idea to his dancers and then ask them to create their own material. A considerable amount of research is carried out before the performance process begins. For example, when his company was preparing *Cinderella*, each dancer was encouraged to create a personal history for their character. Lynn Seymour, who played Sybil (the Stepmother), watched Joan Crawford movies to help her in the task. Her character also bears some resemblance to Cruella de Vil in *101 Dalmations*.

The style of dance may be ballet, contemporary or social dance, generally mixed with a clear narrative and strong characterisation. This is one of the reasons why Matthew Bourne's works are usually classified in the genre of dance theatre rather than ballet or contemporary dance. There is a lot of gesture, pedestrian movement and humour. There are references to other works from dance history and to other choreographers such as Frederick Ashton, Balanchine, Bournonville, Isadora Duncan and MacMillan. For example, in *Boutique*, the intertwining arms in the pas de deux for the Young Man and Barbie are reminiscent of movements in the ribbon pas de deux for Colas and Lise in Ashton's *La Fille Mal Gardée* (1960).

→ Chronology of some main works

Bourne's work as a choreographer is extensive and varied and covers theatre, television and film. Works marked with an asterisk are available on video or DVD.

1988 *Spitfire*	**1992** *Nutcracker! **	**1995** *Swan Lake **
1989 *The Infernal Gallop*	**1993** *Drip – a Narcissistic*	**1997** *Cinderella*
1991 *Town and Country*	*Love Story*	**2000** *The Car Man **
1992 *Deadly Serious*	**1993** *Late Flowering Lust **	**2002** *Play Without Words*
1992 *The Percys of Fitzrovia*	**1994** *Highland Fling*	**2005** *Edward Scissorhands*

→ Fingerprints of Matthew Bourne's style

☑ Bourne is eclectic in his approach to using different styles of dance such as ballet, contemporary and social dance.

☑ His works are popular and strongly influenced by musical theatre and Hollywood musicals with their witty humour and large ensemble numbers. His sets and costumes are lavish and memorable. Bourne believes in entertaining the audience and reaching as wide and diverse an audience as possible.

☑ He uses past ballets and reworks them. In this way he can be seen as a post-modern practitioner as he takes from the past and uses the material to create a meaning relevant for a contemporary audience.

☑ Collaboration is key in his working process. This is evident in his working relationships with designers, composers and technical directors. The dancers have great input into the choreography and characterisation.

☑ He often uses an existing musical score and may adapt it or leave it very close to the original. Sometimes he uses music in an ironic manner to state a point. He uses dancer's counts when choreographing rather than rhythms from the score.

→ Case study 1: *Nutcracker!* (1992)

■ Background

Bourne was invited by Martin Duncan and Nicholas Payne of Opera North to choreograph Tchaikovsky's ballet *The Nutcracker* for a centenary celebration of the work at the Edinburgh International Festival in August 1992. Bourne's *Nutcracker!* was revived by Adventures in Motion Pictures for Christmas in 1993 and 1994 at Sadler's Wells Theatre, London and then by New Adventures in 2002 at the Churchill Theatre, Bromley. The 2002 version is the one recorded on the DVD.

Tchaikovsky's ballet (1892) was based on Hoffman's tale *The Nutcracker and the Mouse King* (1816). Bourne worked on a scenario with Martin Duncan to create a new version of the story. When Bourne was asked to choreograph *The Nutcracker*, Adventures in Motion Pictures had six dancers in the company. This number had to be expanded to eighteen dancers and an additional four actors to provide a big enough cast for *Nutcracker!*

■ Structure

Opening

Bourne made a number of changes to the original ballet. The opening act was originally set in Silberhaus' wealthy home at Christmas time. Bourne wanted to show the dark undertones of Hoffmann's tale and decided to set Act 1 in an orphanage. The influence of the stories of Charles Dickens in such works as *Oliver Twist*, *Nicholas Nickleby* and *A Christmas Carol* can be seen in the drab, austere Victorian setting of Dr Dross' Orphanage for Waifs and Strays.

The set, costumes and lighting show the poverty of the orphans and emphasise the joy they express at the sight of colourful paper hats, which offer some relief from the black and grey that otherwise surround them. The Christmas Tree, rather than being covered with sumptuous decorations, is little more than a leafless twig. The difference in social class and financial status is further highlighted through the contrast between the dull, grey costumes of the orphans and the smart outfits of Matron and Dr Dross (who run the orphanage) and the rich cloth used in the costumes of their two spoilt children, Fritz and Sugar.

The lighting is bright in the opening act and helps to emphasise the contrasts in the set design, for example, in the chequerboard floor with its black and white tiles. The monochrome look of Act 1 is reminiscent of the black and white opening of the 1939 film of *The Wizard of Oz*. The influence of Isadora Duncan can be seen in the scarf dance in Act 1 when the orphans are performing alongside Matron for the Governors.

Christmas is a short-lived affair. After the Governors have departed and the dancing is over, the tree is thrown out of the window by Dr Dross, the presents are locked in a cupboard and the children have to remove the decorations before they go to bed. Clara goes to the cupboard to find her nutcracker doll and here the fantasy begins. It has grown into a life-size man although somewhat robotic and jerky in his movements. The Revolt is led by the Nutcracker, who cracks open the walls of the orphanage so that the orphans can escape.

The Frozen Lake

The audience is transported to the Frozen Lake, peopled with skaters. The characters in the real world of the orphanage each have a counterpart in the fantasy world of the lake and Sweetieland. Many become ice-skaters on the Frozen Lake and central figures have new named characters. Fritz becomes Prince Bon Bon, Sugar becomes Princess Sugar, Matron is now Queen Candy and Dr Dross is King Sherbert. The Nutcracker now has fluid movements and can skate.

References are made to Sonja Henie, who appeared as an ice-skater in films such as *Second Fiddle*. The skaters' fur-edged skirts are based on her outfits and Princess Sugar uses similar charms and smiles to entrap the Nutcracker. The choreography reflects a careful study of skating formations, pathways and steps and is coupled with the use of gesture such as holding the skirts and shaking them to make it look as if the skaters are travelling around the lake in the wind. When Princess Sugar is held up, this is a clear reference to Ashton's *Les Patineurs*.

Clara's friends from the orphanage become the two Cupids, still wearing their glasses but dressed in blue and white striped pyjamas. Clara does not have a new persona or a new name in the fantasy world but she does begin her journey from adolescent to young woman, embarking on a path of sexual discovery.

'The Frozen Lake' from *Nutcracker!*

The Road to Sweetieland

The Road to Sweetieland has similarities with Dorothy's journey along the Yellow Brick Road in *The Wizard of Oz*. Clara sits under a signpost not knowing which way to go. Her hands are held in prayer and this is answered when the two Cupids fly by on a feather. They produce a dress for her similar in style to Dorothy's in *The Wizard of Oz*. After a short trio they all creep off in a stealthy manner holding hands in a line reminiscent of *Coppelia*. The steps are quite melodramatic and can often be seen in silent movies and pantomimes when characters are trying to creep from one place to another without being seen.

Sweetieland

In Sweetieland, the audience is presented with a huge pink mouth, which is the entrance to the club. This is carefully guarded by a bouncer who is dressed as a humbug, the costume large and emphasising the powerful build of the bouncer. Bouncers are renowned for being difficult about letting guests into clubs, often seem disagreeable and rude, and rarely change their minds about allowing someone past them. The Humbug seems to be the correct sweet for displaying these character traits.

In Act 2, the orphan who was smoking out of the window becomes the drug-taking Knickerbocker Glory in Sweetieland. His movements are slow and snakelike, highlighting how he has charm over the innocent. He has a cigarette-holder and smoke seductively circles his body and Clara's. The movement here is reminiscent of the tango from Ashton's *Façade* (1931), in which a gigolo similarly seduces a girl. Clara's other friends become the Marshmallow Girls, the Liquorice Allsorts and the Gobstoppers.

'The Wedding Cake' from *Nutcracker!*

Each of these short dances is a divertissement – a dance intended to entertain its audience. They are diversions from the narrative and use a variety of dance styles.

Princess Sugar has won over the Nutcracker and prepares for their wedding. This begins with a large wedding cake on which dancers sit and kneel and perform a licking dance. Images of greed and gluttony are seen as the dancers perform exaggerated licking and eating motifs.

The wedding cake is layered and is at the centre of the licking dance. It may remind the audience of Busby Berkley, who was famous for his lavish, complicated choreographic scenes in films such as *The Gold Diggers* (1933) and *Ziegfield Girl* (1941).

Ending

The end of the story conforms to the happy ending of many Hollywood musicals when the main character returns home and is with the one she loves. Back at the orphanage, Clara throws the doll on the floor and gets into bed. Pulling back the covers, she reveals the Nutcracker, who kisses her and leads her through the window aided by bed sheets knotted together to form a rope.

Clara has been compared to Dorothy or Alice in Wonderland, going on a journey of enlightenment with temptations placed in her path. Like many fairy tales, *Nutcracker!* works on more than one level and older members of the audience will see the parallels and the sexual allegory as Clara grows from child to adult. Images of masculine potency are evident as the fantasy world takes over reality: the Nutcracker grows from a small doll to a very large man and the tree, which Dr Dross threw out of the window, grows rapidly and breaks the glass.

→ Case study 2: *The Car Man* (2000)

■ Background

The Car Man (2000) is set in a town called Harmony where, ironically, there is a distinct lack of harmonious relationships. The programme notes state that 'The action takes place over a period of nine months in a small Italian/American community' and that it is loosely based on a film entitled *The Postman Always Rings Twice* (1983) by James M Cain. Luca, a stranger, arrives from outside the town and becomes a catalyst for change in the community of mechanics and women who live there.

The 40 minute orchestration of music from Bizet's *Carmen* is by Rodion Shchedrin and was Bourne's inspiration. Terry Davies composed further music based on Bizet's *Carmen*, concentrating on the sections that Shchedrin had not used.

■ Structure

Act 1

Act 1 shows us the garage and Dino's Diner, where the mechanics and their girlfriends/boyfriends eat, drink and have fun. Dino's wife Frankie works in the diner and obviously does not love her husband. Scott Ambler (Associate Director of New Adventures) plays Dino with a strong characterisation of an unattractive,

unpleasant and ill-mannered man. There is a strong use of gesture and pedestrian movement in his creation of the role coupled with amusing facial expressions and a bloody fight scene where he is duped by his wife and then murdered.

There are clear references to the genre of film noir with a femme fatale in the role of Lana, who falls for Luca. Angelo is the character who gives an unexpected twist to the tale as he is in a heterosexual relationship with Rita but is also indulging in a passionate affair with Luca. Angelo becomes the victim in a twist at the end of Act 1 where Lana makes it look as if Angelo killed Dino.

Act 2

Act 2 takes place 6 months later in a club in a city and in the county jailhouse, which is reminiscent of *Jailhouse Rock* (1957), starring Elvis Presley. Now Angelo is in prison.

Bourne opts for a strong linear narrative with one effective use of flashback to the killing of Dino. The audience know all along that Angelo is innocent as they witnessed the murder and now they see the truth revealed to other characters on stage. Bourne uses filmic devices here and creates a strong dramatic edge to the ballet.

Angelo and Lana from *The Car Man*

■ Choreography

The choreography is exciting and there are entertaining ensemble numbers where the dancers react to the stifling heat in Harmony in a sexually aroused way. The audience know from the opening scene where the mechanics are sweating in the garage and later take a steamy shower that they are in for a bit of a romp. Bourne plays on the bisexual theme and Luca is portrayed as an opportunist who causes havoc in the small town community. The dance matches up to the power of the score and allows for dramatic expression to move on the narrative. *The Car Man* is described by Bourne as 'an auto-erotic thriller' and has all the passion, sexual playfulness and revenge of the opera *Carmen* on which it is based.

Shobana Jeyasingh (born 1957)

Shobana Jeyasingh was born in 1957 in Madras, Southern India and spent time in Malaysia and Sri Lanka. Fluent in Tamil and English, she has a BA in Shakespeare Studies and an MA in Renaissance Studies, which reflect her interest in Literature, Language and History.

Jeyasingh began learning the classical Indian dance style of bharata natyam when she was a young girl of seven and when she came to London she was excited by seeing this style of dance in new surroundings. As an adult she has lived in London and her work is a response to the cultural diversity of London in the twentieth and twenty-first century. Whilst this mix of cultural influences is central to her style, she resists the use of the word fusion to describe dance styles that coexist alongside each other or connect with each other. She claims that the idea of fusion is a limiting notion and does not account for the myriad of influences at play when an artist creates work.

'The word "fusion" makes me ill! It is so out-of-date. It presupposes two things coming together, but in my mind I don't feel that there are opposing forces – there are a million influences. What's culturally typical of a person in an age when everyone eats pizza and curry?'

Shobana Jeyasingh

➜ Stylistic development

Dance writer Sanjoy Roy splits Jeyasingh's work into three chronological phases. He calls the first phase 'Dissecting Classicism' and charts its progress from her first piece for her dance company, *Configurations* (1989). It shows the classical solo form being configured into a group piece and appears quite mathematical in its construction. Roy places three other works in this phase: *Correspondences* (1990), *Late* (1991) and *Byzantium* (1991).

The second phase Roy calls 'Journeying from Home' and includes *Making of Maps* (1992), *Romance ... with Footnotes* (1993) and *The Bird and the Wind* (1996). There is a departure from bharata natyam although it can still be seen in these works. The dance form is experimented with and manipulated to offer new perspectives. *Raid* (1995) marks a transition and deals with two broad types of movement: dance and sport. It is based on kabbadi, where two teams invade each other's territory.

The third phase is 'Inventing New Ground' and includes *Palimpsest* (1996), *Intimacies of a Third Order* (1998), *Fine Frenzy* (1999) and *Surface Tension* (2000). Pieces have a greater sense of tension and there seem to be more overlaps of style and form. Other movement sources are used, such as martial arts, and Roy points out that the style of movement is more off centre.

➜ Bharata natyam

Shobana Jeyasingh has had a solo career as a performer of bharata natyam, a dance style performed by women in temples in Southern India and based on religious devotion. The dancers were unmarried women called devadasis, the teachers being known as nattuvanars. The region most associated with this dance form is Tamil Nadu. There is a strong link between the sculptures found in the temples and the shapes portrayed by the dancers in their distinctive costumes.

There are three main components of bharata natyam: nritta, which are the pure dance sequences using rhythmic footwork and hand gestures, nritya, which are face and limb movements used for expression, and natya, which relate to the dramatic telling of a story or representing a theme. The music consists of lyrics and rhythmic constructs. The basic dance steps (adavus) are learned first and are combined into jatis, which are performed to the beating of a wooden block with a stick. The training lasts traditionally for about seven years and the first performance given by the dancer is called the Arangetram, which is like a graduation. The musical compositions by the four brothers of the Thanjavur Quartet (disciples of Muthuswami Dikshitar in the nineteenth century) form most of the repertoire today although new dances are still being added.

Bharata natyam emphasises the importance of shape and gesture.

■ Hand gestures

Mudras (hand gestures) play a very significant role in bharata natyam. There are two types of hand gesture: asamyukta hastah, performed using one hand, either left or right, and samyukta hastah, using both hands. There are 28 single and 24 united hand gestures. There are special hand gestures to denote deities such as Brahman, Vishnu and Shiva; for the different castes such as Brahmana; for different relations such as father or daughter, as well as for the planets, rivers and animals. This is to name but a few. Each mudra has a name in Sanskrit which the dancer learns much as a ballet student learns the French terminology which forms the vocabulary of classical ballet.

→ Fingerprints of Shobana Jeyasingh's style

☑ A style that reflects the diversity of contemporary London: use of contemporary dance and bhararat natyam; use of nritta as a basis for the piece; use of mudras and other forms such as kabbadi and chau.

☑ Non-narrative, multi-layered choreography, and compositional devices such as mirroring, unison, canon, repetition, fragmentation, counterpoint, floor work, contact work, deep knee bends, mixture of both straight back and fluid torso.

☑ Strong relationship between dance and music and close working relationship with composers such as Michael Nyman, Kevin Volans, Glyn Perrin, Alistair MacDonald and Scanner.

☑ Close collaboration with set, lighting and costume designers.

☑ There are recurring themes of migration, identity and crossing boundaries/journeying.

→ Case study: *Surface Tension* (2000)

Choreographer: Shobana Jeyasingh
Music composed by Kevin Volans
Harpsichord by Carole Cerasi
Electronics by Jurgen Simpson
Lighting designed by Lucy Carter
Costumes designed by Ursula Bombshell
Dancers on the DVD: Ameeta Daya, Sowmya Gopalan, Mavin Khoo, Jiva Parthipan, Jasmine Simhalan, Chitra Srishailan

The 2005 DVD of a performance of *Surface Tension* also includes a discussion of various aspects of the work by Shobana Jeyasingh and interviews with some of the collaborators, such as Kevin Volans, who discusses the music. The 27 minute piece is broken down into short chapters which can be analysed and discussed individually.

■ Background

The piece is based on the idea of 'surface' and how we perceive things. Jeyasingh says in her commentary on the DVD that she has always loved Shakespeare's *The Tempest* and that one line stood out to her, where Miranda is being introduced to a young man by her elderly father. Miranda lives on an isolated island and is unaccustomed to seeing young men. Her words on first seeing Ferdinand are: 'There's nothing ill can dwell in such a temple'.

Jeyasingh points out that now, in contrast to Miranda's way of looking at the surface of someone, we tend to be more cynical and do not trust what we see. She recalls the pejorative words connected with the idea of surface, such as 'superficial'. However, dance presents the surface and in her work, which does not follow a linear narrative, the audience have to trust their eyes because the meaning is in what they see.

■ Choreography

Jeyasingh's approach to the choreography was to work with the dancers to find a movement vocabulary for the piece. In classical ballet and bharata natyam, the vocabulary is set and learned before a piece is choreographed. In both dance styles, there is a repertoire of work which the dancers learn and perform. In contemporary dance, however, a new vocabulary is created for each new piece. There are some movements or aspects of other dance styles in the work but they are manipulated and used in a different way from how they were used originally. For example, there is a part of *Surface Tension* where Jeyasingh made up what she calls 'sentences' and 'paragraphs' with a 'full stop' at the end of each. The dancer can be seen bent over with legs straight, feet parallel in second position, with the right hand on the waist and the elbow angular, and the left arm placed straight down with the hand in a mudra. Jeyasingh points out that this is an oblique reference to bharata natyam as the mudra is not being used in the traditional way: it is not facing front. This position is repeated and held at the end of each short section of movement and is therefore like a full stop.

Another part was created by Jeyasingh giving the dancers a phrase to manipulate. Each dancer was asked to use the numbers in their date of birth (in order) to introduce pauses into the phrase. After some experimentation, it was decided that all zeros in the dates should be translated into tens. Depending on the numbers in the birth date, the phrase would be performed in a variety of ways that could look free flowing or fractured. The breaking up of the phrase offered the dancers choices about the pathways they followed and they had different entrances.

Sometimes classical movements are used but in a different way. In a part which Jeyasingh refers to as the 'classical quartet', classical movements are used but rather than being performed facing front, they are performed in profile. In addition to this change, instead of travelling from upstage to downstage, dancers travel from stage left to stage right.

In the harpsichord solo, Jeyasingh experiments with the idea of transitions. There are few transitions in bharara natyam as the movement is created in blocks. The transitions are short and attention is not drawn to them. However, in *Surface Tension*, there are slow movements based on these transitions whose graceful elegance and sustained control are reminiscent of t'ai chi. In contrast to this slow section, Chitra's solo was choreographed in response to the music, which is extremely fast in this section. Jeyasingh has a close working relationship with Chitra and knows her areas of expertise. Chitra is trained in both bharata natyam and kathak styles of Indian dance and is very fast and energetic.

The last section of the piece is a recapitulation of material seen previously in the other two sections. There is a sense of mirroring as two groups work upstage right and downstage left and later repeat each other's material.

■ Music

The starting point for the dance was not an image but an idea about surface. The composer with whom Jeyasingh worked, Kevin Volans, was also preoccupied with the idea of surface and the difference between superficiality and profundity. His music consists of complex rhythms which are to some extent inspired by the elaborate gestures and the complicated hand and feet patterns in Jeyasingh's work. On the DVD, he discusses his composition and you can see the musical score displaying the variety of rhythms he has woven into it. The first section is full of energy and has many changes of rhythm and cross rhythms. The second section has spaces/silences within the music while the third section was originally a long chant which he later interspersed with pauses, 'thinning and thickening it to give it more texture'. Jeyasingh states that sometimes the dance is a response to the emotion in the music; at other times it exists in parallel with the music.

■ Lighting

Jeyasingh worked in collaboration with the lighting designer Lucy Carter. There are practical concerns when lighting a dance piece as the lighting must show the dance and the dancers must be able to see where they are going. The lighting for *Surface Tension* adds atmosphere, changes the mood and has been called 'tropical' by some critics. It illuminates the movement and in the third section takes on a more powerful role when it changes to highlight either two dancers or two groups of dancers pulling away from each other. Jeyasingh calls these moments 'stretch moments'. The lighting helps the audience to dwell on them and appreciate their geometric form.

■ Costumes

The costume design, by Ursula Bombshell, was influenced by Jeyasingh's desire to show emotion. Red was chosen as the predominant colour and there is also blue and purple. The cut and shape of the costume is varied from dancer to dancer so that there is a sense of community without complete uniformity. Jeyasingh recognises that the dancer must be able to dance freely in the costume as well as the costume adding something to the piece.

■ Use of film

As the piece was based on the idea of surface, Jeyasingh wanted to include film in the performance. Two films by Richard Coldman show a dancer performing phrases from the stage choreography. The dancers are dressed in white and the lighting is of necessity low in order for the image to be seen. There are dancers on stage during the second film, but none during the first. The screen is two-dimensional whereas the stage is a three-dimensional area. As a society we take in a lot of information from the two-dimensional screen and Jeyasingh wanted to show a dancing body on the screen.

Lloyd Newson (born 1957)

Lloyd Newson has been an influential choreographer and performer in Britain since the early 1980s. He is well known for his extreme views, his innovative style and his desire to break boundaries. His company is DV8 Physical Theatre and their artistic policy states that their work is 'about taking risks aesthetically and physically, about breaking down the barriers between dance, theatre and personal politics and, above all, communicating ideas and feelings clearly and unpretentiously'.

Newson places a great deal of emphasis on the process and encourages his performers to take risks during rehearsals, which are very private affairs. A new vocabulary of movement is created for each new piece and Newson uses whichever art forms are necessary for the piece – he has pushed these to include, for example, football, rope climbing and clowning. 'DV8' stands for 'Dance and Video 8' and the company retains its original commitment to dance and film. Several works are available on video and DVD.

→ Background and context

Lloyd Newson was born in New Zealand in 1957 and studied Psychology at the University of Melbourne in Australia before becoming involved in dance. He travelled to London on a one-year scholarship at London Contemporary Dance School and then worked as a dancer with Extemporary Dance Theatre from 1981 to 1985. In 1986, DV8 Physical Theatre was founded.

'When we formed the company in 1986 in Europe, nobody that I knew called themselves a physical theatre company. Within two years there were schools in physical theatre in Britain. I thought "I have a hit a – term that is appropriate and a lot of people want to throw themselves into". Then I got very upset seeing all these physical theatre companies emerging who for me weren't physically trained, and I thought that this has lowered the tone of this term, and I don't want to be associated with that term.'

Lloyd Newson

There are, however, many elements of physical theatre in Newson's work and some critics find it hard to see it as dance. A close look at some of the pieces certainly reveals a theatrical side and moments of high drama. Each piece has something new to say, so it follows that each piece should be considered in its own right although some common traits can be detected.

→ Stylistic development

Newson's work is concerned more with content than with the dance style being used. The movement vocabulary is intended to communicate a meaning and not merely to look aesthetic. It is often based on observation of behaviour of people in the real world. This knowledge is brought back to the studio and used to create movement. When working on *Enter Achilles*, Newson asked two heterosexual male dancers to walk along the road hand in hand to see how it felt. When they came back to the studio they had to translate the tension they felt into movement and show how they felt uncomfortable.

Unlike the choreographer of a classical ballet, where each movement is taken from a set repertoire and a set ballet language, Newson endeavours to make a new language for each piece. He may ask the dancer to sing and act as well as move. Newson's work often includes speech, particularly when the choreographer is of the opinion that dance cannot be used to express certain meanings. This can be seen, for example, in the scene in *Strange Fish* where Nigel talks incessantly to fill the void and demonstrate to himself that he is not lonely, while the other dancers show through their movements that they are evading him at all costs, predominantly turning their backs on him and running away.

Newson's dancers are encouraged to experiment and bring movement to the creation of the piece, although he admits that he is the director and the final decision is his. The company is project based and does not have a stage repertoire. That is, DV8 does not remount past works apart from on film, and then the film is significantly different from the stage version and may have a different cast.

→ Chronology of main works

The following is a DV8 chronology according to the programme notes for *The Cost of Living* (2000–2003), although the first work is listed as being created before the company was founded.

1985	*Bein' a Part, Lonely Art*	2005	*Just for Show*
1986	*My Sex, Our Dance*	2008	*To Be Straight with You*
1987	*My Body, Your Body; Deep End; eLeMeN t(h)ree sex*		

Films of DV8's work have been produced as follows:

1988	*Dead Dreams of Monochrome Men*
1990	*If Only ...*
1992	*Strange Fish*
1993	*MSM*
1995	*Enter Achilles*
1997	*Bound to Please*
1997–98	*Enter Achilles* (revival tours)
1999	*The Happiest Day of My Life*
2000– 2003	*The Cost of Living*
2003	*Living Costs* (commissioned by Tate Modern)

1989	*Dead Dreams of Monochrome Men*
1992	*Strange Fish*
1995	*Enter Achilles*
2004	*The Cost of Living*

The film versions are not exactly the same as the stage versions; they are films in their own right. In an interview in the *Sunday Telegraph* in May 2005, Newson outlined how he feels about making films of his pieces: 'It's interesting what translates well into film. Quite often you see pieces that are just dead.'

→ Fingerprints of Lloyd Newson's style

- ☑ Newson's work breaks boundaries, both physical and emotional.
- ☑ Newson's work takes physical risks and uses acrobatics.
- ☑ Newson auditions and assembles dancers when he is about to start a new work, when he has something to say. He therefore creates a new movement vocabulary for each piece and this deals with taboo subjects, involving personal and political issues.
- ☑ He uses unusual sets which are sometimes custom built; he transfers some works into films which are quite different from the original stage productions; he uses multimedia on stage along with speech.
- ☑ Much of his work uses pedestrian movement. Unison is used to make a point rather than to present an aesthetic image.
- ☑ Draws on an eclectic range of styles and approaches to create his own distinctive style.

→ Case study 1: *Enter Achilles* (1995)

Enter Achilles

The film of *Enter Achilles* is set in a pub called 'The Plough' somewhere in London. We see a red double-decker bus go up the busy street where the pub is situated. The action takes place in and around the pub, using locations such as the roof and yard and a path by a canal or river.

■ Structure

This piece starts with a scene showing male dancers moving in slow motion, first clothed and then with bare upper torso. The men resemble sportsmen or spectators at a sports event in the way they are cheering, jeering, punching their arms upwards and looking aggressive and intimidating. There are occasional flashes of light as if from a camera recording the spectacle.

Surprisingly, the men look through a window and we see a man in bed, waking up with a sudden start, perhaps from a nightmare. He has a plastic blow-up doll which he appears to be using for a sexual purpose but seems to be romantically involved with it as his gestures are gentle and loving. Even when a girlfriend leaves a message on his answerphone to say that she has been waiting for him outside a cinema, he drowns out her voice by turning up his music. Clearly he prefers an inanimate object to the real thing. The movement in the scene is disturbing and prepares the audience for a dance piece which questions male behaviour and male attitudes to homosexuality.

There is a violent undertone that runs through the piece and rears its ugly head when the men clash over an issue. Towards the end of the film, the plastic doll is 'raped' and slashed with a broken bottle in order to hurt the man who owns it.

■ Choreography and music

The choreography is dynamic and challenging. In the pub scenes the men go through various stages of a night of drinking. They fall to the ground, tumble over each other all the while managing to hold on to a pint glass of beer. With incredible dexterity, they balance the glass so that little beer is spilt in the opening scenes. Themes of loneliness and isolation emerge as we witness what happens to the outsider, how the strongest man bullies the others and how the behaviour of the pack and its leader dictates the lives of the men in the pub. They are easily threatened by newcomers who do not fit in with their social mores such as drinking beer (the outsider drinks red wine) and playing football, darts and billiards.

Newson rarely uses unison and certainly not to create movement which is pleasing to the eye. Here, though, he shows the men walking in the same way, in time with each other. Acrobatic movements and daring jumps, rolls and falls are employed in a fast-tempo sequence which uses the surfaces available in the pub, such as the bar and the billiard table, to create an exhilarating show of masculine bravado. This is contrasted later with scenes of humiliation such as the shaving of one man by the side of the canal and pulling down each other's trousers and underwear. It seems the men will stop at nothing to taunt each other and prove their own masculinity – whatever that is. There are many allusions through the movement to sexual acts, performed in a crude and aggressive manner, including a mimed rape.

The outsider, who is played by Juan Kruz de Garaio Esnaola, is picked on by the other men. It appears that he is going to receive a beating when suddenly he starts to whirl around in an astonishing and quite humorous way whilst stripping off his outer layer of clothing and revealing a Superman outfit. His movement is always in contrast to the other men's as he is sinuous and smooth with one movement flowing into the next. He dances to *Staying Alive* in a camp way, and offers some comic relief for the audience.

The soundtrack for the film is a mixture of music styles and keeps the pace quite upbeat.

→ Case study 2: *The Cost of Living* (2000)

The set is a large sloping 'grass' hill reminding the audience of a park where people meet and have relationships of different types. However, in the film (2004), the set becomes a seaside location: Cromer on the Norfolk coast. A number of characters also differ in the film. It is nearing the end of the season and the opening scene is a clown show on a pier. We witness a choreographed routine of the clowns' heads wearing bright-red curly wigs. The movements are comical and at times ridiculous as the clowns lean their heads back and shake their wigs to the accompaniment of Eddie's angry monologue.

■ Characters

Eddie is a disaffected clown who takes off his wig and mask following an outburst of rage but being a professional, he continues with the dance routine from the neck upwards. He abuses the audience and scolds them for being late, eventually calling off the show and telling the other clowns to take a break. Each clown comes out of his box to reveal the rest of his body and then walks off, apart from the last clown, David Toole, who shocks the audience by revealing that he has no legs and therefore has to transport himself using his arms and hands. Thus from the outset of this piece, the audience are made to question the role of the disabled dancer and the function of dance in the modern world. They are forced to face up to their prejudices and reassess their attitudes towards the place of others in society.

Newson makes his audience question not only the role of the body in dance, but also the age of the body. His dancers do not necessarily conform to the stereotypical age of a professional dancer in the classical ballet world. For example, Diana Payne-Myers appeared, aged 63, in *Strange Fish* (1992), as well as in the stage version of *The Cost of Living* in 2000.

In the stage version, Diana Payne-Myers introduces herself to the audience, stating her age (71) and admitting to having had several young lovers. Her age is clear from her skin, which is exposed as she is wearing a bathing outfit. As a society we question whether it is acceptable for older, post-menopausal women to have sexual relationships with virile young men.

Diana Payne-Myers and David Toole are not the only performers to make us question our values, beliefs and attitudes. Lawrence Goldhuber is fat, weighing 330 lb, and one female dancer is unusually tall. Another male steps up to the line and tells the audience that he has AIDS. In this way, the performers have not hidden away and put on a mask. We see them for what they are on the surface and we learn a little about their lives.

This piece challenges not only our preconceptions about society but also our expectations of a dance piece. The body shapes and heights are not uniform and there is a mixture of able-bodied and disabled dancers in the cast. However, David Toole's range of movement surely makes us question the use of the label 'disabled'. Newson uses trained dancers and performers and expects a great deal of them, as he wants them to bring their skills and experiences to the collaborative process. David Toole is no exception to this rule.

'This piece is about what we think we are, and what we think we ought to be. We camouflage ourselves in conformity, put on a mask, smile, hide and pretend, so we too are invited. But what happens to those who don't get invited, who aren't perfect, who can't pretend?'

Lloyd Newson talking about *The Cost of Living*

David Toole and the company
in *The Cost of Living*

'What I've had to find over the years, was ways I could create structures, and this is the collaborative nature, where I would be able to explore and maybe exploit their movement, and facilitate what their body says, their history. Every person you see has a history that they are walking with, if you are observant enough. For me I want to bring in that history and not do what dance often does and unify everybody and say everybody is the same.'

Lloyd Newson talking about *The Cost of Living*

■ Structure (2004 film version)

1 Clowns on the pier. We meet Eddie Kay (Scottish accent) and David Toole (disabled, no legs).
2 Girls dancing on the lawn outside and Eddie and David's flat – sets up contrasts between the girls' long legs and strong muscular leg movements and David's lack of legs but use of strong arms.
3 David and Eddie put on make-up in a shared mirror as if preparing to perform.
4 Wheels.
5 Queue to get in the club – 'If I don't have a job, I'm nothing'.
6 Dancing in the club – a duet with Eddie Kay and Rowan Thorpe and a lot of head pecking.
7 David's direct address to camera/monologue in the club Part 1.
8 Eddie meets Vivien Wood.
9 David's monologue Part 2 – 'It's small but it's peachy'.
10 Vivien, Eddie and David.

11   In front of the garages, Rowan Thorpe dances to a Cher track and Katreena Oates shows off her skills with a hula hoop.
12   David on the lawn being interviewed by a male voice and a camera – intimidating, overpowering with very personal questions.
13   Unison ensemble piece on the lawn which highlights the strength of David's movements.
14   Rowan hula hoops down a ramp and tries to court Katreena.
15   David on wheels travelling fast down a hill with Eddie in control and causing havoc at the bus stop.
16   Ballet class – David performs duet on the floor with female dancer.
17   David, Eddie and Vivien walk to bus shelter
18   The beach at night – three men enter the toilets. Chest to calf shots, then hands but no faces, which make the scene very sinister. Then the dancers are seen from the back and their faces are shown in the half-light. Urinals and the sound of running water. Eddie greets Tom in a threatening manner.
19   Daytime on the pier and a gang of lads are watching Katreena perform. The lads become menacing but Katreena walks off holding hands with Rowan.
20   David and Eddie are on deckchairs on the beach – 'Let's get outta here. D'ya wanna lift mate?' Extraordinary image of Eddie walking along the beach with David on his back.

Each dancer finds his or her place; for some this means moving on. In the programme notes for *The Cost of Living* the piece is summarised as follows:

'DV8 presents a piece about perfection and pretence; about how society measures individuals and how we, in turn, value ourselves ... the cost of living.'

From *To Be Straight with You*, 2008

Drama Practitioners

Caryl Churchill (born 1938)

Caryl Churchill, Britain's most successful living female playwright, was born in London in 1938. She wrote plays for BBC radio in the 1960s, after studying English at Oxford University. Her first professionally produced play, *Ants,* was written shortly after she had completed her degree. She intended it for TV, but her agent saw its real potential as a radio play, and it was subsequently broadcast by the BBC. Churchill wrote another seven plays for BBC radio. During the 60s and early 70s she also wrote plays for stage and for TV.

Her style varies, but her best-known plays are often Brechtian in the way they represent characters and settings. Her work tends to explore how language is used to communicate and plotlines are focused on characters struggling to achieve success in a rapidly changing society.

Churchill has collaborated with particular theatre companies to create some of her major plays. She was appointed Resident Dramatist at the Royal Court Theatre in 1974–75, which led to significant collaboration with the feminist group Monstrous Regiment and Max Stafford-Clark's Joint Stock, where discussion and workshopping were an important part of the process. Rather than simply taking the script from pages already finished by the playwright, the actors were able to develop the play with the director and playwright in rehearsal.

Such collaborative methods are taken for granted today but at the time they were very new. Censorship of stage plays had ended only eight years earlier, in 1968, so the freedom to construct a play without having to obtain government approval before performing to the public was new also. Churchill's experience of that freedom (after ten years of writing under the censor) and collaboration with socially committed directors and actors gave much impetus to the next decade of her work.

→ Stylistic trends in mature works

Churchill's work is often perplexing for an audience, but this reflects the post-modern world views that have influenced her writing.

She takes risks with unconventional structures to explore current issues. As a playwright she does not explain or justify her stance. This requires the audience to think for themselves to make sense of her approach. For example, the second act of *Cloud Nine* moves about a century forward in time from the first, while the characters themselves appear to have grown only a quarter of that. It appears to be an entirely different play without a clear direction until the conclusion, which powerfully links both halves of the piece.

Churchill often manipulates and breaks down both language and dramatic structure. This is most extreme in the language of *Blue Kettle* and the structure of *Cloud Nine*. She has found inspiration in collaboration with a wide range of performance practitioners, including political and feminist theatre groups, ordinary people in the community theatre that led to *Fen*, and operatic and dance experimentation with Ian Spink in *Lives of the Great Poisoners*.

Her concern with gender issues is often (but not always) present. Social values, taboos and norms are often broken, sometimes to extremes. Including and exploring cross-gender, cross-race and varied sexuality was an essential part of the working process to create *Cloud Nine*.

Caryl Churchill's work shows a powerful social commitment in the way she explores interpersonal power play, gender and social change. There is an evident political stance without a clear political allegiance, and Churchill herself rejects being categorised in this way.

'If someone says "a socialist playwright" or "a feminist playwright" that can suggest to some people something rather narrow which doesn't cover as many things as you might be thinking about.'

Caryl Churchill

There are several examples of the political dimension of her dramatic writing. Revolution in Cromwell's England is the theme in *Light Shining in Buckinghamshire* and revolution at the end of Ceaușescu's Romania in *Mad Forest* (1990). Gender relationships are at the core of *Vinegar Tom*, *Cloud Nine*, *Fen* and *Top Girls*.

→ Experimental and other work since the 1980s

Churchill's collaborative ventures extended into dance theatre in 1986, when she worked with Ian Spink on *A Mouthful of Birds*, based on the Greek work *The Bacchae* and the idea of 'exploring fruit as a way of destroying and eating, tearing something up that would detach it from pain and guilt…'. There are echoes of Val and Frank from *Fen* in this.

A Mouthful of Birds was followed by *Lives of the Great Poisoners* (1991), developed with Ian Spink's experimental company, Second Stride, and combining dance and operatic song with the historical characters of four famous poisoners, Crippen, Medea, Madame de Brinvilliers and Thomas Midgeley. Bringing together of historical figures, the key device used in *Top Girls*, is blended with other performing art forms to new effect.

The Skriker (1993) is drama but now juxtaposing ancient, metaphorical and supernatural characters with modern urban living to explore the forces which appear to taunt, tempt and drive us from deep inside our culture. The language is again experimental, almost poetic, but constantly shifting like the Skriker character himself.

In *Heart's Desire*, the first of the one-act plays in *Blue Heart*, the scene never progresses beyond a few minutes before stopping apparently randomly and resetting to the beginning and replaying a new variation of the action. At its 1997 premiere audible discontent amongst the audience almost disrupted the performance within minutes of the start of the play. Manipulation and fragmentation of language is used. At its most extreme in *Blue Kettle*, the second half of the original performance and companion to *Heart's Desire*, it suggests the failure of verbal language to communicate meaning by the replacement of words with repetitive and valueless ones. This heightens the significance of intonation, expression and physical action. The gradual disintegration of language turns English into a foreign language by degrees.

→ Fingerprints of Caryl Churchill's style

- ☑ Structural devices used to continually shift the action and so change the audience's perspective, such as nonlinear time, episodic action.

- ☑ A concern with language and attempting to get nearer 'real-life' communication, e.g. *Softcops* and *Top Girls*, or experimenting with the function of language itself, especially in later works, e.g. *Blue Heart*.

- ☑ Plotlines exploring the relative power, status, sexuality and moral/political stance of characters. Problems thrown up by 'success' in historical/political periods of rapid change.

- ☑ Questions of moral and social judgement often raised by the characters directly within the dialogue, engaging the audience to make their own judgements on the likely outcomes.

- ☑ Main characters struggling to convince themselves and others of their moral superiority.

- ☑ Exploration of the wide range of roles played by women in both historical and contemporary society in order to reflect current issues.

- ☑ Stage images that have visual impact which is more important than words, especially at some key moments in the development of the plot.

- ☑ The use of historical and allegorical characters to locate and dislocate the audience's perspective, e.g. *Top Girls*.

- ☑ Representational staging and acting style, explored to the extreme in some works, e.g. *Cloud Nine*.

- ☑ Churchill's use of dialogue often overlaps to capture the nature of real conversation, in which sentences seldom finish neatly.

1972	*Owners* (Royal Court)	1982	*Fen*
1974	*Objections to Sex and Violence*	1987	*Serious Money*
1976	*Vinegar Tom*	1991	*Lives of the Great Poisoners*
	Light Shining in Buckinghamshire		(with Orlando Gough and Ian Spink)
1978	*Softcops*	1993	*The Skriker*
	Cloud Nine	1997	*Blue Heart*
1980–82	*Top Girls*	2001	*Thyestes* (translated from Seneca)

→ Case study 1: *Light Shining in Buckinghamshire* (1976)

■ Background

Churchill was at her most exploratory in looking for new ways of creating theatre when writing this play. She and the Joint Stock director, Max Stafford-Clark, worked together to find a subject. *Light Shining in Buckinghamshire* was the result, created through three weeks of workshops with the actors, followed by nine weeks when she wrote a script, then a six-week rehearsal period. This way of working was new to British theatre in 1976, which had been freed from government censorship only eight years earlier. Churchill commented later that working with Joint Stock permanently changed her working methods.

■ Plot

The plot of the play is based on known historical events of the 1640s, but intended to reflect some of the rapid social change taking place in Britain in the late twentieth century also. The characters Claxton and Cobbe are based on known figures but are not intended to be historical representations. The king has been overthrown, and the people believe they have commonwealth, a kind of non-political communism. The Putney Debates, which led to the setting up of parliament, are represented, and differences of opinion develop about what should constitute freedom and government. Starvation ensues, new landlords are established from among the people, and the poor realise they are enslaved again – this was a false dawn.

■ Key themes

The destruction of old order and creation of new forms of authority make widespread freedom seem possible, only to be followed by the breaking of that spirit as new order imposes new restrictions leading ultimately to disillusionment. There is a clear focus on what is now often considered most characteristic of Churchill's major work: the problems generated for the individual by rapid social change, and a concern for those at the lower end of society. There is little doubt

PERFORMANCE CONTEXTS 1

UNIT 2

that she was considering the new social freedom of the 1960s followed by political difficulties in the 1970s when she wrote in 1978 of the play:

> 'For a short time … anything seemed possible, and the play shows the amazed excitement of people taking hold of their own lives, and their gradual betrayal as those who led them realised that freedom could not be had without property being destroyed … The simple "Cavaliers and Roundheads" history taught at school hides the complexity … We are told of a step forward to today's democracy but not of a revolution that didn't happen: we are told of Charles and Cromwell but not of the thousands of men and women who tried to change their lives … their voices are surprisingly close to us.'

■ Style

The basic, representational staging in this play was a new device at the time, but was established as typical of Churchill's work.

The devised roots of the play are evident in the many voices. Brechtian influences are apparent: announced titles of scenes, and the intention that they are not dependent on one another, but can be taken to stand alone. The characters are not intended to be played by the same actors each time they appear. They are intended to be a voice or attitude in that place in that moment, and the sequence of scenes builds into a montage from which the audience can construct their own interpretation of the significance of events.

The character voices can be traced through their hopes and aspirations. Star, a corn merchant, begins with hope in religious salvation in the kingdom to come, but a harsh present:

> 'Life is hard, brothers, and how will it get better?'

In Act 2 he says enclosure of land is 'to bring down the price of corn', which sounds well meaning, but in context of the starvation that is happening because of those enclosures, his words show he is becoming as detached as the old landlords. Children suffer especially. This is picked up by the audience in the montage effect of references across several scenes.

Another Brechtian feature of Churchill's complex vision is evident in this: the events in the play are not just a parallel to the present, but also a root cause of where we are today. The difficulties in grasping this dual image should provoke discussion among the audience, leading to a better understanding of the issues.

> 'The play was performed with a table and six chairs, which were used as needed in each scene. When any chairs were not used they were put on either side of the stage, and actors who were not in a scene sat at the side and watched the action. They moved the furniture themselves. Props were carefully chosen and minimal.'
>
> Caryl Churchill

→ Case study 2: *Top Girls* (1980–82)

■ Background

Top Girls is probably Churchill's most frequently studied play. It draws together a number of ideas that had preoccupied her over a period of some years. The bringing together of powerful women from history such as Dull Gret, Lady Nijo and Pope Joan to discuss their lives in a social setting originated in notes she had made more than a decade earlier. The discussion between the women from history is placed within a play about the new women of the late twentieth century who could – and did – run businesses for themselves, but without seeking to empower other women. This turns the mirror back on to the feminist movement to reflect on its achievements.

■ Plot

The plot of the play is unconventional in the way it includes characters from history in the first scene, celebrating the success of Marlene, a businesswoman in the 1980s who runs an employment agency, Top Girls. Later we see Marlene's sister Joyce, struggling to get by in poverty in rural Suffolk, and Angie, a resentful 16-year-old who appears to be her daughter. Later we discover Angie is Marlene's daughter, left behind with Joyce, enabling Marlene to focus on her career. The final scene brings the two sisters together in a family argument. The play is uncomfortably and deliberately incompletely ended with Marlene saying goodnight to Angie, who still believes she is 'aunty Marlene'.

■ Key themes

The key themes are built on issues of power and powerlessness. The play takes an oblique perspective on the rapid movement for equality for women. It focuses on the wide differences in women's roles that were evident. It shows how changes were happening unevenly, and that where women moved into the work roles traditionally taken by men, some, like Marlene, were prepared to use other women and sacrifice family life to achieve their own personal success.

■ Other stylistic elements

The Brechtian representational style reminds the audience that this is a play for judgement not for the pleasure of a story. There was no attempt to make the blonde Lindsay Duncan, who played Lady Nijo in the original production, darken her hair to appear Japanese: the purpose was to represent the character not to generate the illusion that she was really present.

Typical features of Caryl Churchill's concern with ordinary people and the way language communicates can be seen in the final scene in the dialogue, when Marlene visits Joyce in the rural countryside where they both grew up.

> **Marlene** I don't believe in class. Anyone can do anything if they've got what it takes.
> **Joyce** And if they haven't?
> **Marlene** If they're stupid, lazy or frightened, I'm not going to help them get a job, why should I?
> **Joyce** What about Angie?
> **Marlene** What about Angie?
> **Joyce** She's stupid, lazy and frightened, so what about her?

Marlene's social success makes her persuasive and convincing in her opinions, but Joyce's straightforward and caring practicality leaves the audience struggling to decide which side to take. The concern is with how stronger members of society exploit weaker ones. They discuss the prime minister of the time, Margaret Thatcher.

> **Marlene** Who's to drive it on? First woman prime minister. Terrifico. Aces. Right on. / You must admit. Certainly gets my vote.
> **Joyce** What good's first woman if it's her? I suppose you'd have liked Hitler if he was a woman. Ms Hitler. Got a lot done, Hitlerina. / Great adventures.

The sentences are broken up with '/' to direct the actors to overlap speech as real-life characters do; and Marlene's language structure is broken up with short, slangy utterances, trying to convince by force of will, not argument: 'Terrifico. Aces. Right on.' Joyce's replies are short, weighted with experience.

Asterisks in the script indicate places where the speaker is replying to something that another character has said earlier. Churchill aims constantly to construct speech that matches real-life dialogue.

> **Joyce** Aah. *Just don't go on about mum's life when you haven't been to see her for how many years. / I go and see her every week.
> **Marlene** It's up to me. *Then don't go and see her every week.

Churchill's style assumes that the audience will understand the topical references. Margaret Thatcher is identified as 'Maggie', putting the audience in the time period of the play. The effect is of a play which exists always in the present moment rather than one which views the situation from a historical perspective.

Joyce has four cleaning jobs to get by, and expects no better future for Angie even with a change of government:

> **Joyce** …I expect her children will say what a wasted life she's had. If she has children. Because nothing's changed and it won't with them in.

Lindsay Duncan as Lady Nijo with Gwen Taylor (Marlene) and Selina Cadell (Pope Joan) in the original Royal Court production of *Top Girls*

Harold Athol Fugard is the most significant and prolific South African playwright of the late twentieth and early twenty-first century, and the first to gain international recognition. He was born in Cape Province, South Africa in 1932. His father was descended from English immigrants, his mother from Dutch pioneer settler families. Underprivileged, living in a barely literate sector of mixed white society, Fugard knew poverty. He was educated in English rather than Afrikaans but speaks both. He took a course in motor mechanics but gained a scholarship to the University of Cape Town. He became strongly atheist in his views at this time: religious characters are usually portrayed as well meaning but helpless in his plays.

Fugard did not complete his degree but dropped out to travel the world working on a steamship for a year. This expanded his views, and in his own eyes, freed him from prejudice. He became more fully aware of the extreme racism in his society, but also experienced guilt and remorse, evident in his plays, notably for an incident in which as a child he had spat in the face of a black family servant. This is echoed in *Master Harold … and the Boys*, written decades later.

On his return Fugard got a job as a journalist. He chose to write in English although many of the characters in his plays would more naturally speak Afrikaans, or Xhosa. At times character voices 'translate' into English to make his multiracial work understandable to a world audience while maintaining a sense of the many languages of South Africa. He started a theatre workshop group and began to write short plays. However, it was only when Fugard worked in the Native Commissioner's Court that he experienced at first hand the gross inequality and oppressive pass laws the black races lived under. He saw what he knew few whites were aware of or concerned about, and this was his turning point.

→ Stylistic trends in mature works

Fugard dedicated himself, as a white playwright, to working with black actors to create plays to bring about change in a time of strict segregation. His plays tend to be concise, naturalistic and intended for minimal staging, set in simple spaces between a small number of characters. The intensity of the relationships drives the action, balanced sometimes by unexpected moments of ironic comedy. His earliest work is some of his most direct and engaging. *No-Good Friday* (1958) is regarded as his establishing play. The raw simplicity of the action is sudden and shocking.

Athol Fugard appeared as a character very similar to himself in his play, *Valley Song*, at the Royal Court in 1996 (here with Esmeralda Bihl as Veronica).This post-apartheid work reflects on political and personal transition: an old man's dreams for what South Africa might one day become are interwoven with the hopes of a young girl with that future already in her hands.

The success of this play, among the poor black township audience in the first instance, was due to its portrayal of the injustices suffered by dispossessed people. It projected Fugard forwards significantly. He had played Father Higgins, a well meaning but powerless white mission priest who tries to aid black families. However, when a liberal white venue invited the company to perform there, Fugard was unable to play Higgins, as the segregation rules forbade a white man to participate on stage with blacks. The actors – all working men themselves – were outraged and were set to turn down the performance, but Fugard persuaded them to play it with a black Higgins, as a political act, to bring awareness of the townships to a white audience who were ignorant of them.

Fugard's success as a playwright was established in the 1960s through his protest plays, intended to inform white South African and international communities of a political system that was powerful and intolerant. After a televised screening of *The Blood Knot* in Britain in 1967, Fugard's passport was withdrawn. In 1971, after a public petition, it was returned, enabling him to direct *Boesman and Lena* in London at the Royal Court Theatre. His public popularity with liberal whites did not give him security. *The Island* refers to the prison colony where political prisoners, including Nelson Mandela, were held. To prevent state interference, the play had to have the working title *Die Hodoshe Span,* meaning *The Carrion Fly*. This was code for a particular prison warder reputed to be persistent and ruthless in destroying the spirit of prisoners.

Not long after *The Island*, Fugard's approach to plays and theatre took a new direction. In 1962 he had written an open letter to British playwrights which led to a boycott stopping performances of their work in the segregated theatres in South Africa. In 1974 he changed his stance, because he felt that people were culturally deadened and unable to access the material that would politicise them to work for change. In his notes he records:

> 'Anything that will get people to think and feel for themselves, that will stop them delegating these functions to politicians, is important to our survival. Theatre can help do this.'

His experience of long-term apartheid made him believe that theatre in segregated venues was better than none at all, and that white audiences should be addressed more directly. In his plays, he now focused less directly on the situation of black South Africans and more on use and abuse of power in his own, white sector of society. He stopped working collaboratively and his plays instead started to explore the conflict between the guilt which leads to not participating in society and taking responsibility for society's wrongs. Fugard's writing found more favour when he began to write what are now sometimes termed memory plays based on his own past.

Notable for specific and clearly political portrayal of life on the margins of the South African apartheid system, his later work is less devised with performers and more reflective of his own earlier life experiences. *Exits and Entrances* (2004), for example, portrays the relationship between a young budding playwright and an ageing, disillusioned actor.

→ Chronology of main works

1958	*No-Good Friday* (Bantu Men's Social Centre, Johannesburg)	**1982**	*Master Harold and the Boys* (Yale University, USA)
1961	*The Blood Knot* (Dorkay House Centre, Johannesburg)	**1989**	*My Children! My Africa!* (Market Theatre, Johannesburg)
1966	*The Coat* (first read at Dunne Hall of the Hill Presbyterian Church, Johannesburg)	**1992**	*Playland* (Market Theatre, Johannesburg, following USA tryouts)
1969	*Boesman and Lena* (Rhodes University, Grahamstown)	**2001**	*Sorrows and Rejoicings* (McCarter Theatre, Princeton, USA)
1972	*Sizwe Bansi is Dead* (The Space Theatre, Cape Town)	**2004**	*Entrances and Exits* (Fountain Theatre, Los Angeles, USA)
1973	*The Island*, under the title *Die Hodoshe Span* (The Space Theatre, Cape Town)		

→ Fingerprints of Athol Fugard's style

☑ Plays usually set in one location with little/no scene changes, minimal props. Limited character numbers focus the action on their personal struggles to assert identity and self-worth; guilt and conscience are also frequent elements.

☑ Physical intensity creates the theatrical and dramatic power of the action. Moments of sudden and unexpected brutality intended to shock the audience.

☑ A need to 'bear witness' to real events and to tell the story of those events. Debate and argument are used to communicate political viewpoints.

☑ Humour and comic action in adversity heighten the sense of marginalisation. But a sense of relentless movement towards tragedy drives the earlier plays; later plays are driven by the necessity of considered choice and working towards a better future.

☑ Main characters are usually on the margins of society, in earlier plays especially. They are often based in reality, parts created for specific actors or based on Fugard himself. There is a racial mix of characters in most

plays which is significant to the action, though some white roles are 'unseen' in the period of segregation.

☑ Fugard takes an atheist stance, but includes religion as supportive of political struggle.

☑ Highly collaborative approach up to and including *The Island*; introspective, reflective and more conventional playwriting method after *The Island*.

☑ Active interplay between the local action and universal themes through reference or symbolic allusion to classical theatre and religious imagery.

☑ The plays have to be performed with a specific audience in mind. There is a recognition that the message to a European/American audience is not the same as to a South African one; the context of theatre performance is different, and South African audiences participate in the performance in a way that European ones do not; debate and interaction with the stage action is part of the performance.

→ Case study 1: *No-Good Friday* (1958)

■ Background

No-Good Friday is regarded as Fugard's establishing play, and it projected him significantly in South African theatre. It was played first with Fugard's own amateur theatre company, and was written with specific actors in mind for the characters. At first its success was among the poor black township audience, who would have recognised the action as a dramatic representation of their world. It was later played to white audiences, to whom it was a first insight into the lives of those who did their manual work.

No-Good Friday is located in Sophiatown, on the edge of the city of Johannesburg, where, unusually, blacks were allowed to own land. The small freedoms afforded them in this township generated a sense of community. The experience of working with township actors on this first significant play created a model which Fugard continued to follow but with smaller numbers on stage, reflecting the need to have a core of secure performers – the social difficulties in the townships increased uncertainty for larger casts.

■ Plot

The setting is the good-natured poverty of black workers working towards Friday – pay day – which is also the day a township protection-racket gangster, Shark, collects his money. At the end of the second scene he orders the instant and brutal knifing of Tobias, an innocent and naive new arrival from the countryside, in front of a crowd of onlookers for not comprehending why he should pay. The raw simplicity of the killing shocks audiences. It intentionally breaks the conventions of a plot built on the complication of the lives of characters who the audience feel they have come to know.

The letter Tobias was due to send home has a simple poetry which prompts the main character, Willie, a more educated worker, to realise what has been lost by coming to the city. He takes a stand and refuses to pay any more, feeling complicit in the murder they have all witnessed. The play ends with him awaiting Shark's return. As he waits alone he is joined by a blind man, Moses, who knows he can be with him to the last as he cannot be called as a witness to the killing.

The white 'Baas' is discussed but only to frame the main action. This is typical of Fugard's work. Mention is made of the pass laws, the corrupt police, and Pinkie's forced apology over the tea voucher.

■ Key themes of the play

This play portrays the injustices suffered by dispossessed people. The characters are both symbols and easily recognisable types showing the way people struggle to exist.

The past becomes significant in the play without being discussed. Tobias brings memories that are a catalyst to Willie. Moses has a memory too, but it is out of date. It cannot be connected to the present.

Willie's stand against the protection racket can be interpreted in a variety of ways, but the self-sacrificial Christian parallel is evident alongside the political message, despite Fugard's atheism. Self-advancement through study is shown to be a dead end; his relationship is also sacrificed to a greater cause.

The one white character in the play, Father Higgins, is a reminder of the standard of justice these characters were denied. Religion is not depicted as entirely valueless – for many of Fugard's audience it was their hope. It is his very helplessness that allows Moses to bear witness, accompanying Willie and intending to give him a few extra moments of advance notice to prepare himself for the death that must come soon.

→ Case study 2: *The Island* (1973)

■ Background

The Island is one of Fugard's most collaborative plays. The script was written down only after it had first been performed. His two actors, John Kani and Winston Ntshona, devised the play through improvising the work of two prisoners in the Island penal colony. The living plight of Robben Island prisoners juxtaposed with the ancient classical Greek storyline enabled Fugard to draw parallels between universal tragic themes and the real South Africans who, like Antigone, took a moral stand knowing they faced heavy punishment.

■ Plot

Two prisoners are shown, on Robben Island. The play begins with a siren that raises the sleeping men. The playhouse becomes the prison, and the audience are visitors. Endless tasks are intended by the Hodoshe to break the prisoners' spirit and dehumanise them: their energy and togetherness raises them above the work and reasserts their humanity.

In this play at last there is triumph in adversity rather than heroic failure. The message is that the brotherhood of the nation will remain strong. When Winston pulls off his wig in scene 4 and speaks the last lines as himself it is clear he has finally understood.

■ Style

The actors use their own first names, John and Winston. This intentionally breaks the standard convention of improvisation work to remind the audience that there is a reality here that is not usually present in theatre.

Minimal staging reflects reality. A shared blanket, a tin, and a bucket of water were as much as real prisoners were allowed. Prison dress of shirt and shorts creates an image of children, reinforced by the mime and energy shown, but the image is deliberately misleading and the shock of sudden shift of action to the second mime is a recognisable Fugard trait. A whistle is blown, and the two are suddenly handcuffed at wrists and ankles and forced to run together. One mutters a prayer, the other a rhythm for the run. The dramatic conciseness here shows how they respond differently. The prayer may sustain John's mind but will not help the action; the rhythm established by Winston will support them both. Fugard's atheism and humanitarianism appear in this moment.

The frenetic exercise brings real sweat and pain. The actors do not just perform, they experience in actuality what prisoners underwent daily. This is not just making theatre, but a dramatic re-enactment.

> *They do not run fast enough. They get beaten …Winston receiving a bad blow to the eye and John spraining an ankle. In this condition they arrive finally at the cell door.*

The day's work done, *The Island* shifts its action again. This forces the audience to rethink these men and how they can want to perform for the pleasure of those who beat them. There is no explanation: for the black races this represents the daily degradation of their existence.

John's struggle to teach Winston the story and his lines adds a comic but ironic twist. As the lines unfold, the audience hear the parallels between the play and the South African laws.

> **John** Now look, Winston, we're not going to argue. Between me and you, we know she's Not Guilty. But in the play she pleads Guilty. Get that straight.
>
> **Winston** No man John! Antigone is Not Guilty….

The struggle to teach and persuade Winston becomes the direction of the action. But as the play appears to be settling into a clear line, there is a new and critical shift, evidence of the improvisations that led to the creation of the plot. John is to leave the Island in a matter of months. Suddenly the full weight of Winston's life sentence is clear. Winston begins to experience a torment akin to Antigone's, and he lashes out at John.

> **Winston** You stink, John. You stink of beer, company, of *poes*, of freedom…Your freedom stinks, John, and it's driving me mad.

The power and status struggles typical of Fugard's exploitation theories are most intensely explored here. Soon John sinks to the floor, unable to answer Winston any more, but:

> *…Winston seems almost to bend under the weight of life stretching ahead of him on the Island. For a few seconds he lives in silence with his reality, then slowly straightens up. When he speaks again, it is the voice of a man who has come to terms with his fate, massively compassionate.*
> Nyana we Sizwe!

In this action Winston genuinely expresses the dignity in suffering of the entire black nation. It is a demanding challenge for any actor, and probably the most electric moment of all Fugard's work.

> 'I used to joke that I was any disruptive kid's nightmare, I was a 17-stone drama teacher with a PhD.'
>
> John Godber in introduction to Bouncers–1990s Remix

John Godber was born in Upton in West Yorkshire in 1956. He came from a mining family and trained as a drama teacher. He became Head of Drama at the school he had himself attended, but became disillusioned with the education system and ended his teaching career after six years. He is one of Britain's most prolific playwrights, with over 50 plays to his name since the 1970s, and reputedly the third most performed British playwright, after Shakespeare and Ayckbourn. His immediate and accessible style, low comedy and adaptable staging contribute to his considerable popularity. There is an autobiographical focus on the perspective of working-class, downmarket characters. Situations are developed from places and events he knew well. The characters in *Bouncers* are drawn from his own sporting activities, including rugby, weightlifting and bodybuilding. These provide a springboard to the action rather than the plotline.

Godber took over Hull Truck, which had been a touring political theatre company, and has been its artistic director since 1984. He moulded it into a company which tours extensively across provincial England, often playing less prestigious but popular venues. His skill is in combining a fast paced, demanding and physical style, playful but sharply focused use of language and a political stance with an apparent simplicity of action – the 'slice of life' situations easily recognisable to any audience.

While still a teacher he was also writing for TV, including *Chalkface*, *Grange Hill*, *Brookside* and *Crown Court*, and the discipline of writing short, episodic and emotionally revealing language is worked into his plays. Stylistically his work is a blend of TV dialogue style and the simple practicality of a drama teacher – physically sharp, lively, economical and always entertaining.

→ Stylistic trends in mature works

Mime and heightened body language, gestures and facial expression communicate character directly. Dialogue is used in a wide range of ways to support the rapidly changing action and roles played by the performers. Music is also used in transitions and to create the atmosphere of the location. Appropriate lighting to represent the locations – e.g. bar, supermarket, girls' homes in *Shakers* – is not specified. Technical production is left to the performance company staging the play, and even the interval is identified only as 'possible' before scene

PERFORMANCE CONTEXTS 1

UNIT 2

10 in *Shakers*. Godber intends the control of the practicalities of staging to be devolved, in Brechtian manner, to remake the play in a way which will work for that audience in that place.

Language is the other pillar of the action, blending punchy TV-style short lines with theatrical diversity. Godber taps into the wide range of British social types (foreign characters are rare in his earlier works). Narrated or related action, description, wit, voice and accent, dialect terms (e.g. 'twagging', in *Teechers*, for 'truancy'), reflective monologues, stock phrases, crude language, choral speaking and the pre-echo which undercuts (e.g. in the TV producers scene in *Shakers*): these are some of the most readily identifiable language devices Godber uses.

Action and dialogue are focused on delivering a social or social/political message – Godber's writing is concise and economical, avoiding using any language device for its own sake. The events in the plays generate opportunities for the action. For example, drama lessons in *Teechers* prompt re-enaction of the story by the pupils, using drama techniques learned. The typical good time/bad time night out in *Bouncers* explores the many moments in such an evening. The apparent glamour juxtaposed with the actual drudgery and exploitation of the *Shakers* girls is in many ways a celebration of the energy and optimism of the working classes balanced by the disappointment in the limited opportunities society is willing to provide for them.

The style also mirrors working-class life: the four actors in *Bouncers* have to work physically and strenuously using mime and stylised body language on stage to deliver a wide range of characters. It draws on Italian *commedia dell'arte* semi-improvised plays, the low-comedy styles of Shakespeare and Ben Jonson, and ancient theatre devices such as narrator characters – e.g. in *Bouncers* – apparently not the most appropriate to be telling the story, because of their lack of education. It put audiences at ease. They were listening to characters who were witty and entertaining, commenting sharply on popular culture without belittling the audience. There is mockery of the educated classes too: a college-student beer race in *Bouncers*, and the producers in *Shakers*.

Godber's approach is unashamedly anti-elite. Characters are not psychologically complex and are revealed through their own words. Godber stated his intention to expand audiences. In writing *Bouncers* he wanted to overcome the lack of interest in theatre he had experienced from adults and 'school kids', and wanted to 'create a piece of theatre that spoke to a generation of clubbers rather than theatregoers'.

However, his style is not simple. The illusion frequently shifts, but always with signposts which ensure the audience do not get left behind. These are varied – characters with identifying names, spoken as they adopt their body language, or a semi-Brechtian announced introduction, e.g. 'one brace of TV producers'. The casting is flexible, with a core of developed characters and many other stock types or stereotypes. There is built-in flexibility to make the piece contemporary, with current fashion and pop music. The setting is created, moved on, and is entirely dependent upon using the physicality of the performers, as Godber also states: 'They do not have a set or cups and saucers to rely on, they cannot be contextualised by flapping scenery.'

→ Chronology of main works

John Godber is an extremely prolific writer. These are some of his most significant works.

1982 *Happy Jack* (National Student Drama Festival, performed by John Godber and Jane Thornton)

1983 *Bouncers* (Hill Rotherham Arts Centre, performed by the Yorkshire Actors Company)
September in the Rain (National Student Drama Festival, Bretton Hall College, Wakefield, performed by John Godber and Jane Thornton)

1984 *Up'n'Under* (Assembly Rooms, Edinburgh Fringe Festival, performed by Hull Truck Theatre Co.)

1985 *Shakers* (Spring Street Theatre, home of Hull Truck Theatre Co., co-written with Jane Thornton)

1987 *Teechers* (Assembly Rooms, Edinburgh Fringe Festival, performed by Hull Truck Theatre Co.)

1991 *Shakers Re-stirred* (Spring Street Theatre, performed by Hull Truck Theatre Co.)
Bouncers – 1990's Remix (Spring Street Theatre, performed by Hull Truck Theatre Co.)
Happy Families (49 simultaneous amateur performances throughout the United Kingdom and one in Tel Aviv)

1995 *Lucky Sods* (Spring Street Theatre)

1999 *Thick as a Brick* (Spring Street Theatre)

→ Fingerprints of John Godber's style

☑ Influenced by experiences as a drama teacher, then writing for TV sit-com drama and soaps, e.g. *Grange Hill*. Unashamedly anti-elite and eclectic dramatic style combining elements from popular TV entertainment, German expressionism, Brecht, Dario Fo, Berkoff-type mime.

☑ Easily identifiable and familiar working-class perspective of characters, locations and situations; higher-class characters are usually comic and two-dimensional. Accessible, 'slice of life' reflection of working-class everyday reality, often exploring the conflict between their aspirations and the limited opportunities for the characters.

☑ A core of central characters who develop dramatically, played by a small set of performers who multi-role. A wide range of 'thumbnail' social stereotypes identified by specific features, e.g. typical language and physical manner.

☑ Fast-paced action, short scenes, snap scene changes announced by performers, minimal props/staging. A highly physical style, frequent use of mime of props and actions.

☑ Comedy often based simultaneously on visual and verbal parody, including cross-gender and cross-generation contrast, e.g. adults playing children in *Teechers*.

☑ Character development moments through soliloquy or monologue, often poignant social observation.

☑ Multi-use of music: to change action, define a location or time period, or to generate emotion.

☑ Overt theatricality, drawing attention to the mechanism of the drama, e.g. in audience address or third-party comment on the action, announced scene changes, verbal or visual gags.

☑ Some manipulation of chronological action, use of freeze and nonlinear progression, e.g. flashback or jumping forwards in time. Potential to bring the piece up to date by using contemporary music and costume.

→ Case study 1: *Bouncers* (1983)

■ Background

One of Godber's earliest attempts at a social-comment play was performed at the Edinburgh Fringe Festival in 1977. This was reworked later into the successful four-man version of *Bouncers* performed in 1983, expanded by his knowledge of the types who became bouncers for a living. Godber calls it a memory play, and he states that in some ways he simply recorded what he saw on Friday and Saturday nights. It sets out to 'illustrate the sort of thing that happens late'. This line defines the intention. It also shows that there are two types of audience members – the ones who will see a mirror of the social life they know and those who will see into the world of the late-night, on-the-town revellers that they stay away from.

■ Plot

The play takes place over a single evening, following four bouncers in their work. The punters are also portrayed, using multi-role acting. They have earned this night out, but there is an increasing sense of lack of ambition and aspiration in the characters observed by the bouncers. As the night wears on, the language becomes coarser. There is also an increasing lack of dignity as the drink takes over, with later scenes focused on the debris at the end of the evening: fighting, cheap fast food, sex, sick and a queasy taxi ride home to watch a dirty video.

■ Key themes

Godber identifies the theme as a universal one: 'Men after beer after women, and the beat goes on'. He is exploring and revealing a social class which is below many theatregoers' cultural radar – the ordinary, working-class people which most British playwrights have avoided writing about, often because their higher levels of education separate them from the shop, mining and factory workers Godber knows well. But the play is not just a recording of life. There was rapid change happening – pubs turning into clubs and wine bars, a new bright-lights social scene with jobs attached. Godber is observing a social group adjusting to change. There is excitement but it has an edge of sadness to it, mixed carefully around the comedy. The energy, humour and enjoyment of a night out is mirrored in the rapid progression of the play, tracking the rhythm of a Friday night. This includes the sudden switch from bouncers into college students:

> **Eric** Here we go Justin. Beer race. Une, deux, trois.
> **Les** My go. *(Eric and Les pour beer over their heads)* Now your turn Justin …oh, he's fluffed it. Get them down, Justin.

(Judd [Justin] has fluffed the exercise and consequently has to take his trousers down to the Zulu warrior song)

Throughout the piece Godber plays with theatre conventions, mixing styles almost recklessly. The four bouncers introduce the play in a verse prologue which becomes a rap, blending classical and popular culture. They suddenly switch into female stereotypes in a hairdresser's, switching back in an instant on the choral command 'Barbers'. The cross-gender scene seems to satirise Shakespeare's ladies, all of whom were played by men, reducing them to the commonest types. The choral moment is almost a blink-of-an-eye parody of a Greek chorus narration. The audience do not need to know this: they simply enjoy the sharp pace and vivid comic images. The rapid staccato dialogue and mime was new to and delighted its audience:

Ralph Come on, let's get down there, pick something up. Right.
All Right.
Eric Hang on.
Les What?
Eric Piss call.
All Right.

(They all turn their backs as if peeing and then turn back to face the audience)

The snappy dialogue and instantaneous shifts are balanced by one other main device, the character monologue. This also serves to define the bouncers as very different people. Ralph's solo speeches are just announcements to the crowd. Les observes in short bursts, but does not reach conclusions. It is Eric who shows sensitivity in observing and realising, partly understanding, that the girls who get drunk are wasting their youth in drink and sex:

Pure and dirty, innocent and vulgar, it all withers, washes away. Eighteen, going on thirty-five, because they think they've got to, because they're forced to … I dunno.

Judd, the fourth bouncer, hardly reflects at all. The play ends as it began, with the bouncers' rap, telling us it will be going on next weekend, presumably for ever, in an endless social trap.

WE'LL BE DOWN HERE, YES, WITH YOU
AND YOU
AND YOU
AND YOU….

Les Thank you and good night.

→ Case study 2: *Teechers* (1987)

■ Background

Godber's foray into the world of school in *Teechers* is heartfelt, reworking the issues explored in his early, much angrier play *EPA* (Educational Priority Area). It is personal, autobiographical and deeply sympathetic to the pupil characters, but they are lightly drawn. We can know them, like real pupils, only through what we see of them at school.

This is a play whose effect is almost unique in British theatre. Its satire works differently depending on whether it is played by school-age teenagers or by adult performers, and to what audience. The frequent multi-role shifting from pupil to adult means one or the other will be parodied. It is unique in unifying the audience by portraying something each audience member has experienced: school education. Nixon is the one character to be played 'straight', as an innocent discovering an irregular world on the other side of the teaching fence.

The play is a three-hander, where Salty, Gail and Hobby multi-role to the point where it is almost unclear whether they are telling the story or it is telling them. It is precisely constructed but has a directness which delights the audience.

■ Plot

Teechers begins with the end of schooldays for the pupils, retelling the events leading up to their leaving and the departure of their popular drama teacher, Mr Nixon.

The young and idealistic teacher discovers the poor facilities of the ordinary school compared with the wealthy one, staffroom politics and pupils with no expectations of a meaningful career. It is through playing tennis, at which Nixon secretly excels, with the staff that he routs his enemies. As a theatrical device this has the feel of one of Godber's TV dramas, but he may be recycling a real-life anecdote of his own sporting prowess.

■ Key themes

This is a play about the neglect at the poor end of the educational system. Here wealth is not parodied as it is in *Bouncers* and *Shakers*. The focus is the educational entitlement which is denied to the children of Whitewall High School.

The play is highly diverse in exploring language and how it is used for control, in the recurrent 'Stop running, Simon Patterson!' and the stock lines such as those Mrs Parry wields:

> **Parry** I know that was the bell, Simon Patterson. The bell is a signal for me to move and not for anyone else.

Disempowerment is built into the system. Nixon asks simply:

> **Nixon** Well, where should you be?
> **Gail** Sir, I don't know, I can't work it out on my timetable. I'm in tutor group ID. But I'm in teaching group IY5 and I should be in block 43B doing Biology. But 3YY6 are in there…

Salty's delight in saying 'knackers' aloud at the opening of the play, on the day he is leaving, is his way of expressing the restrictions on speech in school: he at last has the freedom to say whatever he wants.

The other level of action in this play exploring control and manipulation is in the power struggles between teaching staff – and the caretaker, whose officially low status is contradicted by the power he wields in his possession of the hall after school.

Sex, the driving force of *Bouncers*, is a satirical not a political element, seen in Oggy Moxon, cross-gendered and spoken through Gail. The same performer delivers it in Jackie Prime's description of herself:

> **Prime** Jackie Prime was tall, suntanned, bouncy and an expert at netball and tennis … She was developing dance in the gym and took an interest in all games.

It exists also in Nixon's infatuation, but it is unrequited. Mirroring school life, sex is not the purpose of the action, so it is not developed into an element of the plot.

Character is delivered through examples such as those described, and through the narrated sections, where the performers speak more as if reading aloud a classroom essay than a playscript:

> **Whitham** You've had it now', said Maureen Whitham, scale-two humanities, as she sat listening and thumbing through the Times Ed. Old Basford will make your life a misery…

This enables the action to shift between past and present tense without any clear joins. Godber's ease in time shifting is seen in some manipulation of time and chronology, using flashbacks and freezes.

The poignancy typical of a Godber play is delivered at the end in the pupils' pleas for him not to leave: not for them, but for the younger pupils. It is a political statement about the state of education.

From the 1999 production of *Teechers* by Hull Truck Theatre Co.
Photo: Adrian Gatie

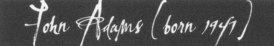

John Adams (born 1947)

John Adams is America's most frequently performed living composer. Adams' output is prolific and includes opera, orchestral music, chamber music. His style is eclectic and varies considerably between individual pieces. As a result, it is difficult to define as he draws on elements of Minimalism, popular music and orchestral music.

→ Early days

John Adams was born in the town of Worcester, Massachusetts in February 1947. He had an enthusiasm and aptitude for music from an early age and began composing from his teens. His first full-scale work was a *Suite for String Orchestra*, produced when he was only 13. Gaining a scholarship, he went on to study music at the prestigious Harvard University, which he left in 1971 having stayed on to complete a Master's degree.

For a graduation present, Adams' parents gave him a copy of John Cage's *Silence*, a series of philosophical writings about music that outline Cage's unique perspective on music. Inspired by Cage's ideas, Adams decided to move to the other side of the country from America's East Coast to take up residence in San Francisco, where he has lived ever since. Adams was firmly of the view that the culture and atmosphere of the West Coast would give him more scope to explore radical music ideas.

Between 1972 and 1982, John Adams taught at the San Francisco Conservatory of Music and began to compose professionally whilst there. His early works date from his time at the Conservatory and include *American Standard* and *Christian Zeal and Activity,* both from 1973. Just as the Minimalist composer Steve Reich had done ten years earlier, he also experimented with electronic music, but abandoned this after three years, just as Reich had done.

→ Work in San Francisco

Adams was already familiar with the style of Minimalism but in 1974, he rediscovered it through hearing a live performance of Steve Reich's *Drumming*. This music was very different to the experimental music of John Cage and Adams quickly decided that it offered him an approach to composition that was genuinely American. The music of the two most important Minimalist composers, Steve Reich (born 1936) and Philip Glass (born 1937), was tonal and rhythmic, two aspects of music that had not been encouraged in Adams' study at Harvard and which he had not encouraged in his students in his teaching at the Conservatory.

Adams has spoken of this point in his career as a 'diatonic conversion', in other words, the point at which tonal and rhythmic music became the most significant aspects of the way he wrote music. Reich and Glass both used these elements in writing short units (often consisting of between eight and twelve notes) that repeated incessantly, changing only very gradually over time. The music would change so slowly that, as Steve Reich pointed out, it was more like watching the minute hand on a clock rather than the second hand.

Phrygian Gates (1977–78) and *Shaker Loops* (1978) are both examples of how Minimalism has influenced Adams' style, although if you compare his approach with that of Reich or Glass you will hear some differences. Adams has said that his music is 'emotionally committed' whereas the style of the 1960s Minimalists can sound very austere. Adams' most significant difference, however, is the way he wrote for orchestra or, to some extent, the fact that he wrote for orchestra at all.

As a conductor and performer, he was more in touch with the tradition of European classical music and much of his work has been written for full orchestra or chamber ensemble, rather than his own ensemble. The musical scores for most of his compositions are readily available, ensuring that they can be performed without Adams himself needing to be present.

John Adams' first large-scale orchestral work is *Harmonium* (1981), a setting of various poems, which also uses a large chorus. This was performed by the San Francisco Symphony Orchestra and was responsible for bringing Adams' music to the attention of mainstream audiences who went to orchestral concerts. It was quickly followed by other pieces that have also become widely performed within the orchestral repertoire, such as *Harmonielehre* (1984–85) and *Short Ride in a Fast Machine* (1986). You can hear in these two pieces how Adams combines the repetitive language of Minimalism with the more expressive style of the late Romantic period that you might associate with the symphonies of Gustav Mahler (1860–1911). You can hear this diversity in much of Adams' chamber music.

→ Adams as a political composer

John Adams did not set out to become a composer of opera or one who intended to make political statements through his music. Yet he has ended up doing both, largely through his first two operas, *Nixon in China* (1985–87) and

President Richard Nixon meets Chairman Mao Tse-tung, the inspiration for John Adams' opera *Nixon in China*.

The Death of Klinghoffer (1990–91). Adams worked with the same team for both: the librettist Alice Goodman and the director Peter Sellars. Both operas build on the musical styles Adams was developing in his instrumental works. The subject matter of both consists of events from recent American history, and in neither case do these seem at first sight to be of particular significance.

Nixon in China is about the visit of the then USA President Richard Nixon and his Secretary of State Dr Henry Kissinger to Chairman Mao Tse-tung (Zedong) in Beijing in 1972. The visit was significant in changing the relationship between China and the USA, and the opera focuses on the political way in which the characters act towards each other. Nixon referred to the event as 'the week that changed the world'.

The Death of Klinghoffer is more politically charged in its subject matter and deals with the Arab–Israeli conflict. The action takes place on board the cruise liner *Achille Lauro*, which was taken hostage by Palestinian gunmen, resulting in the death of Leon Klinghoffer, an American Jew dependent on a wheelchair for mobility. The opera was premiered in Brussels in 1991, during the first Gulf War. Since the opera deals with the psychological motivations of the characters, it does not offer judgements as to who is right or wrong and a number of performances in America were cancelled after the events of 9/11.

➜ Adams as a post-modern composer

The diversity of John Adams' style can make it difficult to gain an overview of his output or understand the significant differences between individual pieces. You may find the following fingerprints checklist helpful in identifying trends in the composer's work, especially as you look through the chronology of his works. Think of these as being fingerprints by which you can identify Adams' involvement in his music.

→ Chronology of main works

John Adams is a prolific composer. This list includes his most significant works, in chronological order. Listing them in this way will show you the diverse musical ensembles for which Adams writes.

1973	*Christian Zeal and Activity* (for unspecified chamber ensemble)	1994	*John's Book of Alleged Dances* (for string quartet)
1978	*Shaker Loops* (for string septet)	1995	*Road Movies* (for violin and piano)
1979	*Common Tones in Simple Time* (for orchestra)		*I Was Looking at the Ceiling and Then I Saw the Sky* (songplay in two acts)
1980–81	*Harmonium* (for chorus and large orchestra)		*Lollapalooza* (for orchestra)
1982	*Grand Pianola Music* (for two pianos, three female voices, winds, brass and percussion)	1996	*Gnarly Buttons* (for clarinet and chamber ensemble)
			Slonimsky's Earbox (for orchestra)
1984–85	*Harmonielehre* (for orchestra)		*Century Rolls* (for piano and orchestra)
1985	*The Chairman Dances* (foxtrot for orchestra)		*Hallelujah Junction* (for two pianos)
1985–87	*Nixon in China* (opera in three acts)	1997–98	*Naive and Sentimental Music* (for orchestra)
1986	*Short Ride in a Fast Machine* (fanfare for orchestra)	2000	*El Niño* (a Nativity oratorio)
1988	*The Wound-Dresser* (for baritone voice and orchestra)	2002	*On the Transmigration of Souls* (for orchestra, chorus, children's choir and pre-recorded soundtrack)
1990–91	*The Death of Klinghoffer* (opera in two acts)	2003	*Dharma at Big Sur* (for electric violin and orchestra)
1992	*Chamber Symphony*	2004–05	*Doctor Atomic* (opera in two acts)
1993	*Violin Concerto*	2006	*A Flowering Tree* (opera in two acts)

→ Fingerprints of John Adams' style

☑ Adams is eclectic in his approach to using different styles of music. You can see this as being a typically post-modern approach to composition as he uses aspects of the music of the past but in a new way. For example, his orchestration is often reminiscent of the nineteenth century.

☑ Aspects of Minimalism are evident in many of Adams' earlier works. This is less severe than the rigid systems used by Steve Reich and Philip Glass.

☑ Well crafted orchestration is a key feature that links Adams to the mainstream of orchestral composers.

☑ Engagement with the culture of contemporary America, particularly America's place in the world, and its political role.

☑ The importance of popular music styles as well as classical ones. See, for example, his use of Gospel music in *I Was Looking at the Ceiling and Then I Saw the Sky*.

☑ His collaborations with particular performers in writing pieces for them, e.g. *Century Rolls* (1996) was written for Emanuel Ax. His collaboration with Peter Sellers underpins several stage works.

→ Case study 1 – *Shaker Loops* (1978)

■ Background

Shaker Loops is one of John Adams' earliest works. The composer's notes in the published score state that it was written in late 1978 and first performed in December of that year, conducted by Adams himself. There are two versions of the piece, the original version for string septet and a revised version for string orchestra, produced in 1982. The revised version lasts 26 minutes in performance.

The inspiration for the piece was the worship style of the Millennial Church in New England. The Church was more commonly known as the Shakers because of the ecstatic shaking and trembling that was a common part of their worship. There is no real musical link with the Shakers – there are no hymn tunes or Shaker melodies used. Adams makes the link with the Shakers by imitating their frenzied trembling in the way he writes for the string parts. He uses musical loops (short snippets of music, repeated over and over again) throughout the piece, and employs a number of techniques to capture the trembling style of Shaker worship.

■ Structure

The piece is in four sections, each of which follows on directly from the previous one without a break. Adams' intention is that each of the four sections calls for a particular style of string playing.

Part I	Shaking and Trembling	Rapid tremolo movement, with the strings using a fast, shaking bow. Several styles used (the score contains directions such as spiccato – off the string, sul tasto – on the fingerboard)
Part II	Hymning Slews	Slow movement that makes extensive use of glissandi
Part III	Loops and Verses	Melodic section, with the cellos playing an extended melodic line
Part IV	A Final Shaking	Rapid tremolo movement, with the strings using a fast, shaking bow

Unlike the earlier Minimalist composers, John Adams had an interest in writing for traditional orchestral instruments. He had been working with groups of string players for some months before the composition of *Shaker Loops*. Unlike many contemporary composers, he was able to work with performers from the San Francisco Conservatory to try out the string writing to make sure that it was technically playable and musically effective. Through this working process, Adams developed the repetitive, modular structure of the loops, the most significant structural component of the piece. These string loops are similar to the tape loops used by the Minimalist composer Steve Reich in his tape pieces *It's Gonna Rain* (1965) and *Come Out* (1966). In the septet version of *Shaker Loops*, the conductor determines how many repetitions of each loop are played and when the parts enter. In the orchestral version, the repetitions are all written out.

Rhythm and tempo

The tempo changes between each of the four sections, although there is very little change of speed within any of the individual movements. This is typical of the Minimalist style of the 1960s, which very often made use of the same tempo through an entire piece. The rhythms of each of the four parts are determined by the types of loop that Adams uses in that part. For example, in Part I, this loop is played for 28 bars by the second violin:

JOHN ADAMS

Melody and harmony

Although Adams had experimented with more avant-garde styles of music, *Shaker Loops* marks his return to tonal music. However, it is not always clear which key the music is in at any one point and there is some ambiguity between different tonal centres. The opening of the first movement, for example, seems to combine elements of C major, G major and E minor. One of the best examples of Adams' use of sustained chords is at the opening of Part II, where the harmony literally 'slews' from chord to chord, even though there is very little in the way of chord changes in the traditional sense. The harmony here creates a real sense of stillness and Adams is able to use this as a complete contrast to the shaking of the first movement.

→ Case study 2 – *Short Ride in a Fast Machine* (1986)

■ Background

This piece was first performed on 13 June 1986 by the Pittsburgh Symphony Orchestra, conducted by Michael Tilson Thomas. By the standards of Adams' other works, it is relatively short, lasting for approximately 4 minutes. However, it is scored for a large orchestra, and studying it has its own complexities.

The piece is a fanfare, and forms one half of a set of two fanfares, the other one being *Tromba Lontana*. Although both were first performed in 1986, the two pieces were commissioned separately. *Short Ride in a Fast Machine* was commissioned by the Great Woods Festival. *Tromba Lontana* was commissioned by the Houston Symphony Orchestra and was first performed on 4 April 1986.

■ A Minimalist fanfare

Short Ride in a Fast Machine is a fanfare. This type of piece is hard to define in terms of form. Fanfares are generally short and often intended for ceremonial occasions, perhaps to rouse the mood of a crowd and lift their spirits in expectation of a civic or military event. The use of brass instruments, especially the trumpet, is characteristic and ideally suited to outdoor performance, although not all fanfares are intended to be performed outdoors. Adams' decision to write a fanfare sets his style apart from the music of the earlier generation of Minimalists such as Steve Reich and Philip Glass, who did not write for orchestra in this manner.

■ Structure

The piece is a continuous whole and does not divide easily into contrasting sections, although there are points where there are some clear changes in the music. The style of Adams' early music was strongly influenced by Minimalism and this can be seen in the repetitive features of the music. It is the extent of the repetition that makes it difficult to divide the piece into sections. It is worth considering the various elements of the music as part of the way that Adams structures the piece. The clarinet parts at the opening set the tone of incessant repetition that pervades the rest of the piece.

Opening of *Short Ride in a Fast Machine*: clarinet parts.

JOHN ADAMS

■ Rhythm and tempo

There is a constant beat played on the woodblock throughout although this is not always regular. The nature of a fanfare demands that the music should be fast and percussive, so it is not surprising that Adams structures the piece around a continuous rhythm. The majority of the piece is loud and there are points where it becomes even louder.

The tempo hardly changes throughout the piece. The tempo is quick (152 beats per minute). This helps to reinforce the joyful and celebratory nature of a fanfare, and depicts the exhilaration of the 'passengers' as the machine hurtles along. There is one exception to this, between bars 138 and 181, where the speed is a little slower, but the original tempo is resumed for the last eight bars to create a triumphant ending.

The rhythm sounds more and more mechanical as it presses on. Although the pulse remains broadly constant, the time signature changes frequently – this may not be obvious to the audience, however. The music alternates mainly between 3/2 and 4/2 with some bars in the irregular time signature of 7/4. The effect of this is to help create a sense of breathlessness as the machine hurtles rapidly through the changing rhythmic groupings this creates.

■ Melody and harmony

There is very little in the way of melody, and this is typical of fanfares, which usually rely on short motifs (generally played by trumpets and other brass instruments) rather than extended melodies. There is a good example of this type of writing at bar 138, where two trumpets play this short melody:

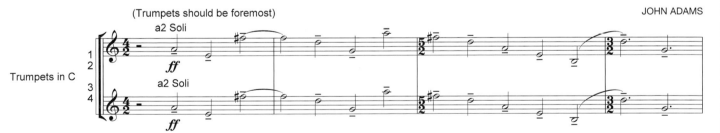

The harmony is also clearly influenced by the Minimalist style and there are no chord progressions in the music. In fact, the lack of change in the harmonies helps to give the impression of a single long-delayed cadence. In other words, it is as if the chord changes are so minimal that they seem to have no effect on the music, except to prolong the time before the end of the piece arrives.

The Beatles are generally acknowledged to be one of the most significant bands in the twentieth century. The group's four members – John Lennon, Paul McCartney, George Harrison and Ringo Starr – made a contribution to the development of British and American popular music that steered it in a new direction. Their albums were particularly significant in establishing the place of British music in the USA. The band was a huge commercial success and had  numerous Number 1 hits. By 1985 it was estimated that the Beatles had sold over one billion recordings, and the earnings from their recordings as being around £100 million.

Their success was both musical and social. The songs captured the spirit of the 1960s with its questioning of accepted social norms. As teenagers became more financially affluent they were able to afford recordings and were influenced by songs that questioned authority, made reference to the taking of drugs and were explicit about tensions in family life and relationships. In addition to their musical output, the Beatles also made a number of films but these are not discussed here as we are concerned only with their musical output.

→ Starting in Liverpool

All four Beatles came from the city of Liverpool. John Lennon had formed a band called the Quarry Men in 1956 and over the next two years met Paul McCartney and George Harrison, both of whom subsequently joined the band. The name was changed from 'The Quarry Men' to 'The Beatles' in 1960 and the band included Stuart Sutcliffe on bass guitar and Pete Best on drums. The group played a number of gigs, most notably at the Indra Club in Hamburg's red-light district and the Cavern Club in Liverpool. It was at the Cavern where they were heard by Brian Epstein, who became the band's manager and was successful in obtaining a recording contract for them with Parlophone in 1962, by which time the familiar line-up of Lennon, McCartney, Harrison and Ringo Starr was finalised. This introduced the Beatles to the producer George Martin, who ran the Parlophone record label.

The band had its origins in skiffle (a style of music made popular in 1950s Britain by Lonnie Donegan), but the Beatles (as the name reflected) developed themselves as a beat band, a stylistic development that they led in the early 1960s. Beat music became known for its straightforward good-humoured songs, which generally had memorable tunes and vocal harmonies moved along by driving rhythms and normally led by a guitar line-up.

Having been introduced to George Martin, the songwriting team of Lennon and McCartney set to work to produce songs that would establish the band's reputation; George Harrison's songs were to become significant in the band's later period. The Beatles undertook a national tour of Britain in 1963 and it was the impact of this tour, together with subsequent TV appearances in the USA, that gave the band the break they were looking for and brought their music to a worldwide audience. It produced an unprecedented level of record sales on both sides of the Atlantic, which was sustained during the next two years, aided by the release of the feature films *A Hard Day's Night* and *Help!* in 1964 and 1965 respectively.

The Beatles in performance in 1964

→ Developing style

The Beatles' songs began to change in style during 1965. There was an obvious move away from the upbeat emotionally simple songs of the beat music style in favour of a more complex and involved musical style. As with many successful bands, they were able to recognise shifts in the music industry and adapt their style to reflect this. Initially, this was through comic imitations of other styles, with soul music being parodied on the 1966 album *Rubber Soul*. This was quickly abandoned in favour of music that began to reflect the growth of drug culture amongst pop musicians. By 1967, the band had developed a new, psychedelic style that acknowledged, amongst other things, the significance of hallucinogenic drugs such as LSD. This is most noticeable in the surreal imagery and musical contrasts of the song *Lucy in the Sky with Diamonds*, from the 1967 album *Sgt Pepper's Lonely Hearts Club Band*. The use of contorted images and surreal memories reflected the imagery used in the songs of Bob Dylan.

Brian Epstein died in August 1967 and this had a negative impact on the future of the band. Relationships between the band members were increasingly sour but nevertheless the Beatles stayed together until 1970, when the four went their separate ways as solo artists.

→ Chronology of main works

The Beatles' musical legacy is contained largely within 12 albums, produced between 1963 and 1970.

1963	*Please Please Me*	**1968**	*The Beatles [White Album] (Disc 1)*
	With The Beatles		*The Beatles [White Album] (Disc 2)*
1964	*A Hard Day's Night*	**1969**	*Yellow Submarine*
1965	*Help!*	**1970**	*Let It Be*
	Rubber Soul		*Abbey Road*
1966	*Revolver*		
1967	*Sgt Pepper's Lonely Hearts Club Band*		
	Magical Mystery Tour		

→ Fingerprints of the Beatles' style

☑ Simple but memorable melodies that capture the mood of the lyrics. *Michelle* and *Hey Jude* are excellent examples of slow sustained melodies; *Penny Lane* is a jaunty air, a nostalgic recollection of growing up in Liverpool.

☑ The contrast between songs with a comic theme (e.g. *When I'm Sixty-Four*), sentimental ballads (e.g. *Hey Jude*) and songs with a serious intention (e.g. *For No-one*).

☑ Differences in style between the early songs inspired by beat music (often simple love songs) and the more emotionally complex songs of the later albums which pursue issues such as drugs, suicide, old age.

☑ The use of narrative in songs (e.g. *She's Leaving Home*) and the use of musical devices to reflect the story (e.g. syncopated (off-beat) rhythms to emphasise the instability of the character in *Eleanor Rigby*; changes in tonality during a song to reflect the changes in mood of the lyrics).

☑ Use of varied instrumentation – particularly the differences between songs: 'standard' instrumental line-ups such as guitar, bass and drums (e.g. *Help!*); orchestral instruments (e.g. in *Penny Lane* or the string quartet in *Eleanor Rigby* or the use of an orchestral glissando in *A Day in the Life*); Eastern influences (e.g. the use of the sitar and the combination of swarmandela with cellos and brass in *Strawberry Fields*).

☑ The use of particular instruments to create contrasting moods (e.g. comic, serious or sad). Examples include the use of high notes on solo piccolo, trumpet and flute to describe 'blue suburban skies' in *Penny Lane*; the use of synthesisers (e.g. the newly invented Mellotron in *Strawberry Fields*).

☑ The influence of the use of orchestral instruments on later bands, such as The Verve.

☑ The influence of music technology, such as the experimentation with multi-track recording in *A Day in the Life* or the use of multi-track recording technology to create the effect of larger combinations of instruments; the placing of microphones in unconventional places to create effects; the use of vari-speed recording.

→ Two songs from *Sgt Pepper's Lonely Hearts Club Band* (1967)

The A-level specification requires you to study four contrasting songs by the Beatles. Two are included here to demonstrate how this should be approached and what you need to know.

■ Background to the album

Sgt Pepper's Lonely Hearts Club Band is the eighth of the Beatles' 12 albums and is considered by many to be the group's finest. It was released in June 1967 and marks the point at which the group concentrated almost exclusively on studio recording rather than live performances.

Each member assumes a new identity in a made-up band with the title 'Sgt Pepper's Lonely Hearts Club Band' (Ringo Starr is Billy Shears, the band leader). The songs on the album were originally intended to form a 'concert' by that band but in reality only the first two have anything to do with each other. The very well known album cover pictures the Beatles in military-like uniforms surrounded by a large number of well known people ranging from Oscar Wilde to Marilyn Monroe and including the German avant-garde composer Karlheinz Stockhausen.

The songs cover a range of social issues, such as family breakdown and drugs, and use a wide range of styles, a diverse range of instruments as well as innovative recording techniques.

The album contains 13 songs, in this order:

1 *Sgt Pepper's Lonely Hearts Club Band*
2 *With a Little Help from My Friends*
3 *Lucy in the Sky with Diamonds*
4 *Getting Better*
5 *Fixing a Hole*
6 *She's Leaving Home*
7 *Being for the Benefit of Mr Kite*
8 *Within You Without You*
9 *When I'm Sixty-Four*
10 *Lovely Rita*
11 *Good Morning Good Morning*
12 *Sgt Pepper's Lonely Hearts Club Band* (Reprise)
13 *A Day in the Life*

→ Case study 1 – *She's Leaving Home*

This is the sixth song on the album. The three verses were written by Paul McCartney and the chorus by John Lennon. Inspired by a real story in the *Daily Mirror*, the song deals with the social issue of a young girl who had left home and was missing. The structure divides the story so that the verse tells what is going on as if it was being reported. The chorus has a similar effect to the chorus in a Greek tragedy, as it comments on what is going on. There are two vocal lines in the chorus and these overlap (as shown in brackets below).

■ Structure

Verse
Wednesday morning at five o'clock as the day begins
Silently closing her bedroom door
Leaving the note that she hoped would say more
She goes downstairs to the kitchen clutching her handkerchief
Quietly turning the backdoor key
Stepping outside she is free.

Chorus
She (We gave her most of our lives)
is leaving (Sacrificed most of our lives)
home (We gave her everything money could buy)
She's leaving home after living alone
For so many years. Bye, bye

Verse
Father snores as his wife gets into her dressing gown
Picks up the letter that's lying there
Standing alone at the top of the stairs
She breaks down and cries to her husband Daddy our baby's gone
Why would she treat us so thoughtlessly
How could she do this to me.

Chorus
She (We never thought of ourselves)
is leaving (Never a thought for ourselves)
home (We struggled hard all our lives to get by)
She's leaving home after living alone
For so many years. Bye, bye

Verse
Friday morning at nine o'clock she is far away
Waiting to keep the appointment she made
Meeting a man from the motor trade.

Chorus
She (What did we do that was wrong)
is having (We didn't know it was wrong)
fun (Fun is the one thing that money can't buy)
Something inside that was always denied
For so many years. Bye, bye
She's leaving home. Bye, bye

The song is a clear narrative in which the hope and optimism of the girl leaving to start a new life contrasts with the despair of the parents reading her note announcing her departure. The song is in a steady 3/4 waltz time and in the key of E major, both of which emphasise the upbeat outlook of the girl.

■ Melody and harmony

The song is strophic (the same music is used for each verse) and the verse itself divides into two sections of three lines each. The first line moves almost entirely by step to the next note with a leap on the sixth note of the melody (on the word 'five' in verse 1); lines 2 and 3 have the same melody.

First line of She's Leaving Home

Words & music JOHN LENNON & PAUL MCCARTNEY

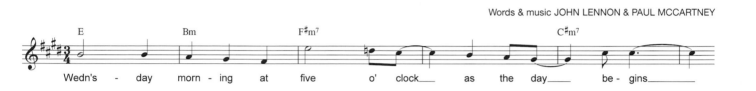

Wedn's - day morn - ing at five o' clock___ as the day___ be - gins___

The second half of the verse (lines 4–6) repeats this pattern. Verse 2 has the same structure, but the third verse has only three lines, emphasising the way in which the girl's relationship at home with her parents has been cut short. The harmony is interesting and forms a contrast to the standard three chords so typical in pop songs of the period, the harmonic progression consisting of a nine-chord sequence:

$$E - B\text{ minor} - F\#\text{minor} - C\#\text{minor}^7 - F\#^7 - B^7\text{sus}^4 - B^9 - B^7\text{sus}^4 - B^9.$$

This sequence accompanies the first three lines of the verse, and is repeated for the second three lines (except in verse 3). By contrast, the chorus has ten bars with a held chord of E major, perhaps commenting on the way in which the parents wish to hold their daughter at home.

■ Instrumentation

There is a varied use of instrumentation and the examples here are a few of the many that could be used. In addition to the string quartet, the opening four bars make use of a harp playing arpeggios. The strings play detached chords, perhaps emphasising the detachment of the characters, but contrasted with the scale-like legato cello melody at the end of the first line. The string parts are used again to bring out this character relationship at the start of the second verse. As the father lies snoring in bed, the cello plays a heavy detached arpeggio figure. The story culminates at the words 'Daddy our baby's gone', where a triplet figure is used in the string parts to heighten the drama of what has happened.

➔ Case study 2 – *When I'm Sixty-Four*

This is the ninth song on the album. It was written by Paul McCartney (but also credited to John Lennon) and was composed several years before the release of *Sgt Pepper*, apparently dating back to the performances in the Cavern Club. The theme is apparently about growing older and it is possible that the coincidence of Paul McCartney's father turning 64 might have been the inspiration for including it here. Interviews with John Lennon highlighted the satirical nature of the lyrics as they poked fun at their parents' generation rather than glorified their own ageing.

■ Structure

When I get older losing my hair,
Many years from now.
Will you still be sending me a valentine
Birthday greetings bottle of wine?

If I'd been out till quarter to three
Would you lock the door,
Will you still need me, will you still feed me,
When I'm sixty-four?

You'll be older too,
And if you say the word,
I could stay with you.

I could be handy, mending a fuse
When your lights have gone.
You can knit a sweater by the fireside
Sunday mornings go for a ride,

Doing the garden, digging the weeds,
Who could ask for more.
Will you still need me, will you still feed me,
When I'm sixty-four?

Every summer we can rent a cottage,
In the Isle of Wight, if it's not too dear
We shall scrimp and save
Grandchildren on your knee
Vera, Chuck & Dave

Send me a postcard, drop me a line,
Stating point of view
Indicate precisely what you mean to say
Yours sincerely, wasting away

Give me your answer, fill in a form
Mine for evermore
Will you still need me, will you still feed me,
When I'm sixty-four?

The song has a jaunty light-hearted mood throughout and is performed in the style of a swing number; this use of an older style helps to make it seem intentionally written for an older generation. It is in the key of C major and the brief move to A minor for the chorus does not change the overall mood. The brisk tempo remains constant throughout.

■ Melody and harmony

Following a six-bar introduction, the melody is quickly established. It is extremely well known and highly memorable, although the dotted rhythms in the performance are not normally written out as such. The style harks back to the swing era of the 1930s and 1940s, as befits the subject matter of the lyrics. The harmony is based largely on tonic–dominant chord progressions between C major and G7.

Melody of When I'm
Sixty-Four

Words & music JOHN LENNON & PAUL MCCARTNEY

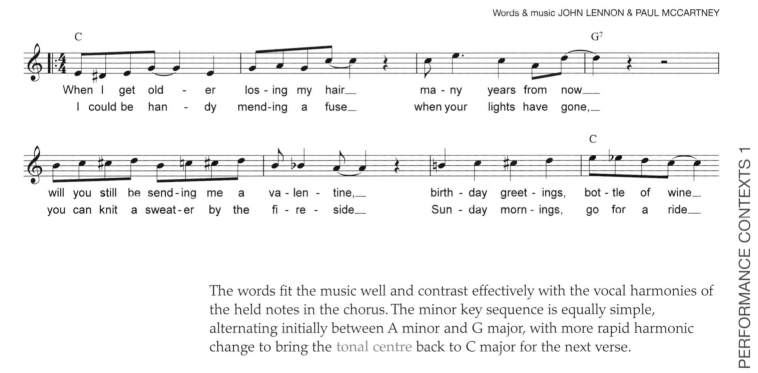

The words fit the music well and contrast effectively with the vocal harmonies of the held notes in the chorus. The minor key sequence is equally simple, alternating initially between A minor and G major, with more rapid harmonic change to bring the tonal centre back to C major for the next verse.

■ Instrumentation

The instrumentation is relatively straightforward, the most noticeable aspect being the use of three clarinets (two soprano and a bass). These help to identify the song with the swing era of Benny Goodman and the distinctive timbre of the trio sounds through the texture. The use of chimes – perhaps to signify the passing of time – is also out of the ordinary.

George Gershwin (1898–1937)

George Gershwin is one of the most significant American songwriters of the early twentieth century. His songs have memorable tunes, pulsating rhythms and capture the spirit of American songwriting in an era when live performance was far more common than recorded music. He wrote hundreds of songs and a large number of them have been recorded by several different artists over the last 70 years or so. One of the signs of the greatness of Gershwin's songs is that they exist in so many different versions because different singers have produced their own interpretations. As well as songs, Gershwin wrote a small number of concert works such as *Rhapsody in Blue*. Although significant pieces of music, they are not discussed here as we are concerned only with George Gershwin as a songwriter.

→ Gershwin as a songwriter

■ Tin Pan Alley

George Gershwin (1898–1937) was born in New York. As a child he showed a strong interest in music and when his parents bought a piano in 1910, Gershwin quickly demonstrated an aptitude for playing it. At the age of 14, he began lessons with Charles Hambitzer, who introduced him to the nineteenth-century European piano repertoire of such composers as Frederick Chopin (1810–49) and Franz Liszt (1811–86).

Although this interest in serious composition for the piano remained with him for the whole of his musical career, in 1914 Gershwin left high school and took work as a song plugger for Jerome H. Remick & Co. This required considerable musical skill in performing songs for prospective singers, most obviously the ability to play them on the piano, transposing as appropriate for the soloist he was accompanying, as well as demonstrating the song as necessary. The firm was based in the area of New York known as Tin Pan Alley (between 29th Street and 6th Avenue), so called because of the jangling noise created by so many song pluggers plying their trade in close proximity to each other.

■ Approaching Broadway

The experience of working on Tin Pan Alley created in Gershwin an ambition to write his own songs rather than simply demonstrating the songs of others. His aspiration was to work on Broadway, geographically close to Remick & Co., but artistically a long way away. Nevertheless, within a year, Gershwin had begun to publish songs for shows on Broadway and by 1919 composed the full score for the show *La La Lucille*, with lyrics by Arthur Jackson, B. G. DeSylva and Irving Caesar.

Throughout his career, there was always a tension between the requirements for successful songwriting and the ability to compose the music for entire shows. George Gershwin's enduring fame and popularity rest firmly on his ability to craft tuneful and memorable songs rather than his attempts to create dramatically satisfying musicals in which the songs complement the action. The songs that have become famous have tended to do so independently of the shows they came from. Gershwin himself was not averse to considering moving a song from one show to another in the case of a potentially successful song in a show that had flopped commercially.

Al Jolson was responsible for the popularity of Gershwin's *Swanee*.

Gershwin's strengths as a songwriter can be seen in his earliest achievements. His experience as a song plugger had introduced him to a strict formula for writing songs that would prove commercially successful. His first hit was *Swanee*, recorded by Al Jolson in 1920, and written in the style that owed much to Tin Pan Alley: a short piano introduction, a melancholy verse in a minor key, a longer, tuneful and more memorable chorus in a major key, a repetition of the chorus. The structure of the chorus was repetitive and made effective use of short musical motifs that were easy to remember.

It was probably Jolson's performance of *Swanee* that accounted for its great success and Gershwin knew the importance of making good contacts in the world of the Broadway musical. Between 1920 and 1924, he worked with the well known impresario George White to produce music for White's famous annual musical revues, known as *George White's Scandals*. This in turn led to his writing scores for shows in London as well as New York.

At this point, George Gershwin had collaborated with a number of lyricists, including his brother Ira Gershwin. By 1924, Ira was George's preferred lyricist and the brothers' first mature show, *Lady, Be Good*, was produced that year. The show contained a number of individual songs that went on to become famous, including the title song *Lady, Be Good* as well as

Fascinating Rhythm, The Half of it, Dearie, Blues and *The Man I Love*. The last of these is analysed in detail later in this unit (pages 93–95).

The shows for which Gershwin produced music were closely related in style to the revue – a loose collection of songs held together by a fairly basic plot. The book musical, where the plot is closely related to the music and dance of the show, began in earnest about this time, but most of Gershwin's shows are more influenced by earlier styles such as vaudeville, burlesque and revue. In common with many American songwriting partnerships of the early twentieth century, the Gershwin brothers set words to music rather than the other way round. European classical composers had normally set the existing words of poets to music, which allowed them to capture the meaning of the words in the way the melody was shaped.

■ Success as a songwriter and move to Hollywood

Gershwin was highly successful as a songwriter and in the 13 years between 1924 and his death in 1937 produced hundreds of songs for shows such as *Oh Kay!* (1926), *Funny Face* (1927), *Rosalie* (1928), *Girl Crazy* (1930), *Of Thee I Sing* (1931), *Pardon My English* (1933) and a work that Gershwin referred to as an 'American Folk Opera', *Porgy and Bess* (1935). This was based on the novel *Porgy* by DuBose Heyward, with whom the Gershwin brothers came to an arrangement to produce the opera. The show had the closest links between the songs and the drama, and was the best crafted of Gershwin's works for the stage. It contained some of the brothers' best songs, such as *Summertime, I Got Plenty of Nuttin', It Ain't Necessarily So* and *I Loves You, Porgy*. Nevertheless, like two previous shows, *Pardon My English* and *Let 'Em Eat Cake*, it was not a commercial success

The varied success of the shows did not affect George Gershwin's fame and fortune. He was in high demand as a performer but felt the need to work with film studios in Hollywood rather than writing for the Broadway stage. In the event he was there less than two years, his most significant work being the music for the film *Shall We Dance*. Whilst this had the same type of flimsy plot and improbable scenarios as many of the earlier Broadway shows, it contained some of his most mature songs. Three in particular – *They Can't Take That Away from Me, They All Laughed* and *Let's Call the Whole Thing Off* – have proved some of his most enduring.

→ Chronology of main works

George Gershwin wrote the music for a large number of musical comedies, dating from 1924. Here is a list of the most significant.

1924	*Lady, Be Good!*	**1928**	*Rosalie*
1925	*Tell Me More*	**1929**	*Show Girl*
	Tip Toes	**1930**	*Girl Crazy*
1926	*Oh, Kay!*	**1933**	*Pardon My English*
1927	*Funny Face*	**1935**	*Porgy and Bess*

→ Fingerprints of George Gershwin's style

☑ Many of George Gershwin's songs reflect his early career as a song plugger in Tin Pan Alley, where songs were written to 32-bar melodies divided into four phrases of eight bars each – the overall pattern was normally AABA. *Swanee* is a good example of this influence.

☑ Gershwin's music was composed before the lyrics therefore examples of word painting are due to the skill of the lyricist. The rhythm of the words always matches the rhythm of the music although a fair criticism is that the words sometimes make little sense.

☑ The melodies of the songs make extensive use of pentatonic scales and are generally highly memorable, particularly the choruses. The verses are often omitted in performance.

☑ Gershwin's melodies often use blue notes to capture the style of African-American singers; his later melodies have greater chromatic complexity.

☑ In performance many of the rhythms would be given a rubato treatment, especially in slower songs.

☑ Ira Gershwin's lyrics are witty, often with an internal rhyme scheme, and reflect the style of Gilbert and Sullivan.

☑ Songs are normally written for piano and voice but there are a variety of different piano styles in different songs.

☑ The songs normally have strong harmonic progressions: in the early songs these are often based around standard progressions such as I–VI–II–V, but later songs have greater harmonic complexity.

The A-level specification requires you to study four contrasting songs by Gershwin. Two are included here to demonstrate how this should be approached and what you need to know.

→ Case study 1 – *The Man I Love* (1924)

Background
When was the song written? 1924
What show is it taken from? *Lady, Be Good*
Who wrote the lyrics? Ira Gershwin (the 'book' was by Guy Bolton and Fred Thompson)
Where does it fit in Gershwin's output? It was the first really successful show that he worked on with Ira Gershwin as a lyricist and the style shows how far he had moved on from Tin Pan Alley. It is a slow song, with subject matter typical of yearning for love.

■ Structure
The song consists of a short verse of only eight lines, followed by a chorus of more than twice that length. The refrain is repeated, making it very significantly longer

than the verse. The subject matter is typical of many other songs of the time: a sad, melancholy verse leading to a hope-filled refrain.

Verse
When the mellow moon begins to beam,
Ev'ry night I dream a little dream,
And of course Prince Charming is the theme,
The he for me.

Although I realize as well as you,
It is seldom that a dream comes true,
To me it's clear
That he'll appear.

Refrain
Someday he'll come along,
The man I love;
And he'll be big and strong,
The man I love;
And when he comes my way,
I'll do my best to make him stay.

He'll look at me and smile,
I'll understand;
And in a little while
He'll take my hand;
And though it seems absurd,
I know we both won't say a word. –

Maybe I shall meet him Sunday,
Maybe Monday, maybe not;
Still I'm sure to meet him one day,
Maybe Tuesday will be my good news day.

He'll build a little home,
Just meant for two,
From which I'll never roam,
Who would – would you?
And so all else above,
I'm waiting for the man I love.

Although the lyrics have been written to fit the music, they do this fairly well. Occasionally, there is a sense of Ira Gershwin straining to make the words fit, such as in the fourth line of the verse ('The he for me') and the penultimate line of the chorus ('And so all else above'). For the most part, the rhythm of the words is reflected in the rhythm of the melody. The stresses of the words generally fit well with the stronger beats of the melody. This is obvious from the first line onwards. The tempo change at 'Maybe I shall meet him Sunday' is also reflected in the change of mood of the words.

■ Melody

The melody of the verse is in the key of Eb and is simplicity itself. Each of the first lines takes the same rhythm as the previous line but starts two notes higher. This produces a sequence in the melody. Each line helps to raise the pitch until the melody reaches its climax on 'Prince Charming is the theme' and then falls back in the fourth line. The second verse takes a similar shape but modulates to Bb before returning to the home key, ready for the chorus.

The refrain is much more interesting in its use of melody. It consists of four sections, three of which use the same melody. The third section has a jaunty melody, in contrast with the main tune, which makes use of blue notes, a favourite device of Gershwin. These are reflected in the chromatic harmony of the piano part, which gives a melancholy, yearning feeling to the music as if to reinforce the weariness of the woman waiting for a lover to come along.

Opening of refrain of The Man I Love

Words by IRA GERSHWIN   Music by GEORGE GERSHWIN

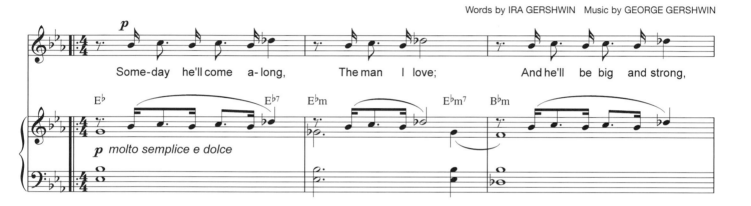

The middle section is more lively and reflects the hope that 'Maybe I shall meet him Sunday'.

→ Case study 2 – *They Can't Take That Away from Me* (1937)

Background

When was the song written? 1937

What show is it taken from? It was written for the film *Shall We Dance*.

Who wrote the lyrics? Ira Gershwin (the screenplay was by Allan Scott and Ernest Pagano)

Where does it fit in Gershwin's output? The songs that George and Ira Gershwin wrote for the film *Shall We Dance* represent their most mature and successful approach to songwriting. Although George Gershwin was uneasy about the way his songs were used in the film, it contains some of his best work, particularly the songs *They Can't Take That Away from Me*, *Let's Call the Whole Thing Off* and *They All Laughed*.

■ Structure

As with Gershwin's earlier songs, the verse is significantly shorter than the refrain. The refrain is repeated in total, thus making the imbalance even more marked. In contrast with many of the earlier songs, the verse of *They Can't Take That Away from Me* is as well known as the refrain and the song tends to be performed as a single entity. This may be accounted for by a musical sophistication of both verse and refrain that was less typical of Gershwin's songs from the 1920s.

Verse
Our romance won't end on a sorrowful note,
Though by tomorrow you're gone;
The song is ended, but as the songwriter wrote,
The melody lingers on.

They may take you from me,
I'll miss your fond caress.
But though they may take you from me, I'll still possess:

Refrain
The way you wear your hat,
The way you sip your tea,
The mem'ry of all that,
No, No! They can't take that away from me!

The way your smile just beams,
The way you sing off key,
The way you haunt my dreams,
No, No! They can't take that away from me!

We may never, never meet again
On the bumpy road to love,
Still I'll always, always keep the mem'ry of

The way you hold your knife,
The way we danced till three,
The way you've changed my life.
No, No! They can't take that away from me!
No! They can't take that away from me!

The song has a yearning, emotional quality, far removed from the contrived emotional utterances of Tin Pan Alley. There are some poetic touches in both the verse and the refrain; phrases such as 'The song is ended, but as the songwriter wrote, the melody lingers on' show a depth and maturity in Ira Gershwin's lyrics that complement his brother's music well. There are a number of phrases that are repeated to help create a strong structure. These include the phrase 'The way you …' and the repeated 'No, No! They can't take that away from me!' As in some of the earlier songs, the mood changes in the middle of the chorus, at 'We may never, never meet again', and then returns to a more positive mood for the final five lines.

■ Melody

The song is in the key of Eb major although this is clearer in the refrain than in the verse. The opening of the verse is highly chromatic and produces an interesting and varied melody, which moves in and out of the key of Eb major. This is much more developed than the verses of many of Gershwin's songs and the harmonies in the piano part complement this perfectly. By the end of the verse, despite a considerable amount of chromatic movement, the melody leads back to the home key for the refrain.

First four lines of They Can't Take That Away from Me

Words by IRA GERSHWIN Music by GEORGE GERSHWIN

The refrain makes extensive use of a motif consisting of the note Eb, repeated five times, to the words 'The way you [wear your]', with the last two words changing for each statement. Some performers treat this motif as being syncopated, others sing it exactly as written. Whichever way it is performed, it is significant for its repetition.

There is a contrasting style in the three-line section 'We may never, never meet again ...'. The melody here is in the key of G minor and provides a melancholy reflection on the transient nature of love. The message of the song is reiterated at the end by repetition of the title line of the song.

Examination Practice:
Sample Questions

In the written examination, you will need to answer two questions, each from a different section. You will have 2 hours to do this. Here are some examples that you may find it useful to work through with your tutors.

■ Section A

Matthew Bourne

Discuss the issues of gender representation raised by Matthew Bourne's work.

Shobana Jeyasingh

Shobana Jeyasingh claims that her aim is 'to create exciting and engaging performances that tell the story of our time.' How does she do this?

Lloyd Newson

What physical challenge does Newson's work present to a performer? Base your answer on two roles from a piece by Newson.

■ Section B

Caryl Churchill

With close reference to one play, discuss the way in which Churchill comments on contemporary society.

Athol Fugard

Select a central character in one of Fugard's plays and discuss the way you would shape the physical and vocal dimensions of the role.

John Godber

Discuss the approach to dialogue in one of John Godber's plays.

■ Section C

John Adams

'A rich mix of American influences.' With close reference to one piece by John Adams, discuss the extent to which such influences may be seen.

The Beatles

How did the Beatles challenge the culture and society of the 1960s in their songs?

George Gershwin

Discuss George Gershwin's use of chromatic harmony in his songs.

UNIT 3
Performance Contexts 2

→ Why study a topic?

In the previous unit, the focus was on studying a single piece of dance, drama or music in detail. The reason for doing this was to draw out the most important approaches used, trends followed and influences on the practitioner who devised the piece. In the present unit, the reverse is the case. The focus is on a broad topic, and the purpose of the study is to investigate how the different aspects of the topic can be seen in nine varied examples. These examples should be split equally between dance, drama and music. You may choose to draw these examples from the same practitioner in each art form, or you may choose to look at up to nine different practitioners. Whichever you choose, this study is more advanced as some of the examples may conflict with each other and the picture may be complex and even confusing. However, there are generic trends that unite the works and these emerge through a careful study of the richness of the topic.

The four topic options are

● **Post-Modern Approaches to the Performing Arts since 1960**
● **Politics and Performance since 1914**
● **The Twentieth-Century American Musical**
● **Approaches to Performance in the Far East.**

To encourage an in-depth study of the topic, you will study only one of these four options.

Remember that when you answer questions in the examination, you can make **passing reference** to the practitioners you have studied at AS level in *Unit 2: Performance Contexts 1*, but you **cannot** study these practitioners in detail at A2 level in this unit. However, there may be practitioners listed in the AS unit which you did not study, and so you could choose a work from one of those practitioners to look at in this unit.

Post-Modern Approaches
to the Performing Arts since 1960

Until the middle of the twentieth century, styles and movements in the performing arts seemed to evolve into one another and this made it easy to identify a more-or-less clear line of development. Since the 1960s, this has become increasingly difficult as it has no longer been so straightforward to label a work as being 'in' a particular style. There are many reasons for this.

There is no longer a sense of linear progression from one style to another. Instead of looking for a new style, practitioners may choose to rework performance styles from the past to create a new performance work. Rather than working in isolation, they might choose to create work that incorporates other art forms. For example, dance companies may use physical theatre, dialogue and film in their pieces. Drama companies might rely on physical theatre to replace or work alongside the spoken word. Real and virtual worlds can be mixed in the theatre space. In some cases, the intricate and skilful use of puppetry has become so sophisticated that the audience forgets what is animate and what is not. The use of video with music, or music as an ingredient of sound installations, or music as downloads or ringtones has become widespread and prevalent. All of this is typical of the eclectic world of post-modern performance.

Allan Kaprow invented the term 'happening' in 1957 as a way of referring to artistic work and collaborations which at the time defied conventional description. The Happening movement thrived during the 1960s, especially in New York. The image below comes from a 1964 happening created in New York by American choreographer Yvonne Rainer and (behind the board) sculptor Robert Morris.

There have been many attempts at defining post-modernism, which is not surprising given the complexity of the topic. Post-modernism is quite different from all earlier styles because it attempts to embrace the whole diversity of performing arts styles. This very diversity means that there is no longer a single artistic movement that can be easily defined or labelled. Eclecticism is the order of the day: practitioners may take and borrow from past styles, conventions or techniques; conflicting elements may be used in the same work, and there is no restriction on the subject matter of works.

→ An eclectic mix

There is no longer a clear distinction between high and low art in any of the art forms. It is not uncommon, for example, to see eclectic work in which ballet is mixed with street dance in the same piece. In drama, Shakespearean language may be entwined with street language or even a

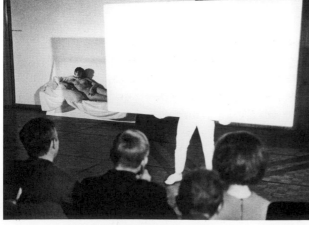

foreign language. In music, medieval plainsong could be interspersed with ambient music or another contemporary style. There are simply no stylistic guidelines to follow, although this does not prevent individual artists defining their style closely, or companies producing artistic policy statements.

In breaking down the barriers between art forms, post-modern practitioners often work in collaboration. Even if the work was not produced collaboratively, it may still be used as such. The music of Steve Reich, for example, is used by a number of choreographers although very little of it has been written specifically for dance. The development of the genre of physical theatre has provoked a number of debates as to the distinctions between drama and dance.

→ The use of styles from the past

A feature of much post-modern work is the use of artistic work from previous generations. A practitioner might borrow from the past, or indeed the present, and mix the two together so that history no longer has any meaning. According to this view, post-modernism spells the end of history since there can never be another new style. New approaches are simply bringing together old ones in a different way.

For example, in *Cross Channel*, Lea Anderson takes fashions from past eras and mixes them together. In her work *Flesh and Blood* the intertextual references include Carl Dreyer's 1928 film *The Passion of Joan of Arc* (reflected in the dancers' short haircuts and the emphasis on the facial expression), as well works such as *Reptiles* (1943) by graphic artist M. C. Escher (1898–1972), with the dancers moving in a two-dimensional manner inspired by his flat drawings. Contemporary musicians and DJs sample from past recordings and recycle samples in a new way, sometimes giving a respectful nod to a past melodic line in the form of a quotation, at other times parodying it to create humour for the listener.

Some practitioners specialise in creating pastiche or parody. This may be a simple reworking of an existing score, script or dance, which can include more than one style or have various styles or forms juxtaposed within it. Whatever content is used carries no value judgement with it: all historical and contemporary work is deemed to be of equal value by the post-modernist practitioner. Styles that might now appear dated (such as comedy of manners) might be used ironically.

→ Technology

The development of technology since 1960 – and the recent development of digital technology in particular – has made possible a number of things that would have been inconceivable in previous generations. Live performance in proscenium hall theatres or concert halls is simply one possible performance arena. The dissemination of performance work to the 'iPod generation' is as likely to be through internet sources, MP3 players, YouTube and other social networking sites, reinforced by free-access encyclopedias. Musicians can work independently of record labels and produce their own albums that can reach the public as downloads.

Theatrical productions are becoming increasingly sophisticated as technology offers a wider array of options for those designing sets, props, lighting and sound. Innovative ways of portraying creatures on stage has led to imaginative use of puppets. In Nick Stafford's adaptation of Michael Morpurgo's *War Horse*, for example, the horses are large puppets designed by Basil Jones and Adrian Kohler. They are operated by puppeteers, but are so well designed and move so like real horses that the audience accept them as living creatures. This is an example of hyperreality.

Life-size puppets of horses feature in *War Horse* at the National Theatre.

→ Fingerprints of post-modern style

☑ Post-modernism tries to make sense of the huge diversity of contemporary styles and the way in which there no longer seems to be any 'direction' in terms of stylistic development. Collaboration between art forms and between practitioners is often a feature of work.

☑ A reassessment of the art of the past – post-modernism marks the 'end of history'. If this view is accepted wholesale, by definition there can be no more styles to follow it. Modernism is, on this view, the last historical style. However, some dance work is now described as 'post post-modern'.

☑ Eclecticism and the reinterpretation of the past. The approach is all about using existing styles in a new context – often these are conventional forms revisited.

☑ Styles are frequently juxtaposed in a way in which they were never intended to be used but this does not matter. This may embrace intertextuality – the use of references to things outside the art form or artefact.

☑ Post-modernism makes no value judgements about the relative worth of different types of art. This raises questions of meaning and 'no meaning' – should there be any meaning to a piece of performance in any case?

☑ The audience as 'consumer', with each person simply choosing what he or she wants to 'consume'. The style is about approaches to reworking, refiguration, recycling/pastiche with large-scale perspective.

The following works are studied in this section and could be used to illustrate the fingerprints of post-modern approaches to performance work. They are listed in the order in which they were produced, but remember what has been said about there being no obvious linear progression with post-modern works. Do not look for developments between one piece and another, but do consider what they have in common, and how they might differ.

1967	Steve Reich – *Piano Phase*	1987	Lea Anderson – *Flesh and Blood*
1973	Edward Bond – *Bingo*	2000	Akram Khan – *Rush*
1975	David Bowie – *Low*	2006	Mark Ravenhill & Frantic Assembly – *Pool (No Water)*
1975	Patti Smith – *Horses*		
1975	Steven Berkoff – *East*	2007	Motionhouse Dance Company – *Driven*

→ Steve Reich – *Piano Phase*

Steve Reich (born 1936) is one of the most significant living American composers. As a student at the Julliard School in New York he was taught to compose in European styles of the early twentieth century, particularly 12-tone music, or Serialism. After moving to Mills College, San Francisco, Reich was taught by the Italian composer Luciano Berio, who finally advised him to turn to writing tonal music. This was a turning point in Reich's career as a composer because it released him from trying to imitate modern styles with which he had no sympathy, and allowed him to use conventional approaches instead, but in a new way. The way in which he went on to use elements of traditional music is a good example of a post-modern approach.

The style developed by Reich and others in the early 1960s became known as Minimalism, although Reich himself was no fan of this title. The group of four so-called Minimalist composers also included Philip Glass (born 1937), Terry Riley (born 1935) and LaMonte Young (born 1935).

■ Phasing

The most noticeable feature of Reich's style is its intense and incessant repetition. It has also been referred to as systems music or repetitive music, both of which are probably more accurate descriptions than 'Minimalist'. His two earliest pieces were not for traditional instruments but for tape loops. Reich's interest in human speech is obvious here. He made tape recordings of people speaking and, having selected a snippet he liked the sound of, used it as a repetitive loop. Before sampling technology became commonplace, the only way of creating this type of loop was physically to cut the tape and stick it together.

In *Come Out* (1966), Reich had sampled the voice of a young man who was being framed for a murder he did not commit. The short speech snippet of Daniel Hamm saying the words 'come out to show them' is used as a tape loop and played against an identical loop of the same sample. As the tape recorders that Reich was using were of low quality, the loops began to move out of phase with each other and produced a very interesting musical effect. The technique became known as phasing, and was a discovery that Reich had made the previous year when working with recordings of a Black Pentecostal preacher in San Francisco who was preaching about the story of Noah from the Bible. The resultant piece, *It's Gonna Rain*, established the principle of phasing.

Reich was determined to achieve the same effect of phasing using human performers rather than tape recorders. He was concerned that it would be impossible to move slowly out of phase in live performance, but discovered that with careful practice it was possible to do so. This led to two significant phase pieces that used live performers: *Piano Phase* (1967) and *Violin Phase* (1967).

■ *Piano Phase* (1967)

Piano Phase is simple in its use of materials: a single phrase of 12 notes (but played with both hands to simplify it). A second pianist plays the same phrase and then very slightly increases the tempo to move it one semiquaver ahead of the first part. This continues until the second part moves again then the process continues until the two parts are back in unison again at the end of the piece. In his 1968 essay *Music as a Gradual Process*, Reich spelt out the importance of these process-based systems to his composition. Once the melodic material was chosen, the system ran itself. The important aspect for the listener was the unexpected musical moments that occur as the parts collide in and out of phase. Reich referred to this as the 'mysteries' of the phase since there was no guarantee that what one person heard, another would also hear.

Opening of *Piano Phase*

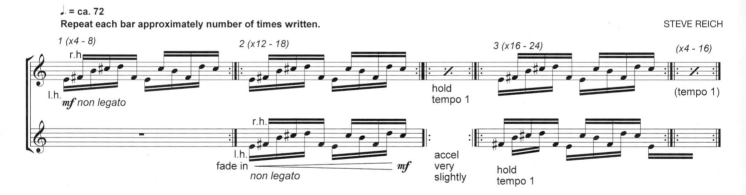

This music is post-modern because it makes use of recognisable musical materials from the past but uses them in a new way. There is nothing new about using a short tonal motif, but the constant repetition and phasing is different to anything that had been done before. As Reich's music developed from the 1970s through to the twenty-first century, the repetitive element remained and the composer was able to reintroduce other elements of tonal music, such as using a series of chords, which had been abandoned by composers in the first half of the twentieth century. *Music for 18 Musicians*, for example, uses a series of 11 chords at the opening of the piece although these are not a traditional chord sequence. The principle underlying Reich's post-modern approach – and that of the other so-called Minimalist composers – is that the musical materials of the past can be re-used in the music of today, but in a different manner to their usage by previous composers. Similarly, Reich's use of World Music influences such as the gamelan or African drumming, identify his approach as being post-modern.

→ Edward Bond – *Bingo*

Edward Bond (born 1937) is recognised as one of the most radical British playwrights of the late twentieth century. As a post-modern practitioner he intentionally provides no personal information in his published playscripts except that he was born and educated in London. Bond was evacuated to the countryside during the Second World War but was in London throughout the Blitz and the V-rocket attacks. Such organised violence and terror perpetrated upon ordinary people had a formative influence on his creative thinking.

He has been a prolific playwright since the 1970s but the controversial content of his works meant he was often in opposition to the theatre establishment. In the 1960s, when censorship still limited what could be shown, he explored on stage the inherent violence in society including the stoning of a baby's pram by urban youths in *Saved* (1965). Other subjects for extreme treatment included Queen Victoria, Florence Nightingale, Princes Albert, Arthur and George in *Early Morning* (1967) and Shakespeare and Ben Jonson in *Bingo* (1973).

He has the reputation of being uncompromising in his theatrical approach. Disagreements over the staging of his plays by the National Theatre and the Royal Court led to some of his work being staged abroad. His popularity has at times been stronger in mainland Europe and he has collaborated with theatres in Paris, Berlin and the USA, but also with a school in Cambridge, near his home. More recently increased recognition of the relevance of his social themes has generated major revivals of his work in the UK.

■ Bond's theatre

Bond aims not just to be post-modern but to define post-modernism and advance it as the mode of thinking required for the time we live in. With the text to some plays he includes essays exploring his thinking. There are detailed notes on post-modernism in *Jackets* and *The Company of Men*, a double bill exploring power codes in eighteenth-century Japan in the first work, and in the modern boardroom in the second. Bond's themes are set out in these notes: the relationship between history and the present state; the relationship between people, technology and authority; how theatre and the arts are part of that relationship. This post-modern manifesto states that meaning cannot be derived from the world but must be given to it. There is also a political dimension to Bond's thought that insists people ask questions about the limits and rules of social experience to make them understandable and act to change them if necessary.

■ *Bingo* (1973)

The opening essay with the text of *Bingo* states that there are two types of 'wrong' in society. Some 'wrong' can be improved upon by doing it less badly, but society can improve on the other type only

John Gielgud as Shakespeare in the Royal Court production of *Bingo* by not doing it at all. Bond means that state violence cannot be done 'better'. Society can be better only by becoming just (providing equally for the needs of all), so violence would have no purpose. As the organisation of society would be just, there would be no need for politics either. He further questions whether the feelings and opinions we have are truly our own, or whether the injustice of society means we express the ones we are persuaded to have.

These are difficult ideas to grasp out of context, but if borne in mind when exploring the play they make the action understandable. Bond uses the past in a post-modern manner. He uses the theme of the enclosure of common and tenanted land in the time of Shakespeare, which gave power to the wealthy and dispossessed the tenants. The majority of the population were not freemen and had to stay within the bounds of their parishes. This social control was seen by those in power as necessary and good; for those who lived under it, it was oppression to be resisted.

A young woman who appears mentally disordered from a previous beating is first punished severely then executed for arson and her body hangs over the stage for the whole of the second act. The only character who appears to have unconstrained feelings is a brain-damaged old man looked after by an old woman trying to restrain him from sexual transgression. She hopes he will die before her, knowing that without her he would suffer at the hands of the authorities for his actions.

There are two types of language used here – the educated 'authority' figures speak in modern English, while the native country people speak accented dialect. The post-modern structure makes no attempt to be true to the period, but sets side by side Shakespearean and modern language. Shakespeare, now retired, finds himself unwillingly on the landowners' side. His image as a great artist counts for nothing. In this place he is simply one local landowner who is persuaded to join others. His art has not touched these people, which suggests we should ask whether it has made any real difference to us either. His increasing weariness leads to despair and ultimately suicide, after a visit from an envious Ben Jonson, who admits his task in the visit is to spy on the work the old master might be writing.

Jonson and Shakespeare get drunk, and Shakespeare passes out. Shakespeare's daughter is more concerned with moral standards and the content of her father's will than his welfare. The play ends with her searching frantically around Shakespeare's bed in the hope of finding a new will as her father dies.

Combe, a modernising landlord, believes that the suffering of the poor is necessary to create a better world for all in future. Bond foreshadows the Thatcherite government that came to power in 1979 some years after this play. One of the ministers of that government used the phrase 'a price worth paying' in reference to the economic upheaval in the 1980s in which manufacturing and mining communities collapsed. Combe is willing to use force to punish those who resist less violently by filling ditches at night. The imbalance of the violence employed by one side against the more passive physical exertions of the other shows the themes of Bond's post-modern manifesto in action.

→ David Bowie – *Low*

David Bowie was born David Robert Jones in 1947 in Brixton, London. In the 1960s he played in bands and released records but it was not until 1969 that he experienced chart success. This was with his Top 5 UK hit single *Space Oddity*, a ballad about an astronaut called Major Tom who became lost in space. This was one of a number of personas that Bowie has adopted during his career, including Ziggy Stardust and the Thin White Duke.

He studied acting, *commedia dell'arte* then mime with Lindsay Kemp and this influenced his performance style in the 1970s. He would invent a character and then kill them off in order to invent yet another. The clearest example of this is in his 1972 album *The Rise and Fall of Ziggy Stardust and the Spiders from Mars*. Bowie is known for his regular changing of style and persona throughout his music career. Although reinvention is not the same thing as post-modernism, in Bowie's case it provides the context for his reinterpretation of earlier styles. In his third album, *The Man Who Saved the World* (1970), Bowie chose a heavy rock guitar courtesy of Mick Ronson over the acoustic sound of the previous album. Bowie also showed his androgynous side on the UK album cover, where he is wearing a dress.

Bowie has appeared in films such as *Labyrinth* and *Absolute Beginners*, stage plays such as *Baal* by Bertolt Brecht, and TV documentaries. He has made outstanding and innovative music videos such as *Ashes to Ashes*.

■ Collaboration

Collaborations between practitioners are common in post-modernism. Bowie has worked closely with Brian Eno and Iggy Pop as well as with producers such as Tony Visconti and Gus Dugeon. Bowie has produced other artists such as the band Mott the Hoople, for whom he wrote and produced *All the Young Dudes*. Along with Mick Ronson, he produced *Transformer* for Lou Reed, who had been part of the Velvet Underground. The band the Spiders from Mars came back together to make *Aladdin Sane*.

■ Borrowing from the past

In 1974 Bowie released *Diamond Dogs*, which was influenced by George Orwell's novel *1984*. This album provides an interesting study of how Bowie took a novel from the past (written in 1948) about a future world (in 1984) and made his own predictions about a dystopian world.

Young Americans (1975) represents another new departure for Bowie's style, demonstrating the influences of philly soul (soul music influenced by funk). After this he found another persona for his performances and recordings, the Thin White Duke, and went on to produce *Station to Station* (1976).

Bowie co-produced *The Idiot* and *Lust for Life* with Iggy Pop. He worked with Brian Eno on what became known as the Berlin trilogy: *Low*, *Heroes* and *Lodger*, significant also for their influence on post-modern Minimalist composer Philip Glass. Another influence on Bowie was Conny Plank, who had a studio in Neunkirchen near Cologne, where he produced/engineered many of the most significant German bands of the 1970s, such as Kraftwerk, Neu! and Holger Czukay. Conny's characteristic electronic sound using droning backing tracks, multilayered synthesisers and dramatic vocal sounds can be heard in the Berlin trilogy.

■ *Low* (1975)

Low is the first album in the Berlin trilogy but much of it was recorded in France. David Bowie intended *Low* to be the soundtrack for the film *The Man Who Fell to Earth* (1976), directed by Nicholas Roeg, but it was not finished in time. Bowie starred in the film as Mr Newton, an alien in disguise who had come in search of water from a planet that was suffering a severe drought. The final tracks were recorded at the Hansa Studios in Berlin and later mixed at the Hansa by the Wall studios. Bowie did little to promote the album's release, which was in keeping with his attitude to keeping 'a low profile'. This was the visual pun displayed by the album cover – a photograph from *The Man Who Fell to Earth*.

The album's track list is

1   *Speed of Life*
2   *Breaking Glass*
3   *What in the World*
4   *Sound and Vision*
5   *Always Crashing in the Same Car*
6   *Be My Wife*
7   *A New Career in a New Town*
8   *Warszawa*
9   *Art Decade*
10 *Weeping Wall*
11 *Subterraneans.*

According to Bowie, the first side of the album is about him and the second is a reaction to the strange situation at that time of West Berlin, which was in the middle of the Eastern bloc, surrounded on all sides. At the time of making the record, Bowie was trying to turn his life around. He had been addicted to cocaine in America and realised that he needed a radical change, so he moved with Iggy Pop to Europe. Bowie became fascinated by German electronic bands such as Neu! and Kraftwerk and their influence can be heard on the album.

The album's producer, Tony Visconti, brought a new gadget called the Eventide Harmonizer to the studio, which could alter the pitch while keeping the tempo. This was responsible for some aspects of the album's unique sound, particularly the way the pitch of the snare-drum was lowered. Whilst Bowie embraced electronic music, he did not want to use synthesisers to replace instruments but rather to manipulate the sounds of real instruments and to create texture. Bowie has indicated that Kraftwerk were a starting point for him as they were determined to move away from commercial music with its stereotypical chord sequences. But whereas Kraftwerk produced robotic music with electronically created percussion that kept a rigid tempo, Bowie used live musicians and was more spontaneous in the studio. Bowie has referred to his work at this time as being a hybrid of the new European music and other forms such as R 'n' B.

Brian Eno used oblique-strategies cards, which offer a random element to the process much like Merce Cunningham's chance method in dance. The musicians would turn over the cards at different moments during the recording session and then follow the written instructions, such as 'Fill every beat with something'. This helped Bowie move away from narrative-driven albums and towards a nonlinear structure and abstract feel – significant aspects of post-modern approaches. The album is predominantly instrumental and atmospheric with few lyrics. The backing tracks were recorded first, followed by overdubs and instrumental solos and, last, the lyrics and vocals.

→ Patti Smith – *Horses*

Patricia Lee Smith was born in Chicago in 1946. She was the eldest of four children, raised in Philadelphia and later New Jersey. She graduated from high school in 1964 and worked in a toy factory, which she despised. She was exposed to music early on by her mother, who bought her jazz records and a Bob Dylan album. Smith says that the music of the 1960s became more poetic, and rather than providing music to dance to, made comments about things that people were rebelling against and questioning, such as the Vietnam War and the lack of civil rights in the USA. Smith was heavily influenced by the poetry of Arthur Rimbaud and began her career reading poetry accompanied by Lenny Kaye on guitar.

Smith had planned to become an art teacher and attended Glassboro State Teachers' College but she would not teach the curriculum, preferring instead to teach about obscure artists and experiment with her own poetry. In 1967, having given up a baby for adoption, Smith moved to New York, found a job in a bookstore and met Robert Mapplethorpe, with whom she had a long and platonic relationship. The cover of her 1975 album *Horses* consists of his photographic portrait of her.

'Three chord rock merged with the power of the word.'
Patti Smith on her music

When she returned from Paris, she found Mapplethorpe ill and moved with him into the Chelsea Hotel, which was a refuge for poor artists and underground figures such as William S. Burroughs. She started to mix with the Andy Warhol crowd, give poetry readings on stage and write music reviews. She had affairs with several men including Jim Carroll (writer of *The Basketball Diaries*) and Sam Shepherd (playwright), with whom she wrote the play *Cowboy Mouth* (1971).

Her first poetry book, *Seventh Heaven*, was published in 1972 by Telegraph and received rave reviews. Frequently described as the Punk Poet Laureate, she performed her poetry in London and back in New York, where Lenny Kaye played guitar accompaniment throughout at CBGBs night club. Later, Richard Sohl joined them as a keyboard player and their first single, *Piss Factory/Hey Joe*, was recorded at Electric Ladyland Studios. After performing as a successful support for Richard Hell's band Television, Ivan Kral (guitarist) and Jay Dee Daugherty (drummer) joined Smith's band. In 1975 Bob Dylan went to see her play and this led to Clive Davis signing her for seven albums with Arista Records.

In 2005 Patti Smith was made a Commander of the *Ordre des Arts et des Lettres* by the French Culture Ministry for her empowering work for women in the arts and for her appreciation of Arthur Rimbaud. She was inducted into the Rock and Roll Hall of Fame in 2007. In an article entitled 'Ain't it strange' in the *New York Times* on 12 March 2007, she questioned whether someone like her who works 'within the revolutionary landscape of rock' should accept 'laurels from an institution'. She decided to accept on behalf of people like her late husband and others who would not be able to receive such laurels.

Patti Smith demonstrates some post-modern traits: her reworking of other writers' songs; her seemingly androgynous look; her fascination with different art forms and how they can merge together; her desire to change and experiment with form and medium and her extraordinary vocals. Her style is a cross between singing and an explosive, angry style of poetry reading, with a roller coaster of emotions ranging through love, anguish and frustration. Her output is peppered with snippets from a wide range of rock songs, and the way this interacts with her own text produces a very dense musical texture.

■ *Horses* (1975)

The album's track list is

1 *Gloria* 5:57
   In Excelsis Deo (Smith)
   Gloria (version) (Van Morrison)
2 *Redondo Beach* 3:26 (Smith, Richard Sohl, Lenny Kaye)
3 *Birdland* 9:15 (Smith, Sohl, Kaye, Ivan Kral)
4 *Free Money* 3:52 (Smith, Kaye)
5 *Kimberly* 4:27 (Smith, Allen Lanier, Kral)
6 *Break It Up* 4:04 (Smith, Tom Verlaine)
7 *Land* 9:25
   Horses (Smith)
   Land of a Thousand Dances (Chris Kenner)
   La Mer(de) (Smith)
8 *Elegie* 2:57 (Smith, Lanier)

Produced by John Cale, *Horses* was released on 10 November 1975 and was praised by *Rolling Stone* magazine and the *New York Times*. It sold 200 000 copies over the next year and reached Number 47 in the charts. It is renowned for its opening line (added by Smith) to the Van Morrison track song entitled *Gloria*: 'Jesus died for somebody's sins but not mine'.

The Smith version of *Gloria* sounds very different from the original and it is often hard for the listener to recognise Van Morrison's song. Smith's unique performance and idiosyncratic vocals demonstrate that she is an artist whose style is hard to pin down, and the way she brings different styles together is typical of post-modern practitioners. Other female artists who followed her, such as Lene Lovich and Siouxsie of Siouxsie and the Banshees, show traits of Smith's experimental vocals with her range of pitch, her growling low notes and high whoops, situated somewhere between a scream and a shout.

Horses marked Patti Smith as the first artist from the New York punk scene to have a recording deal and to release an album. The songs reflect Smith's passions for poetry (inspired by Arthur Rimbaud), protest (inspired by Bob Dylan), jazz and rock and roll (inspired by artists such as Jimi Hendrix, Jim Morrison, the Rolling Stones, John Coltrane and Smokey Robinson).

Smith collaborated on the album with musicians from other bands such as Tom Verlaine from Television and Allen Lanier from Blue Öyster Cult.

The songs on the album are marked by Smith's interest in the power of the poetic word. *Birdland* tells the story of a son whose father has died and left him the farm they used to share. The lines read like stream-of-consciousness writing and it is hard to follow the narrative as the emotions of the deserted son take over. *Land* has become an iconic song in pop history, with its famous line 'The boy looked at Johnny, Johnny wanted to run'. The lines are littered with metaphors and allusions, making a very dense lyric open to a myriad of interpretations.

→ Steven Berkoff – *East*

Steven Berkoff (born 1937) is one of the most innovative contemporary British drama practitioners. The son of a Russian émigré Jewish tailor, as a young man he escaped from the cultural and economic poverty of his home in Stepney, East London into the world of professional theatre. His intellectuality was evident as he developed the stage tones of a professional actor but held on to his cockney vocal manner.

In the early 1960s, he became strongly influenced by French total theatre after reading the work of Antonin Artaud. Feeling that this articulated everything he felt about theatre, he trained further at the Jacques Lecoq school in Paris.

Naturally unconventional, he found it difficult to obtain mainstream roles: he felt he had greatness that was unrecognised and embarked upon creating his own plays – and his own style – to suit his own talents. Nevertheless, he has also acted in a number of films, including commercial successes such as *Octopussy*, *Rambo* and *Beverly Hills Cop*.

■ Berkoff's theatre

Berkoff's work takes place in an unstable world of contradictions, and extreme, sometimes rapidly shifting emotions. The style he developed from his reading of Artaud and Lecoq led to his production of Kafka's *Metamorphosis* (1969). An ideal work for developing his interests, *Metamorphosis* pioneered what became identifiable as a form we now call physical theatre.

Berkoff had a chameleon desire to be many things and to show all of them at once if possible. He combined Kafka's stark prose with Lecoq's highly disciplined physical expression and Artaud's desire to explore extremes of sensory experience. His intention was to awaken the mind through shock. Berkoff intended strong reactions, and has been reputed to delight in members of the audience walking out in distaste at the unconventionality of his performances. It was even rumoured that on occasions he would 'plant' individuals who would leave noisily objecting in mid-performance, in order to provoke a more active experience.

■ *East* (1975)

East is the first of a series of Berkoff's own verse plays. Berkoff has always had a contradictory attitude to his origins, and a need for contradictions to be laid out in order for his work to have the value intended. He has a simultaneous fascination and disgust in the intense familiarity of characters. The post-modern comedy of the piece is based in the diversity of images, rapidly and sharply drawn, a wide range of recognisable contexts, music and language, and sharp satirical messages.

Structural features

East has no linear narrative, a strong post-modern feature. It is a series of 19 free-standing scenes in a 2 hour performance, usually played without an interval. The physical intensity of the action and stamina required is evident in the perspiration of the actors playing Mike and Les in the video of the stage production that toured in the year 2000. Their duo portrayal of motorcycle and rider in scene 12 is a memorable example of Berkoff's use of Lecoq physicality in a new context. The three other characters, Mum, Dad and Sylv, are less demanding, although the part of Sylv requires physical athleticism.

Another post-modern feature is the language Berkoff created in an echo of his own training as an actor. This brings together the cockney assertiveness and self-perceived heroism which he found matched the assured manner of the characters of Shakespeare. Using not just the verse style and language but recognisable quotations for the audience to identify intertextually, he mock elevates the action. For example, 'he doth bestride the world like a colossus', from the Roman world of *Antony and Cleopatra*, is spoken with cockney tones and swagger, and projects the East End psyche to an audience who might never venture to the theatre.

The use of diverse music in *East* is another post-modern feature. There are sung transitions of *My Old Man*. Silent-film music accompanying scene 2 supports a French Lecoq-style comic mime in which the audience rather than silent film is portrayed. Dad salutes the National Anthem as his family push past him. A well known blues piano riff accompanies the courtship strutting when the minds of Mike and Les turn to sex, but in comic conjunction with their exaggerated manner and stylised chat-up lines. There is a speech melody in the cockney expletive 'Fuu …ckinell', which is always sung rather than spoken.

Characterisation

Dad pre-dates and predicts the formation of the British National Party. An East End fascist of the pre-war kind, he is not dangerous only because he is ignored, as in the dinner scene, where his monologue pales behind the frantic shovelling of food.

The character of Mum is comic but with a social/political edge, serving as a warning to any young woman growing up in a poor community. Played by a man, she is a faded reference to the pantomime dame, weary and stripped of any sexual manner. She nonetheless discusses with a snoring Dad whether they are having sex or not, to audible squeals from the audience. In her ensuing monologue she leads the audience in an extended comic gag of the bluest variety. For the duration of this Berkoff skilfully creates in the theatre the feel of a working men's club.

Berkoff implies that Sylv is a precursor to Mum. Mike and Les are interested in her only for her physical attractiveness but are prepared to go to considerable and comic lengths, using mime to illustrate their need, to persuade her to have sex. Her extended monologue is a pre-feminist declamation, angry, assertive but ultimately hopeless: she can never 'be a fella'.

The London Theatre Group in the original production of *East*

Mike and Les are post-modern heroes. They have no ambition, only the desire for pleasure. There is no evidence of any education but they have a classical Shakespearian manner – they know everything they need to, and always have a ready answer. They will fight each other brutally over a girl then carry each other to hospital to be patched up. An attractive girl is a challenge to give their all for, triumph over, and abandon. They are anti-moral and succeed where conventional morality states they should be examples of failure.

Ultimately, this is the contradiction of the world of *East*: a society which according to moral standards should cease to function defies gravity and has a strength of its own making.

→ Lea Anderson – *Flesh and Blood*

Lea Anderson graduated from the Laban Centre in 1984 and formed the all-female company the Cholmondeleys (pronounced *Chumleys*) with Teresa Barker and Gaynor Coward. Their first public performance was at the Edinburgh Fringe Festival. One of their pieces was based on a seventeenth-century painting in the Tate Gallery of the Cholmondeley Sisters and the name stuck. Anderson also created an all-male counterpart company, the Featherstonehaughs (pronounced *Fanshaws*), whose name was taken from a book on the pronunciation of old English family titles.

Lea Anderson

Sometimes the two companies perform together in the same work (for example, *Cross Channel*, 1991) and sometimes they perform each other's repertoire (*Double Take*, 2004). The way in which they play with the idea of gender fits well with the post-modern approach to performance. There is no hierarchy between dancers and no distinction between a chorus and prima ballerina/principal male. Each dancer is equal in status with the others in the ensemble.

To celebrate the twentieth anniversary of the Cholmondeleys, Anderson put on a show called *Double Take* where the two companies performed each other's work. The Featherstonehaughs, the all-male company, performed *Flesh and Blood* in the females' costumes and brought to it a strange, almost sinister feel. The original score was performed live by Steve Blake and his band the Victims of Death. The DVD of *Double Take* is set in a large warehouse and begins with a speeded-up version of the set being created and the floor being laid. It has several quirky short numbers such as *Elvis Legs* and *Greetings* and shows Lea Anderson being playful with her subject matter.

■ Anderson's style

Lea Anderson recycles images from the past, mixed with an eclectic range of music and pedestrian movement, to create pieces to be performed in many different settings, from traditional to non-conventional. This helps secure her place as a post-modern practitioner.

From the 2006 production of *Yippeee!!!*

She has made pieces for all sorts of venues, including a public car park (*Car*), a derelict warehouse and the inside of a cathedral (*Flesh and Blood*), and the stage. She values dance on film as much as dance on stage and uses the multiple

perspectives offered by the camera to juxtapose scenes, groups of dancers and times of day.

Anderson uses many different types of stimulus material to inspire her work and her visual-arts background is clearly evident in many of her pieces. She has collaborated with Sandy Powell for costume designs and with Steve Blake and Drostan Madden for sound and music. Her pieces are usually episodic in structure and are quite often made up of short scenes. There is humour in her work, often quirky and not always readily accessible. She is well known for using a mixture of body types and heights in her company and for a focus on minute detail rather than grandiose movement. Each piece has its own movement vocabulary, which is developed in a collaborative way with the dancers in the company.

■ *Flesh and Blood* (1987)

Performed by the Cholmondeleys, *Flesh and Blood* was presented on stage and reworked for film.

The eclectic choice of sets for this piece, the recycling of images from the paintings of Bosch and Escher, the iconic use of images from religious statues from past ages, the use of contact work, ensemble sections and duets, the strong unison work and equal status of the dancers help to place it in the post-modern genre.

The piece begins outside on a derelict wharfside with a contact duet between two female dancers both facing the camera. They are dressed in long liquid silver jersey dresses, which offer a strong contrast to the bleak landscape in which they are placed. One dancer appears to be trying to trap the dancer in front, who is trying to escape. The dynamic of the movement is strong and powerful with sudden drops to the ground.

The art works of Escher and Bosch influence the second section. It takes place in a dance studio with a black floor and the dancers performing floor work, symbolising insects crawling. The dancers are on their backs and use the palms of their hands to help them travel short distances at speed. They twist from the waist and look helpless, like beetles stuck on their backs, unable to flip themselves over.

The third section is based on the Carl Dreyer film about Joan of Arc . It places great emphasis on the upper half of the dancers' bodies as they perform a series of small movements including use of the eyes. The make-up and short hairstyles accentuate these movements, which work well on camera. The dancers experimented with writing letters with the tips of their noses to create some of the small movements. This section demonstrates that large movements are not always necessary in dance although it is easier to see eye movement and facial expressions on film than on stage.

The fourth section is situated in an ornate cathedral with natural light coming through from the left-hand side of the performance area. Dancers perform duets consisting of a series of weight-taking movements and drops to the floor coupled with lifts where the toes and hands 'twinkle'. Simultaneously another set of dancers are lying on the floor and performing small gestures with their feet or toes. The music and the movement mirror each other's gentle and slow dynamic to create a tranquil and serene mood.

The final section is more upbeat and brings the dancers to a standing position facing front and showing the geographical difference between heaven and hell with their last position of the hands and fingers.

→ Akram Khan – *Rush*

Akram Khan was born in London in 1974. His mother was a dance teacher who introduced him to Bengali folk dancing and to Sri Pratap Pawar, who taught him kathak. In 1994 Khan went to study for a Dance degree at De Montfort University, Leicester, and subsequently to the Northern School of Contemporary Dance. His work covers a range of dance styles including contact improvisation, physical theatre, Graham and Cunningham as well as what has become known as contemporary kathak. Like Shobana Jeyasingh (see pages 42–46), Khan refuses to use the word 'fusion' when talking about how he uses different styles in his work. However, the notion of fusion is central to a discussion of post-modern practice, and Khan represents many post-modern trends in his choreography.

Kathak is derived from the Sanskrit word *katha*, meaning 'story'. It is a form of Indian classical dance originating from North India. Some of its key features are fast footwork, spins and a strong, upright torso. There are three major schools of kathak. Akram Khan works in the Lucknow gharana tradition, in which abhinaya or expressional acting is part of the style. The combination of abstract rhythmic elements (nritta) and the expressive and narrative aspects of movement (nritya) make the style exciting and entertaining. The style works by moving through stages of increasing dynamic and tempo.

■ Drama and film

Khan's talents extend beyond the dance world. When he was only ten years old he worked as an actor in a production of *The Adventures of Mowgli*. Later, in 1988, he was in Sir Peter Brook's play for the Royal Shakespeare Company *The Mahabharata*. Khan has also worked on dance in film and choreographed a short solo piece called *Loose in Flight* (1995), which was filmed for Channel 4 in 1999. He received a Time Out Live Award in 2000 and was the subject of an episode of *The South Bank Show* on ITV in October 2002. In common with other post-modern choreographers, Khan has collaborated with other well known artists, such as Anish Kapoor, who made the designs for *Kaash* (2002), and Hanif Kureishi, whose narrative texts were used in *Ma* (2004).

■ *Rush* (2000)

Rush was Khan's first work for his newly formed company, the Akram Khan Company, and won him the Critics' Circle National Dance Award as Outstanding Newcomer for his unique style, which had been described by dance critics previously as 'contemporary kathak'.

Akram Khan has also produced choreography in response to Steve Reich's 'Variations for Vibes, Pianos and Strings' (2005).

The preparatory work for *Rush* took place in Anne Teresa de Keersmaeker's Performing Arts Research Training Studios in Brussels, Belgium. Ann Joseph was the lighting designer. The piece was premiered in the Rosas Performance Space in July 2000 and the UK premiere was in October 2000 at the Midlands Arts Centre, Birmingham.

A post-modern approach

Lasting for 30 minutes, *Rush* is about a parachute jump and the feelings experienced by the jumper during free fall, particularly those relating to the five senses. The choreography, sound design, lighting, set and costume work closely together to produce a unique piece of dance. There is little feeling of narrative, although the jump from the plane clearly is an event.

The programme for the performance describes the piece as

> *'A purely abstract work inspired by the observation of paragliders in "freefall" – a physical state between tremendous speed and serene stillness. A rare Indian cycle of nine and a half beats is the choreography's basic structure for movement, space and music.'*

There are key positions in the piece that relate directly to positions which can be experienced during free fall: for example, a position where the body gently sways with the feet parallel and slightly apart and the arms held to the sides, bent in a right angle at the elbow with the underarm parallel to the ground and palms facing forward. Another significant position is the dancer leaning forward with legs straight and arms flung back into a V shape.

The dancers had to experiment with different types of falling. Khan's method of working was to call out a certain part of the body, which then had to become heavy and lead the action. In the piece there are sudden falls to the floor into rolls that are unpredictable, reflecting the nature of a parachute jump, in that the jumper does not know where the eventual landing will take place.

The success of the piece hinges on the timing of the movements in its unusual counting pattern, which is strange to dancers who are used to counting in eights. This perhaps contributes to the feeling of anticipation of what is to come next which the audience may experience when watching the piece. Boles or rhythmic syllables are used to count the beats.

Stylistic materials

Other ingredients of this piece include naturalistic pedestrian movement and some actions that result in percussive moments. The piece is choreographed for a trio and the material is not gender led. There is some unison work but the dancers drop in and out of this. Some triangular formations are reminiscent of the front of the plane or merely the formation of free fallers. Diagonals, lines and curves are used in the pathways. The dynamics of the movements cover a wide range depending on whether the movement is being performed at a fast or slow speed. There are sudden movements, which might reflect the sudden pulling of the parachute, and there is an extraordinary section where Moya Michael swings her extended arm in a circular motion faster and faster until it can hardly be perceived, much like a propeller.

Sound and lighting

The stage is bare and the lighting is blue and white. Fades, blackouts and sudden flashes are used as at the beginning when the dancers walk purposefully on to the stage and take up their positions. The music is created in two sections – the first is atmospheric, using scrap metal and a thunder sheet to make sounds and then slow them down. Section 2 is a contrast as it is rhythmical. The pulse is divided into 6 versus 5 and does not share the nine and half beat Indian cycle.

Khan brings a new dimension to the world of contemporary dance by using different forms and styles in his work. In *Rush* he chose a very unusual starting point – the parachute jump and free falling – and broke boundaries by finding movement to convey the emotions experienced in free fall. He collaborated closely with the lighting designer and the composer to create an integrated performance piece with a very strong and bold movement vocabulary based on the contrast between extreme speed and serene stillness.

→ Mark Ravenhill & Frantic Assembly – *Pool (No Water)*

Mark Ravenhill was born in 1966 and studied English and Drama at the University of Bristol. His career as a playwright began in earnest following the success of a short piece called *Fist*, which led Max Stafford-Clark to commission Ravenhill to write a full-length piece. This was performed in 1996 with the provocative title *Shopping and Fucking*. Since then, Ravenhill has produced *Faust is Dead* (1997), *Handbag* (1998), *Mother Molly's Clap House* (2001), *Totally Over You* (2004) and *Pool (No Water)* (2006).

The Frantic Theatre Company was formed in 1991 and became Frantic Assembly in 1994. One of the significant features of Frantic Assembly's performance work is that it not only sees movement, design and music as being of equal importance but also values text as an integral part of the devised piece.

Mark Ravenhill

■ *Pool (No Water)* (2006)

This collaborative production between Frantic Assembly, the Drum Theatre, Plymouth and Lyric Hammersmith Production was first performed in September 2006 at the Drum Theatre.

Pool (No Water) has a script written by Mark Ravenhill about a famous artist who invites her old friends to a party at a house where she has a new swimming pool to show off. The friends celebrate together, get drunk and the famous host suggests skinny dipping before bedtime. They all tear off their clothes and the host jumps into the pool first but unfortunately the pool boy has drained the water away. The narration at this point is poetic and reads like blank verse, which helps to slow down the pace and highlight the disbelief of the friends and the audience, who use their imaginations to picture the accident and its aftermath.

> There was no splash. There was
> The crack
> The cracking of her body.
> The harsh crack of her body against the concrete.
> Then there was silence.
> Then there was her groan and her squeal and her screams of pain.

What makes this play so unusual is that the host is never seen as there is no one playing this role. The audience must imagine the character and what happens to her through the narration of events and the physical theatre created by the four actors on stage.

The host survives but is in a coma and we watch how the friends treat her in hospital. They start to take photographs of her twisted and swollen body. They even rearrange her limbs to make the composition better. They take many photos on a daily basis and then suddenly, after eight weeks, she comes out of the coma. They show her the photographs and she wants to carry on photographing her healing process. She takes over the project and the friends become jealous of her drive, her talent and her artistic skills all over again.

The friends have a party, take drugs, drink, dance and let their inhibitions go, which leads them to destroy the hard copies of the digital images they took of the woman who used to be one of the 'group' but became famous and removed herself to another country.

Use of narrator

There is some optimism at the end as one of the old friends narrates the conclusion of the story from her point of view. She is grateful that eventually the injured host told the friends the truth: that she had always known they hated her and were jealous of her. She does not care, however, as she knows that she is stronger than them and will always survive. The old friend has now stopped taking heroin and is happily married with two children. She looks back on the night when the host discovered her photographs destroyed as the happiest night of her life. The use of the narrator makes the play seem like a long flashback so the narrative structure can be described as nonlinear.

Rehearsal methods

One of the techniques employed to try to find different voices for the characters was to ask the performers to imagine that they were being interviewed for a documentary on the artist. The script looks like a monologue on the page and has no characters assigned to the lines. In rehearsal, the four performers had to experiment as to who should deliver the lines. In the show, the characters never address each other. They address the audience as if confessing their past sins. The audience has to engage with the feelings of the characters and understand why they behaved in such a despicable manner.

The piece is a good example of physical theatre. The physicality of the action speaks louder than the words and shows the darker side of each character when they individually visit the injured woman in the hospital. The characters perform vile acts on her injured body, sometimes so extreme that we cannot be sure if they are really doing what we think they are doing. This makes the audience consider the abusive nature of photographing the woman's body when she is in a coma and widens the discussion of what is acceptable subject matter for any photograph. The combination of the physical theatre with the fast pace of the music gives the play an intensity and speed, which reflects the anxiety of the characters as they experience strong emotions towards the host.

Set design

The set is very important to this production as the swimming pool with no water serves as a hospital waiting room as well as the house where the party takes place. There is lighting in the roof of the set to illuminate the back room and show the party. The set is clinical and the audience would struggle to escape the main preoccupation of the production: the accident in the waterless pool and its consequences.

While *Pool (No Water)* was in rehearsal, one of the things that impressed Mark Ravenhill was the 'genuine sense of fear and surprise' that Frantic Assembly's physical commitment could create.

Post-modernist fingerprints

There is a close collaboration between the writer, the choreographers/directors, the performers, the set and lighting designers, the film maker and the composer of the music. Each art form is equal in status. There is a strong relationship between Frantic Assembly and the two theatres which co-produced the show.

Frantic Assembly challenge the audience on contemporary issues and debates and do not shy away from controversial and shocking themes.

The drama does not use the traditional structure of acts and scenes but employs what looks like a monologue on the page but is delivered by the four performers on the stage in a confessional format. Physical theatre, movement, speech and music all play equal roles in the drama and technology is used to enhance the production. The set is integral to the play and become a visual metaphor for the unwelcoming friends and the themes of isolation, loneliness and pain.

There is a possible intertextual reference to J. B. Priestley's *An Inspector Calls*, in which the dead girl is never seen nor is her photograph, but she is central to the drama and a catalyst for the action.

→ Motionhouse Dance Theatre – *Driven*

This company was founded in 1988 by Louise Richards and Kevin Finnan with the aim of creating work that combined dance with visual/physical theatre. Their education pack states that their vision is 'to create startling, passionate dance theatre that profoundly moves people to a new place and understanding'.

■ Approach to making a work

The company's approach to making a work is based on collaboration. Kevin Finnan asks the dancers to improvise around a task individually or together and then bring their ideas and material back for reworking. He might change the space they perform in so that the movement becomes restricted or he may ask the dancers to focus on the speed at which their feet move with the music. He acknowledges that there is still a hierarchy, with a director who has devised the original concept and has an intention for the piece. However the role of the choreographer is far more collaborative than in traditional ballet. The dancers work with him to produce the material.

The movement is generally created before the music. The music then works rather like a film score, highlighting certain moments and creating emotion for the audience. Once the music has been created, the two elements can be put together and the movement can be adapted. The music is not treated as an entirely separate entity.

The costumes are designed to be practical and hardwearing for long tours and heavy physical dance theatre. They reflect the places the characters find themselves in, such as nightclubs, but they need to be adapted for special requirements such as a flying harness.

The lighting is added last and is used for a variety of reasons ranging from making areas of the stage brighter or dimmer for different purposes or working with or against the film.

■ *Driven* (2007)

Driven was premiered in January 2007 at Warwick Arts Centre, Coventry. It was conceived, choreographed and directed by Kevin Finnan. It is typical of

Motionhouse Dance Company's approach in its significant use of collaboration, with each person involved in the creative process being credited for their work. The piece is 75 minutes long and has no interval. It is action packed and rarely do the five dancers seem to stop.

The eclectic mix of styles of dance and music found in *Driven* also place it in the post-modern genre. The music is a mixture of original composition and sections of well known pre-recorded music such as a piece of Bach. Close analysis of the 15 sections shows the complex nature of the movement language. A variety of relationships are explored, from solos to ensemble, covering a range of styles.

Synopsis

Finnan wanted to make a piece about being driven. He has stated that '*Driven* is about how easy it is for us to live our lives at such a pace that it is hard to find the time to consider if, in fact, this is the way we want to live'. We witness the characters dancing together in a club, working together in an office, forming different relationships and then one character suffers a terrible accident. There follows an agonising scene in a hospital where the other characters wait for news and show different reactions to the accident. It is not clear if the victim is dead or not, maybe he is in a coma. He appears to come back to life later in the piece but some audience members read this presence as a ghost. The piece is open to interpretation so these different readings are equally valid.

Structure

The structure of the piece is dictated to some extent by the physical space of the stage area. The set is integral to the work, so much so that it is often made early on in the process and is used in the studio during improvisation. For *Driven*, the set has to allow film to be shown, have a steel framework so that flying with a harness can take place, include a series of revolving doors painted black on one side and white on the other, and allow enough space for stools, tables and last but not least, the dancers. Finnan is known for his site-based performance work, including *The Edge* (June 2004), an event on the beach at Watergate Bay in Cornwall.

Driven has a narrative but it is not necessarily linear and could be better described as episodic. The narrative is fragmented and one scene is juxtaposed with another so that there is no sense of flow but rather a mood of tension and apprehension. These characters seem to be living life at a hectic pace and soon something will stop them in their tracks.

The piece starts with a film set in a bar followed by a fast-paced section including athletic movement, catching and throwing of dancers, difficult lifts and constant changing of direction, dodging and performing with a partner. This high-energy section for the ensemble is juxtaposed with a solo performed by the Cleaner, who is suffering from an obsessive-compulsive disorder. She spends much of the solo on the floor trying to clean a very tiny area of the floor and refuses to give in. She uses all parts of her body to rub the floor clean as well as using her mop. Above her two dancers perform aerial work but nobody notices her.

Another solo is performed by Rachel McDermott, who does not seem to be able to decide whether to take her coat off or put it on. Underneath she is wearing

'You feel the soar of flight in your chest and the tug of gravity in your gut' is how one reviewer described the experience of watching *Driven*.

underwear and has clearly taken off her dress. She is in a dilemma about whether to reveal herself or not and she enacts a battle with her coat while rolling and flailing on the floor. The solo reflects her feelings of confusion and frustration and rouses sympathy for her feelings of isolation.

Other sections use the stools in the office to travel the stage and to hang off and curl around. The flying sections often look dangerous as the stage area is small – one wrong move and the fliers look like they will collide.

Style

Motionhouse push the boundaries within a limited space to see what is possible. The work is integrated and contains physical risks, high energy and a fast pace. The movement vocabulary is devised in relation to the set, themes and subject matter. There is a lot of contact work in trios and duets as well as acrobatics and circus-inspired actions.

The use of physical theatre with dance as well as new forms such as aerial work shows a desire to break boundaries and experiment with new ways of performing while retaining some original features from the past. The eclectic mix of music and the use of multimedia with live performance help place this work in the post-modern genre.

Politics and Performance
since 1914

→ What's the point of politics?

Politics is not just about the way that countries are run: there are political dimensions to all human activities, from the way that society is ordered through to the way in which power games dominate human relationships. Political performance seeks to raise awareness and influence the audience's thinking about the political dimensions of whichever issue forms the subject matter of the performance they are watching. Most important, it seeks to challenge, persuade and change attitudes and actions. Issues may take a variety of forms ranging, for example, from the way society is governed or controlled, and the impact this has on people's lives, to the sexual politics that dominate many human relationships. Political performance may also include works that reinforce the attitudes held by those in authority, usually called propaganda.

Political performance is most associated with theatre, but dance and music can be equally political in their intentions. Dance practitioners such as Christopher Bruce have sought to reflect the injustices of society, Lloyd Newson has sought to

Charlie Chaplin in
The Great Dictator

explore the nature of sexual politics in human relationships. Music practitioners have often written pieces or songs that seek to challenge political injustice. The music of Dmitri Shostakovich shows the tensions between the artist's wishes and the Soviet state; the songs of Joan Baez deal with significant issues of civil rights. The purposes of the practitioner in writing his or her work have strong similarities across the art forms.

The combined effect of all the art forms used by the practitioner should be considered, although one form may appear dominant in delivering the political message. Dylan's musical accompaniment and vocal qualities are integral to the effect generated; Bruce's theatrical elements and use of culturally located music underpin the message in the dance, and Berkoff's intensely choreographed action is usually essential to his style of drama.

→ Three stages in the political process

For a practitioner to make an audience politically aware, there is a three-stage process.

1 The practitioner has to communicate enough information for the audience to become sufficiently aware of context to feel they can make a judgement about where the performance is coming from.

2 The practitioner seeks to align the audience's viewpoint with his or her own in order to make them want to change the status quo.

3 Prompted by the practitioner, the audience forms a view as to how change should take place. For many practitioners this is a challenge which includes a specific message. For others it may more open to audience interpretation, as characterised by John Lydon's physical manner and harsh vocals as Johnny Rotten in the Sex Pistols' *Anarchy in the UK*: 'Don't know what I want but I know where to get it.'

→ What does political performance involve?

Political performance is often inventive and unconventional. It intends to reach the most significant audiences – the movers and shakers – and achieve an effect that the forces of authority would not anticipate. This means that the performance locations and the resources available may be quite unconventional. Performance technology is sometimes minimal. Venues and audiences may not be theatre based. For example, Bob Dylan performed informally with guitar and harmonica, and Dario Fo performed in factories to workers. These are important elements in considering the political effect achieved.

Character is central to the delivery of a political performance in all three art forms, especially where the character is given a voice through dialogue. This characterisation is diverse and possibly unexpected in its portrayal, such as the maniac in Fo's *Accidental Death*, or the reptilian figures in *Ghost Dances*.

Political performance often involves the presence of some form of Authority which exerts a force on the action in its absence. Two main categories of character feature. One consists of easily recognisable types, simple mouthpieces or intentionally narrow representations of those the audience expect to see and

From the mid 1960s, opposition to the Vietnam War grew into a major political issue in the United States, with significant cultural impact.

instantly comprehend. The other comprises an indefinably wide variety of more complex and originally conceived roles, from Brechtian representational characters to the fully 'real', as in Robin Soans' verbatim drug addicts in *A State Affair*. In these developed types there must be an element of sympathy, which coupled to an element of the unexpected usually delivers the message of the piece.

The social, cultural and historical context in which practitioners operate is vital to understanding their political output. Political performance exists as a direct and immediate response to its time and place. There would be little useful purpose in creating a political work years after the events other than as a historical record, except where those events can be used as a parallel and to shed light upon the present. Some works are created to 'bear witness' to continuing and unresolved injustice, such as Dario Fo's *Accidental Death of an Anarchist*, Bob Dylan's *Hurricane* and Christopher Bruce's *Ghost Dances*.

Some practitioners may also be post-modern in their approach, and this is relevant where the stylistic features are used to communicate the political message, as given in the fingerprints below.

→ Fingerprints of the political performance's style

☑ A political work may be defined as one that seeks to question the status quo with the intention of persuasion through techniques and approaches that challenge social norms. The practitioner may have adapted his or her work in relation to the political context, such as pre-1968 censorship in Britain or the new freedom to explore and experiment with artistic expression in the subsequent decades.

☑ Political performance offers a critique of the social order – this may be on a micro level (e.g. in a local community) or on a macro level (e.g. challenging corrupt government policies). There may be specific references to real people and past events that locate and justify the message to the audience.

☑ The year 1914 is a useful historical marker for political change across the world although there were a number of other significant political dates in the first two decades of the twentieth century. You need to be aware of the significance of the outbreak of the First World War and the shattering of romantic notions about continuous human improvement.

☑ Use of satire, allegory, humour, black comedy and lampoon as a means of poking fun (particularly at political figures), manipulating audience expectations and influencing audience opinion.

☑ Use of music – especially song – as a means of commenting directly on the political dimensions of a situation.

☑ Language forms used and structural effects present in the language, such as argument, logical devices, verse form, rhetorical questioning.

As examples of political performance, we shall discuss the following, which could be used to illustrate the fingerprints of political performance.

1923	Sean O'Casey – *Shadow of a Gunman*	**1970**	Dario Fo – *Accidental Death of an Anarchist*
1932	Kurt Jooss – *The Green Table*		
1939	Bertolt Brecht – *Mother Courage*	**1984**	Billy Bragg– *Brewing Up with Billy Bragg*
1941	Dmtri Shostakovich – *Symphony No. 7 (Leningrad)*	**2002**	Christopher Bruce – *Hurricane*
		2008	ACE Dance and Music – *Skin*
1963	Bob Dylan – *The Freewheelin' Bob Dylan*		

→ Sean O'Casey – *Shadow of a Gunman*

Sean O'Casey (1880–1964) was born John Casey in a poor area of Dublin and grew up familiar with poverty, although his was of a more genteel class than is often credited. He suffered from poor eyesight, which limited his educational achievement, and worked as a manual labourer before becoming involved in labour movements and Irish nationalism. This was at a key time in the struggle for Irish independence and O'Casey had associations with the paramilitary Irish Citizens Army. However, by 1914 he became less directly involved with politics as the movement for liberation intensified, and turned to writing a few years later.

Shadow of a Gunman (1923) was his first professionally produced work. It is the first of a series of three plays known collectively as the Abbey Theatre plays (performed at the Abbey Theatre, Dublin) that remain his best-known work. The other two are *Juno and the Paycock* (1924) and *The Plough and the Stars* (1926).

■ Sean O'Casey's theatre

O'Casey's style is lively, and he created strong and vibrant roles which made his work attractive to a wide audience, not just those who were seeking a political message. He used a naturalistic style at a time when this was still a relatively new genre in the English-speaking world. In the early twentieth century there was a strong movement in Irish writing for the stage and this provided the British stage with material at a time when English stage writing was comparatively weak. Influences on O'Casey include George Bernard Shaw's concern with causes and effects of social dilemmas and J. M. Synge's interest in Irish culture.

■ *Shadow of a Gunman* (1923)

Shadow of a Gunman was written in 1923 and performed at the Abbey Theatre, Dublin.

Synopsis

This play is set in a tenement building in May 1920, during the time of Irish resistance to British soldiers who were used to put down the struggle for independence. Seumas, a pedlar, and Davoren, a self-styled poet, share the room.

Davoren allows the neighbours to believe he is a Republican gunman in hiding as this has romantic appeal, especially to Minnie Powell, a young and spirited woman.

Mr Maguire, a friend of Seumus, leaves a bag in the room to collect later. Unknown to the occupants he is a real Republican and the bag contains bombs. News comes that Maguire has been killed in an ambush, and as Auxiliary soldiers arrive to search the building, Seumas and Davoren discover the contents of the bag. They panic, but Minnie stays calm and takes the bag to her room, hoping the soldiers will not search there and find it. However, it is discovered, she is arrested and dragged out screaming Republican slogans. Outside there is an ambush and Minnie is shot. Seumas and Davoren do not have the courage to admit to the other tenant, Mrs Grigson, who makes disparaging comments about Minnie, that the bag had been in their room originally, and they thereby conceal Minnie's bravery.

As with other early-twentieth-century naturalism, there is an strong element of melodrama in the sudden dramatic culmination of events, the grounds for which have been laid earlier – Mr Maguire's ominous bag left in the tenement, his reported death, and Minnie's romantic attachment to the idea of a gunman on the run, which Davoren plays on until the crisis where she assumes the role of tragic heroine. However, it is clear that the work transcends these elements, as the audience are left to consider whether Minnie actually put herself forward as willing to die for the cause, or whether events moved too fast for her to save herself. Also, the cowardice of the two men she protected is left unexposed and unpunished. It is a surprisingly modern ending at a time when standard theatre conventions still required resolution of the issues raised by a play.

Kenneth Branagh as Davoren in *Shadow of a Gunman* filmed for television

■ Sean O'Casey's political intentions

Sean O'Casey's concern was to focus on the impact of the Irish Civil War upon the people of Dublin, particularly in the poor areas where he had grown up. This was little known to those who were not directly involved, as there was no radio or TV to bring ready news and the press relayed events in a more limited manner than today but generated bitter determination and conflict in Ireland when events were reported. The raid portrayed in the play was a familiar occurrence to the Dublin people. In that sense O'Casey's work exists as a historical document for a modern audience.

Although his work is political in content and he changed his name accordingly, O'Casey was a powerful dramatist who used close observation of character and attention to detail, evident in the stage directions at the opening of his plays. He focused on the diversity of his characters and the comedy inherent in the language and attitudes of ordinary people.

Sean O'Casey's three political Abbey Theatre plays together point to an appeal for a proper political process by which Ireland might achieve independence. They all end in tragedy, each arguably harsher than the last. The absence of a patriotic message and the bitter words of the dying Bessie in *The Plough and Stars* sparked riots from the strongly Nationalist audience and O'Casey's work was never premiered at the Abbey Theatre again. This leaves a question concerning O'Casey's intentions for the audience to consider: was his message an appeal for a proper political solution or simply a portrayal of the human suffering generated by the struggle?

→ Kurt Jooss – *The Green Table*

Kurt Jooss was born in 1901 in Wasseralfingen, Germany. He attended the Stuttgart Academy of Music, where he studied dance with Rudolph von Laban. They then worked together with Jooss acting as Laban's assistant as well as dancing important roles in his ballets. In 1924 Jooss founded the Neue Tanzbuhne with Aino Siimola, Sigurd Leeder and Hein Heckroth. In 1927 he was appointed director of the dance department at the Essen Folkwang School, which became the Folkwang Tanztheater, later renamed the Ballets Jooss.

In 1933 the Ballets Jooss was in danger of being persecuted by the Nazis, so moved to Dartington in England and later Cambridge. The company stopped working together in 1947 and Jooss went to Santiago, Chile. In 1949 he returned to Essen and the Folkwang Tanztheater was revived until 1953. Although the company stopped working, the school continued and in 1962 Jooss formed the Folkwang Tanzstudio with Pina Bausch. He retired as head of dance in 1968 and died in 1979.

■ *The Green Table* (1932)

The Green Table is Jooss' best-known work, and was the first piece to be fully notated using Labanotation. The piece became Jooss' signature work and has been staged many times, including a production for the Joffrey Ballet in 1967. Jooss' daughter Anna Markard staged it for Les Grands Ballets Canadiens in 1991 and for the Birmingham Royal Ballet in 1992.

Like Brecht's *Arturo Ui*, *The Green Table* is an intensely political work. It offers a commentary on politicians who cause wars but have no thought for their consequences. It criticises the Weimar Republic for its ineffectiveness and political corruption. A year after its premiere, Hitler rose to power, proving that what Jooss said about his dance piece was unfortunately true:

> 'I am firmly convinced that art should never be political, that art should not dream of altering people's convictions ... I don't think any war will be shorter or avoided by sending audiences into "The Green Table".'

Structure, content and style

The Green Table shows the futility of peace negotiations in the 1930s. It has eight scenes and lasts about 30 minutes. It is circular, the first and last scenes both featuring the Gentlemen in Black – ten men dressed in black suits and wearing masks. They are at a negotiating table which is rectangular and covered with a green cloth and appear to be discussing something serious. They form two sides and seem to oppose each other without any physical contact taking place. The style is ballet and contemporary dance mixed together with pedestrian gestures such as pointing, leaning on the table with chin supported by a hand to indicate thinking, and shooting guns. The men dance on the table and jump off it, and appear to be ignorant of the horror and futility of warfare.

Death enters the stage with a skeletal outline on his limbs and a costume reminiscent of a Roman gladiator. He dances a slow sequence in 3/4 to music in 4/4 with very strong and weighted movements. He performs leaps and rhythmic stamps which drive the movement of the scene. He wears a helmet with a plume and very heavy expressionistic make-up to accentuate his eyes and bone structure. This solo provides a transition and introduces the main theme of the piece – war and death.

The following scenes show the different aspects of war indicated by their titles. 'The Farewells' introduces the Standard Bearer, who carries a flag and is dressed in white to symbolise purity. The Young Soldiers follow him without any life of their own. With clenched fists, they march as if hypnotised and set off for war. The women do not want the men to leave and a woman with a white dress holds on to a male dancer as if trying to stop him. Each woman wears a different-coloured dress and head scarf, giving each a different character. The Profiteer, like the Gentlemen in Black, wears gloves, indicating that he does not want to get his hands dirty and will not fight. He wants to make a profit from the war and in the next section we see him stealing from a dead soldier.

In 'The Battle' we witness the soldiers lifting and throwing each other to represent a battle. The flag becomes smattered with blood and the soldiers celebrate their victory just in time before Death comes and takes them one by one.

'The Refugees' shows the women using slow expressive gestures in a beautifully composed tableau. Their outstretched arms show them pleading with each other. The Old Woman runs about in a circle offering a strong contrast to this slow controlled movement. She is frantic and seems to have seen the horror of war whereas the other women remain optimistic but scared. Death appears and the ensemble of women react suddenly in their movement then run off quickly leaving the Old Woman, who uses deep *pliés* and curved arms as she contracts her stomach and bends her head. She seems to be giving in to Death, who carries her away.

'The Partisan' shows a woman dressed in red dancing with a scarf and using juxtaposed movements which are sometimes fast and sometimes slow. She is ready to fight for her cause but is eventually shot by a firing squad.

'The Brothel' shows the Young Girl with her hair loose and using free movement until she is manipulated by the others and pushed about. She holds her hands in front of her face to protect herself. She gives in to a man but then there is a twist and Death takes his place on the floor in a sexual position.

In 'The Aftermath', Death leads all the characters in a procession. Even the Profiteer is finally taken by Death as he is caught up in the rhythm of Death's repeated solo.

Jooss wanted to create a unified piece of work which demonstrates a close collaboration between the designer, the composer and the choreographer. He was meticulous in his working method and made sure that every movement had an expressive value. Jooss calls the style Essentialism. For example, the Profiteer has a cunning nature and needs to act in a stealthy fashion therefore his movements are quick, agile and secretive. Conversely, Death is sharp, direct and angular in his movement to show that he stops at no one, his movement being constantly rhythmic like a clock ticking away the time.

Judi Dench plays Mother Courage in the 1984 Royal Shakespeare Company production.

→ Bertolt Brecht – *Mother Courage*

■ Brecht's theatre

Bertolt Brecht was a well established practitioner by the time he wrote *Mother Courage* in 1939. He had developed a new approach to theatre in reaction to the passive audiences and emotionally manipulative naturalistic theatre developed by Stanislavski. German audiences at the time were being seduced by the all-encompassing Nazi approach, which absorbed the arts into a fictionalised world view in which they placed themselves as the masters to be of a degenerating Europe.

Brecht's style is representational – the performer may create a three-dimensional image but one which exists only in that moment, the here and now. The performer must have the discipline not to 'become' the part and not play for sympathy. The style centres on the notion of *Verfremdungseffekt*, making the familiar unfamiliar, distancing the audience emotionally.

Spass, allowing the audience to talk, eat, drink and comment amongst themselves as part of the entertainment, is also intended to encourage the audience to discuss, disagree and come to a dialectic judgement – one where the truth is tested by discussion. Brecht uses music to break up the action and prevent passivity. The music has a harshness that matches the situation and comments on the action. Characters address the audience directly as part of the *Verfremdungseffekt,* the alienation that keeps the audience's focus at a judgemental rather than a passive level.

■ *Mother Courage and Her Children* (1939)

Background

Mother Courage and Her Children (*Mutter Courage und Ihre Kinder*) is the first of Brecht's major plays. It was written rapidly in 1939 in the early stages of the Second World War, before major hostilities had begun, as a warning to the Scandinavian countries – to which Brecht had exiled himself – not to join the war. In comparison to his earlier political works, there is less overt communism and a more developed intention to entertain: there is a black and ironic humour, often in bleak one-liners. It was first performed in Zurich in 1941.

> *I don't trust him. He's a pal of mine.*
>
> The Armourer in *Mother Courage*, scene 3

The drama is based in the Thirty Years War (1618–48) but the character language is of the social types of the 1930s, to act as an allegory. The action covers the many dilemmas and contradictory situations which may appear absurd to a peacetime audience but which were all too familiar to many who had lived through the realities of war experienced close up.

Synopsis

Mother Courage traces the progress of a woman who makes her living from trading between the armies as the territorial lines shift during the Thirty Years War. In the first scene Mother Courage and her three adult children are attempting to pass a checkpoint where a recruiter and sergeant are trying to find men to enlist. Despite her ingenuity in manipulating the two men, Mother Courage's attention is diverted at the last moment and she loses her son Eilif to the recruiter's bait.

> *Don't tell me peace has broken out just after I laid in new stock!*
>
> *Mother Courage,* scene 8

Over the next several years Mother Courage encounters Eilif again, now favoured by a general for his prowess. She befriends a cook, a chaplain and the prostitute Yvette, and they meet from time to time by chance. In the third scene her second son, Swiss Cheese, who has become an army paymaster, is executed for 'losing' the paybox – he threw it away in fear of his life. His mother attempts to bargain for him but in taking Yvette's advice she loses time and fails. Her fortunes rise and fall in subsequent scenes, and Eilif is eventually executed for a war crime, although the circumstances are not clearly defined and Mother Courage is not told of his death. Kattrin sacrifices herself to warn a town of an impending attack by drumming from a rooftop and is shot. Mother Courage is left to continue to pull her cart alone.

The action spans a period of approximately 11 years, but period and location are intentionally insignificant to prevent the audience from having preconceived views and to focus on the situation in the moment.

There is no plot as such, only a sequence of scenes from which the audience draw meanings. Brecht's theatre drew on popular entertainment in which the audience would think actively: cabaret, entertainment clubs, folk and popular music, even spectator sports such as boxing where the audience would feel they were participants and take sides rather than be drawn into passive unity.

■ Origins and political intentions

Mother Courage has her origins in a famous fictional role from the writing of that period, *Mutter Courasche* by Grimmelhausen. Brecht drew the amorality of Mother Courage from the title character of *Schweyk*, by the Czech novelist Hasek. Other political writing since the Second World War has also explored the inverse world of wartime existence, such as Joseph Heller's novel *Catch-22* and Joan Littlewood's devised play *Oh What a Lovely War*. It was typical of Brecht to draw on well known religious, biblical or folk stories, to generate a sense of familiarity in the audience.

The most central characters in *Mother Courage* have a representative function. For example Kattrin, the half-German daughter, has been brutalised by soldiers before the start of the play and has consequently become dumb. She symbolises those well-meaning German people who had no voice under the Nazis. Her sacrifice is a statement about those who take a stand but are never remembered as heroes.

→ Dmtri Shostakovich – *Symphony No. 7*

Dmtri Shostakovich is one of the best-known orchestral composers of the mid-twentieth century. Born in St Petersburg (known as Leningrad during the Soviet period) in 1906, he knew little of his country before the Russian Revolution of 1917, which led to the establishment of the Soviet Union in 1922. Shostakovich's reputation as a composer is inextricably bound up with his relationship with the Soviet authorities, particularly during the reign of terror inflicted on the country by Joseph Stalin, General Secretary of the Communist Party from 1922 until Stalin's death in 1953.

Without his clashes with the Soviet state, Shostakovich might have been remembered primarily as a Russian composer who wrote extensively for orchestra, producing 15 symphonies. As an art form, the symphony had become something of a spent force by the middle of the twentieth century – the atonal music of composers such as Arnold Schoenberg, Alban Berg and Anton Webern was at that point considered to be at the cutting edge of European composition.

Socialist realism

The prevailing view of the Soviet authorities for a period of around 60 years was that the production of art should be for the greater glory of the Communist state, and that composers and artists were under a moral obligation to produce noble, stirring pieces that revelled in its power and majesty. The production of artistic works was seen as having immense powers of propaganda and there was an expectation that art would reinforce the belief that life in the Soviet Union was immensely superior to that lived in the West. The West was portrayed as decadent, obsessed by the selfish desires of capitalism and the demands of the individual, and reinforced by art that was degenerate and self-indulgent. Any signs of Soviet artists producing such work were quickly stamped out.

■ Shostakovich and Stalin

Shostakovich's career as a composer was typified by his troubled relationship with the Soviet authorities, and particularly Stalin. Early signs of the strained dealings between the two men came with the performance of the composer's opera *Lady Macbeth of the Mtinsk District* in 1934. Initially well received by audiences and the authorities, the opera explores the theme that it is acceptable to murder an evil dictator for the general good of the people. In 1936 *Pravda*, the state newspaper, denounced the opera in an article headed 'Muddle instead of music'. Thus began an uneasy relationship in which the composer was suspected of being less than wholeheartedly committed to the Communist cause. He was questioned by the KGB, and suffered criticism and disgrace. Yet there were also times when he was held up as the champion of socialist realism, as the type of artist that the Soviet Union saw as glorifying their ideals.

Shostakovich's *Symphony No. 5* was completed in 1937 and was described by the composer as 'a Soviet artist's response to just criticism'. It led to a period, albeit temporary, in which he was welcomed back into the Communist fold, as someone able to overcome his previous mistakes, and take forward the ideals of socialist realism. This was confirmed by his response to the wartime siege of his home city, Leningrad.

■ *Symphony No. 7 (Leningrad)* (1941)

The relationship between the Soviet Union and the West in response to the rise of Hitler and Nazism in the Second World War (1939–45) was complex. The resistance of Leningrad to Hitler's advancing armies was, however, one of the defining moments of the war. The city's siege meant that food supplies were cut off and that the population experienced appalling famine, such that thousands died.

Writing a symphony in such circumstances might seem like an irrelevant response, especially since a symphony has no words and can therefore say nothing specifically political. It was the circumstances of its composition, however, that give it such a strong political dimension. The symphony was seen as a symbol of the struggle for freedom and the whole of the first movement is

'Invasion theme', as
played by flutes

dominated by a short motif – often referred to as the 'invasion theme' – that is
repeated over and over again, in the same style as Ravel's *Bolero*.

DMTRI SHOSTAKOVICH

The first performance in Leningrad was particularly poignant. Many of the
orchestra had died of malnutrition before the performance took place, but those
who were there saw it as the greatest moment in their lives in making such a
defiant statement as to the power of the people of Leningrad to resist the spread
of Nazi fascism. Yet Shostakovich's writings seem to suggest, and the views of his
friends seem to reinforce the idea, that the symphony is a much more powerful
piece of propaganda than might have been thought by the Soviet authorities.
Rather than being merely a denunciation of the Nazis, it is in reality a
denunciation of totalitarianism in all its forms – including those of the Soviet
Union. This powerful four-movement symphony is therefore a very subtle piece
of political subversion in apparently reinforcing the ideals of socialist realism
whilst at the same time denouncing them as being no better than Hitler's armies.

→ ## Bob Dylan – *The Freewheelin' Bob Dylan*

Bob Dylan is probably the most influential American popular singer/songwriter
of the second half of the twentieth century. Born Robert Zimmerman in
Minnesota in 1941, he formed a band in high school in the late 1950s. He
dropped out of university in his home state after a summer when he had met the
blues singer Jesse Fuller, the inspiration for his early guitar and harmonica style.
He resurfaced in New York in 1961. There he began introducing himself as Bob
Dylan, taking the name from Dylan Thomas the Welsh poet.

He visited his idol Woody Guthrie, the great poetic and political folk singer, when
he was dying in hospital from a disease which rendered him immobile and
unable to speak. This made a considerable impact on Dylan. He later said of
Guthrie: 'You could listen to his songs and actually learn how to live.' Dylan
obscured his rural origins with varying accounts of where he had come from and
an enigmatic manner, which he has maintained throughout his career, rarely
discussing his work and his intentions openly. He quickly became popular in the
early 1960s in the folk-led anti-war protest movement, but began to feel
manipulated by their treatment of him as their figurehead, and broke away from
the style with an electric backing band in 1965.

Dylan is credited with redefining the role of the vocalist as requiring a
conventionally good voice and thereby opening the field to a more raw style of
singing in 1960s popular music. He both influenced other singers and continued
to draw widely on poetry, literature, folk and blues music. He experimented with

political material in talking blues songs, including a rare comic mockery of right-wing anti-communism in fear of the colour red in *Talking John Birch Paranoid Blues*, but this was not commercially released until much later for fear of offending the John Birch Society, a militant ultra-conservative organisation.

■ *The Freewheelin' Bob Dylan* (1963)

The roughness of his voice matched the seriousness of the social consciousness and protest material in the large volume of material Dylan began to produce from the time of his second album, *The Freewheelin' Bob Dylan*. His first political anthem, *Blowin' in the Wind*, appears on this album. Its melody draws on the traditional black slave song *No More Auction Block*, which Dylan had recorded but not released in 1962. The universal anti-war and human-rights issues inherent in the rhetorical questions asked in the song made it an immediate anthem for his followers. Its visual images and emphasis on sight and seeing were taken up as a banner calling for a change of direction by the US government.

The album also contains the powerful and much covered *A Hard Rain's a-Gonna Fall*, with its melody drawing on the folk ballad *Lord Randall* and a question-and-answer structure which generates images of nuclear war to come. An insistent and building refrain shows Dylan's growing ability to develop musical constructions beyond the traditional models he had utilised.

Dylan has claimed he was not a political songwriter, rather that he just wrote songs. This is disingenuous, but the body of his work shows a willingness to continually explore and leave behind what has already been done, in the manner of *The Times They Are A-Changin'*. His performances show a distaste for repetition, avoiding playing songs in the manner of recorded albums as popular audiences prefer. The insistence that audiences should experience anew and revise their understanding is typical of the active thinking principles of political practitioners.

The Lonesome Death of Hattie Carroll, on the *Freewheelin'* album, has been described as a Brechtian work. It relates the true story of the killing of a hotel maid by a wealthy young socialite without identifying the victim as black and her killer as white, leaving the audience to think actively and make the relevant connections. Dylan's sense of the need for continual change recurs in his greatest anthem, *Like A Rolling Stone* (1965), echoed in its a circular building pattern. Although it obscures its political potential behind the lyrics, it jabs at those who had criticised Dylan's credentials as a protest singer:

> You used to laugh about
> Everyone that was hanging out
> But now you don't talk so loud
> Now you don't feel so proud
> About having to be scrounging your next meal

■ After *Freewheelin'*

After *Freewheelin'* Dylan was secure as a political icon. *The Times They Are A-Changin'* is recognisably his most potent political anthem, titling the album that followed rapidly in early 1964. This song has a more active opening than its predecessor – 'Come gather round people…' – and a more insistent 3/4 beat, popular with folk songs, against the more measured 4/4 time of *Blowin' in the Wind*. Again there is a universal tone and metaphoric images, first of water and swimming, developing an epic scope and using emphatic triple rhyme:

> Come mothers and fathers throughout the land
> And don't criticise what you can't understand
> Your sons and your daughters are beyond your command
> Your old road is rapidly ageing

The call for age to give way to youth was a touchstone of the mood of the early 1960s, but it does not have the passive 'hippy' mentality that was to develop in pop culture within a few years. The mood is energetic and active, more in the manner of a socialist workers' song. The melody is held on a high calling note in the first of these next two lines, using the fall at the end of the couplet to emphasise the title phrase:

> Please get out of the new one if you can't lend your hand
> For the times they are a-changin'

Dylan continued to highlight examples of social injustice, naming the victim and making them representative of a sector of society. *Hurricane* (1975), from the *Desire* album, is a protest tribute to the black boxer Rubin Carter, a middleweight contender for the world title framed for a bar-room murder. *Joey* (also from *Desire)* is a somewhat romanticised story of the death of an apparently kindly Mafia boss.

More recently Dylan has appeared in films, including *Masked and Anonymous* (2003), which has political overtones: he plays a version of himself in a degraded and chaotic America. Just released from prison, he appears bemused by the dissipating energy of those around him. At one point he visits a dying and apparently corrupt leader, perhaps a representation of the US president. His visit seems to be welcomed, but appears to make little difference to the action: perhaps this is Dylan's perspective on his contribution to the politics of his time.

Bob Dylan performing in Sydney, Australia, in 2001

➜ Dario Fo – *Accidental Death of an Anarchist*

Dario Fo (born 1926) is the son of a railway worker and throughout his playwriting career he has voiced a concern for the working class and the class struggle. His career began in comic mime, drawing on traditional forms overlaid with an energetic and highly individual style. Using his considerable appeal he developed his own style as a prominent practitioner in political and social satirical theatre. His audience appeal was often in playing low characters and comic simpletons whose innocence led to apparently accidental exposure of social truths.

His wife, Franca Rame, comes from a family of traditional performers, and together they have developed a number of successful plays in which they both performed. Fo's stance has always been to support the ordinary man against injustice and against uncaring authority. Fascism in Italy became his target. He wrote that political corruption encouraged a taste for satire in the Italian public, claiming that the bourgeoisie were more stupid than in France, Germany and England since there censorship of the entertainment enjoyed by common people had stifled 'vulgar' expression and creativity. This provided Fo with a means of reaching his audiences, and enabling them to participate fully in his work.

■ *Accidental Death of an Anarchist* (1970) *(Morte Accidentale di un Anarchico)*

Origins and political intentions

Accidental Death of an Anarchist was written in 1970 and performed in Milan. It was first performed in English in 1979.

Accidental Death of an Anarchist is Dario Fo's best known and most politically identifiable play. It was created in response to an incident in 1969 when Italy was experiencing terrorist bombings. Italian media sources ignored obvious inconsistencies and supported police accounts that a left-wing anarchist suspect had fallen or jumped from a fourth-floor window in the Milan Police headquarters while undergoing interrogation. Fo wanted to change the public's perception and satirised these events. Using elements of traditional *commedia dell'arte*, he exposed the fraud perpetrated on a willing public who had largely accepted the official version of events.

A decade later three fascist activists, one of them a police agent, were convicted of the crime, pointing responsibility for the attack at the police themselves. The popular appeal of Fo's play effectively prevented the issue from being 'buried' by the authorities, and subsequently made the issue internationally known – but not until the trial was already over. However, the play served as a warning that, although the Italian police were still unreformed, the power of popular theatre could hold them to account.

Synopsis

A character identified as the Maniac arrives at the Milan Police headquarters and makes his way unnoticed into unattended offices. There he assumes the role of a senior magistrate and sets up his own inquiry into the death of the anarchist who 'fell' from the window. In an increasingly farcical manner he exposes the lies and stupidity of the policemen who were involved in the death, and makes them believe that their only option is to jump out of the window themselves.

He then persuades them that their only way to gain public sympathy is to create a new version of the story, which will involve singing an anarchist anthem to show how much they had sided with the victim. A female journalist enters, to interview the police. The Maniac uses several outrageous disguises and eventually convinces her that the police are the guilty party. He then reveals himself and threatens to blow them up using a bomb that had been an item of evidence, telling them he has tape recorded the whole event, providing a record of their effective confessions. The audience are offered two alternative endings – either the bomb explodes and kills the handcuffed policemen, or the journalist chooses whether or not to release them to face justice. The Maniac tells the audience they have to choose which they prefer, and leaves.

Belt and Braces, a touring British 'alternative theatre' company from the 1970s with a committed political pedigree, reached the West End in 1980 with the first UK production of *Accidental Death of an Anarchist*.

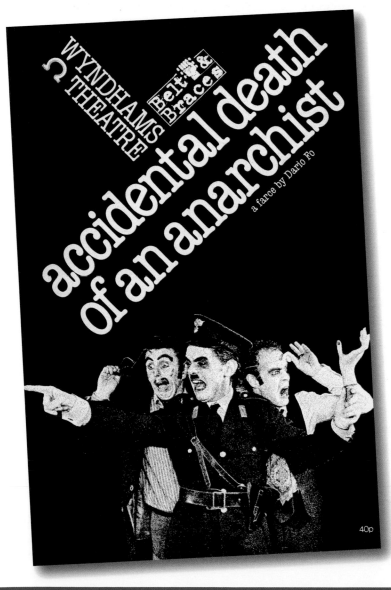

■ Dario Fo's theatre

Dario Fo based his comic role of the Maniac on the eccentric gestures of the Neapolitan clown Toto, who was, Fo wrote, like the Maniac, 'a social outcast who moves, runs, writhes about, shouts, screams, weeps, sneezes, spits and makes obscene gestures in order to succeed precisely in destroying whatever is sacred and essential in power'.

The effectiveness of the comedy is based on clowning in the age-honoured Italian tradition of *commedia dell'arte*. In the action, the apparently foolish character unexpectedly turns the tables on the authority figures and exerts an erratic control over them, destabilising and wrong footing the guilty until the truth is shaken out of them. He terrorises the police with a false arm, a wooden leg and a glass eye that apparently have lives of their own – a technique based on the ancient principles of clowning. Clowning allows Fo to exploit the comic routines and semi-improvised situations that make apparently meaningless mischief suddenly appear purposeful, delighting the ordinary people of the audience who see authority figures on the receiving end.

→ Billy Bragg – *Brewing Up with Billy Bragg*

Billy Bragg is one of the most politically active British singer/songwriters. Born in Dagenham, Essex in 1957, he formed a punk band in 1977, touring London pubs and clubs. He briefly joined the British Army in 1981 but bought himself out after a few months. Always inventive, he managed to get the attention of a record company by pretending to be a TV repair man, and to get a disc played on Radio 1's *John Peel Show* by rushing to the BBC with a mushroom biryani when Peel said on air that he was hungry.

He became increasingly politically prominent as his work was becoming better known, supporting the miners' strike of 1984 then joining the pro-Labour group Red Wedge. After a Conservative government, led by Margaret Thatcher, had been elected twice with less than 50% of the vote, he joined Charter 88 to campaign for reform of the voting system. He travelled to the Soviet Union in the 1980s and there are somewhat humorous references to the icons of cold-war socialism in his songs. He has been outspoken on many high-profile political issues, including national identity with the 2002 album *England, Half-English*. More recently he has been involved in Jail Guitar Doors, which donates instruments for workshops and performance in prisons to encourage rehabilitation.

■ *Brewing Up with Billy Bragg* (1984)

Billy Bragg once said that he realised that to hear the political songs for his time, he was going to have to write them himself, and so set about doing so. From his second album, *Brewing Up with Billy Bragg*, a style for his performing work was established: a solo electric guitar and vocals (although on some recordings a supporting acoustic guitar is also evident) , chiming and clipping chords and inventive riffs underpinning and illustrating a voice which can be harsh and strident or alternately almost sobbing, but always distinctive in its Essex vocal tones. The effect achieved by these riffs is worth some closer analysis, as is the shifting relationship between the voice and the guitar. Atmospheric reverb is used, especially at key emotional moments. The album is a mix of political and bitter love songs. Bragg has always been concerned as much with human experience as political intent, and the human outcomes are invariably the focus in his political songs.

The opening track, *It Says Here*, echoing the street newsvendor's voice, is a challenge to the nation of newspaper readers to be alert to the bias of the predominantly conservative press, with specific references in each line beginning 'it says here'. 'Have you ever wished [that] you were better informed' was the slogan in a major *Sunday Times* poster campaign. The added 'that', which makes the lyric scan, also breaks the illusion of the slogan.

Island of No Return is in the persona of an army squaddie, no doubt drawn from Bragg's brief army experience. A string of drill orders is barked too rapidly to follow, as if to create the sense of panic felt by the novice on the parade ground, whose thoughts juxtapose 'a party way dahn sarf' with fighting fascists in the southern seas 'and in his hand / a weapon that was made in Birmingham'. The song ends with clashing chaotic guitar chords that play out the soldier's combat emotions.

This work established Billy Bragg as a serious solo artist, and his political songwriting strength was acknowledged. He now had the confidence to explore overt politics as well as broken relationships, sometimes bringing the two together.

■ Bragg's later work

Tender Comrade, from the album *Workers' Playtime* (1988), suggests by its title and the sleeve artwork that it is a propaganda song from a lost Soviet political world. However, it is sung unaccompanied as a traditional English folk song, with reflective pauses. Bragg's skill is often evident in his ability to construct a voice which speaks for many and which generates several perspectives on the situation he builds: here looking forward to a time when war will be a memory. *Levi Stubbs' Tears* (1986) uses his other main technique, to narrate in the third person a song which is effectively a short story. This is recognised as one of his greatest songs. It depicts with sharp and telling detail the loneliness of a victim of domestic violence whose accident compensation buys her only isolation from society.

Between the Wars is also a powerful song of the common man, following the *Brewing Up* album in 1985. It demonstrates Billy Bragg's lyrical brilliance. A gentle hymn with echoes of Blake's *Jerusalem*, it recalls the working men born to live their lives in valued trades, undisturbed by the Second World War that would kill so many of them. It has a dual perspective, setting out a charter for peace in a time that we know will end in war:

> Call out the craftsmen
> Bring me the draughtsmen
> And build me a path from cradle to grave
> And I'll give my consent
> To any government
> That does not deny a man a living wage.

The voice now firmly established, in 1986 two political anthems were released on the *Talking with the Taxman about Poetry* album. *There is Power in a Union*, also hymn-like, is probably Bragg's most unembellished political song, calling for action against the Thatcher government's anti-union legislation which sought to end workers' unions as a force to negotiate wages. *Help Save the Youth of America*, only 2¾ minutes long, has an intensity and an apocalyptic authority in its voice which makes it feel longer. With a strong clapping beat and sharp lyrics it refers to TV entertainment, surfer songs and the 1986 Chernobyl nuclear disaster to warn of American insularity, almost exactly 15 years before the 9/11 attacks:

> The fate of the great United States is entwined with the fate of us all
> And the incident at Chernobyl proves the world we live in is very small

A rallying cry in the final refrain warns that if there is war in the cities of Europe again then

> Washington will burn with them
> Omaha will burn with them
> Los Alamos will burn with them

Since the 1980s, Billy Bragg has diversified, working with a number of rock and folk practitioners. Never awed by icons, he wrote new lyrics to *The Internationale*, the socialist anthem, when challenged by the folk singer Pete Seeger, having complained that the existing ones feel somewhat dated. He also worked in collaboration with singer and musician Wilco to bring to life a number of Woody Guthrie lyrics that had no known melodies in the *Mermaid Avenue* album.

→ Christopher Bruce – *Hurricane*

Christopher Bruce was born in Leicester in 1945. As a child he had polio and ballet was recommended as a way of strengthening his body. He joined Rambert School at the age of 13 and then four years later, in 1963, Rambert Dance Company, where he was one of Marie Rambert's protégés.

In November 2002, Christopher Bruce CBE retired as artistic director of Rambert Dance Company after more than eight years in the post. He was associated with the company for over 40 years, both as a dancer and as a choreographer. He is well known for his outstanding performance in Glen Tetley's *Pierrot Lunaire* and for works that he choreographed, such as *Ghost Dances* (1981), *Swansong* (1987) and *Rooster* (1991).

Rambert changed slowly from a pure ballet company to one that employed different styles such as contemporary, and techniques such as Martha Graham's, which was used in class each day. This influenced Bruce's work, which uses a range of styles from ballet and contemporary to folk dance, tap and ballroom. Bruce became associate director in 1975 and associate choreographer before he left in 1987 to pursue a freelance career. He returned in 1994 as artistic director.

Having a strong visual sense, Bruce pays great attention to the set, which might be bare with the lighting playing a key role as in *Swansong* or have a painted backdrop indicating physical setting as in *Ghost Dances* (1981). The second piece is a one-act dance about the dictatorship of General Pinochet in Chile and the disappearance of thousands of innocent people. Three Ghost Dancers await a group of Dead who relive moments of their lives and then pass on. The music is folk, played by the group Inti-Illimani, and helps to create a South American feel for the movement.

> 'I made this ballet for the innocent people of South America, who from the time of the Spanish Conquests have been continuously devastated by political oppression. I would like to give my thanks to Joan Jara for all her help and to Inti-Illimani for the inspiration of their performances.'
>
> Christopher Bruce, *Ghost Dancers* programme note, July 1981

■ *Hurricane* (2002)

Bruce has developed a reputation for making dance pieces based on human-rights issues. Although each piece may be inspired by an event, the suffering of a particular person or group of people, a book or a situation, the message is always universal and reaches out to as wide an audience as possible. The dancers play characters with a strong dramatic technique using facial gesture, costume and make-up to portray the innermost emotions of the downtrodden with whom the audience sympathise.

This piece picks up on the political dimensions of a Bob Dylan song. Bruce heard Bob Dylan's *Hurricane* playing in Camden one day and it became the stimulus for this solo for a male dancer. There is a strong connection with *Pierrot Lunaire* as Bruce employs strong characterisation, clowning, mime and a clown's make-up to show the boxer Rubin 'Hurricane' Carter being framed by the police and wrongfully imprisoned. Using ideas from *commedia dell'arte*, the dancer has his face painted white with very expressive make-up on the eyebrows and around the eyes in the style of a clown or silent-movie actor. Bruce has said that he used the idea of cartoon when choreographing the movement. There are several characters in the narrative and these are denoted by repetition of gesture such as nodding the head coupled with small feminine steps for Miss Patty Valentine.

For more on Dylan's song *Hurricane*, please see page 137.

Structure

The dance tells the story of Rubin 'Hurricane' Carter, a middleweight boxer who was framed by the police in New Jersey for the murder of three men, a murder which he did not commit. He was imprisoned for 20 years after an all-white jury found him guilty. Eventually he was set free and pardoned.

Bruce follows the structure of the song, which consists of 11 verses containing some repetition. The piece starts and ends with the dancer skipping like a boxer in training. There are sections of shadow boxing, punching and falling down as well as walking in a circle to indicate a boxing ring. The solo is about 8 minutes long and is reminiscent of the victim's solo in *Swansong*, although *Hurricane* does not use a chair to show prison bars. There are small intricate steps in each piece reflecting the small dimensions of the cell. Floor work shows entrapment and isolation. Carter sits on the floor in a yoga position with palms showing to mirror the words in the song

> While Rubin sits like Buddha in a ten-foot cell
> An innocent man in a living hell.

The set is simple with a black floor and lighting which at times shows bars or a grid on the floor symbolising prison bars. This image reminds the audience of the injustice done to this innocent victim of a racist police force. Carter was nowhere near the scene of the crime but was driving around town. He was picked up by the police, which was a usual occurrence in the USA at that time:

> If you're black you might as well not show up on the street
> Less you wanna draw the heat.

Hurricane shows a strong relationship with the music, much like *Rooster*, for which Bruce used songs by the Rolling Stones. There are moments in *Hurricane* that remind us of the rooster strut when the character Bello points his feet as he slowly and purposefully walks forward having robbed the cash register.

Political intentions

Bruce believes that good dance theatre should allow statements to be made naturally. The lyrics of Dylan's song make the point clear as the dancer re-enacts the events of the night that led to the ruining of one man's career.

→ ACE Dance and Music – *Skin*

ACE Dance and Music combine contemporary dance with African and Caribbean movement style accompanied by live music and multimedia. The company works with a diverse range of choreographers to create new work, but at the heart of what they do is the work of the founders, Gail and Ian Parmel. The productions of ACE Dance and Music raise cultural awareness and make audiences think about how they behave and react as human beings.

The company's website describes their artistic approach as 'captivating and energetic contemporary dance with African and Caribbean movement style, layering rousing live music scores and multimedia techniques, creating an entertaining and enriching experience which is appealing to all. Pushing the boundaries of contemporary performance, we use new music technology and traditional musical genres to create accessible and exciting dance experiences.'

■ Background to the company

Gail Parmel is the artistic director of ACE. She is a graduate of the Northern School of Contemporary Dance who joined Birmingham-based Kokuma Dance Theatre in 1992 and then worked with Badejo Arts Living Circle. She founded ACE Dance and Music in 1996 with her husband Ian, who is the musical director. Gail Parmel brings her Antiguan heritage and knowledge of contemporary dance to her work.

Ian Parmel has been drumming and playing steel pan since he was a child in Trinidad and Tobago. He was invited to England in 1988 to teach steel-pan music and joined Kokuma Dance Company in 1991. He trained in digital media in Birmingham and works with Soundbeam, a computerised sound package that enables sound to be triggered by interaction with invisible beams.

In partnership, Gail Parmel has choreographed five touring productions for ACE Dance and Music – *The Path, Colours Within, Solitude or Sanctuary, 3 Shades* and *En-Trance* – while Ian has created and directed the music for these productions. Gail has researched and travelled throughout Europe, the Caribbean and Africa. She has participated in the Black Choreographic Initiative and has worked with Batanai, the National Dance Company of Zimbabwe.

■ *Skin* (2008)

Origins and political intentions

Skin –The Spirit of Unity within Different Colours of Life is choreographed for six dancers, and brings together elements of dance styles from Europe, Japan,

Africa and the Caribbean. The staging of the piece calls for extensive sound, light and music, and the extensive score was brought together under the musical direction of Ian Parmel. Gail Parmel worked with two internationally renowned choreographers – Akiko Kitamura (from Japan) and Vincent Mantsoe (from South Africa) – to create a piece in two halves, one half created by each choreographer.

The piece is political in the way it explores what lies beneath the skin and the spirit of unity which human beings can experience, when so many of the world's conflicts have arisen from racial tensions. *Skin* explores how we perceive each other's identity through skin colour. It poses the question: 'From the outside we look different, but underneath, aren't we all the same?' *Skin* is about exploring the identity that lies beneath the skin, and appreciating the diversity of culture in the modern world. Each individual has come from a different experience and background and engages with the present from an individual perspective. *Skin* engages the audience in a debate about living in the present while respecting our roots and traditions, recognising that humanity has so much in common as we all question our identity.

Gail Parmel summarises the project in her artistic statement as follows:

'I strive to root my work in the traditions and movement of the past, and through a journey of exploration aim to express and reflect these roots, while also embracing contemporary ideas and styles. Working with Mantsoe and Kitamura has complemented and enhanced my practice. For this piece I specifically chose to collaborate with International choreographers of the moment who share my desire to "get under the skin" of their traditional cultures and convey what is poignant now, uniting the old and the new.'

A look at the work of Akiko Kitamira and Vincent Mantsoe shows how diverse styles and cultures are brought together within the same piece.

Choreographers

Akiko Kitamura is an acclaimed avant-garde Japanese dancer and choreographer who stimulates the audience's senses using film, lighting, sound and quick movements inspired by high-tech film and video projections. On stage, he uses computer graphics, sound effects and lighting to engage the audience and create an interactive experience.

Vincent Mantsoe is from Soweto in South Africa and has wide experience of African dance and music, having participated in traditional rituals of song and dance. This can be traced back to his imitating street dance on music videos he saw as a boy, as well as hearing his mother drumming every day in her role as a Sangoma or healer. When he began training at the Moving Into Dance Company in Johannesburg, Mantsoe was able to merge his distinct dance forms, which he describes as Afro-fusion. African dance has influences from Zulu dance, Pedi, Xhosa, Venda and Shangaan dance. In addition to this Mantsoe incorporates ballet, Asian dance, t'ai chi, martial arts and Balinese dance.

Mantsoe became the associate artistic director of Moving into Dance Company between 1997 and 2001. He has created work and taught in many countries. His

This image of Marcia Edwards in the 2008 production of *Skin* has been used to great effect in publicity and marketing.

work is featured in the documentary film *African Dance: Sand, Drum and Shostakovich*, which makes some interesting links with Shostakovich's music. (You can read more about Shostakovich's music on pages 133–135.)

Mantsoe uses aspects of African traditional dances, but in order to show respect for these roots he recognises the need to 'ask permission' to borrow from them. To do this, he takes part in a traditional ritual at least twice a year. His respect for the past and for his ancestors is mixed with a desire to engage with the new and move forward in the creative process to produce something of value and to find the real spirit of dance in modern society.

Content and structure

The first half of *Skin* is entitled *Blind Trip* and was choreographed by Akiko Kitamura. The stage looks like a clinical laboratory, with spotlights shining from under the floor, but the dancers explore the skin in a way that science can not. The movement was inspired by the ceremony of fighting. *Blind Trip* looks at how we give out signals and how skin awakens emotions.

The second half of the piece was choreographed by Vincent Mantsoe and is named *Letlalo* after the word for 'skin' in his mother tongue. His choreography explores human power and spirit through the dancers' diverse backgrounds and cultures. As with *Blind Trip*, the choreography explores aspects of the spirit of unity and the things we all share. It shows a journey through time, looking at energy and change.

The Twentieth-Century
American Musical

The development of the musical in the USA during the twentieth century is unique in the way it brought together dance, drama and music: a popular entertainment that evolved into a serious genre. The musical's success grew from its ability to unite the art forms in a way that captured public imagination and to adapt to the changing fashions of the century. In that sense, it is a commentary on America's view of itself and its place in the world. Whilst much of the content is stylised, practitioners worked within the confines of the genre to create stylish and witty pieces, encouraging their audience to enter into a make-believe world in which speech, song and movement were as natural partners as the teams that produced the book, music and lyrics. The genre reached its pinnacle in the middle of the century in what became known as the book musical, where the drama and music are fully integrated and the songs are vital components in moving the drama along.

→ Roots

It is possible to trace the development of the American musical back to the second half of the nineteenth century. There were many genres that finally gave rise to the musical, and whilst all of them were popular entertainments, there were significant differences between them. Operetta had been developed in Europe and became highly popular in the United States, particularly from the late 1870s following many highly successful performances of Gilbert and Sullivan's *HMS Pinafore*. Over the next 30 years many operettas were staged, and in 1907 Franz Lehár's *The Merry Widow* became the most influential European operetta to be produced in the United States. Whilst operetta was a popular form of light entertainment, it nevertheless contained significant elements of drama, particularly character and plot.

By contrast, the other influences on the development of the musical were less dramatic and also less sophisticated. Burlesque and vaudeville also had their roots in European forms and both exploited the popularity of music and spectacle. Whilst vaudeville was targeted at family audiences, burlesque was unashamedly adult entertainment; both were concerned with the notion of showmanship and entertainment. In both, song-and-dance routines, often with spectacular troupes of dancing girls accompanied by professional dance bands, provided audiences with escapist entertainment that was visual, memorable and made few demands on the intellect.

Although an essentially British form of popular entertainment, music hall was akin to vaudeville in its aspirations. It included singing, dancing and comedy routines as well as acrobatic entertainment, all introduced through a chairman who acted as the master of ceremonies for the show. By contrast, minstrel shows were a specific type of vaudeville performance which involved groups of white performers blacking their faces in supposed imitation of the minstrels of the previous centuries. This became an accepted part of nineteenth-century American culture, and was the inspiration for many of the songs of Stephen C. Foster (1826–64), one of America's most significant songwriters of the nineteenth century.

The early decades of the twentieth century were a time when the traditions of operetta and variety entertainment came together to establish the earliest musicals. Whilst there are works such as *Little Johnny Jones* that date back as early as 1904, the form gained its maturity by the early 1920s. By that stage, the ingredients of the musical play were in place – a loose plot, well crafted songs and spectacular dance numbers – but the links between them were flimsy. The plot was generally predictable and songs and dance routines could be taken out and placed at a different point in the show, or even in a different show, if this was deemed to be commercially expedient in pleasing the audience.

→ The book musical

The most important aspect in establishing the musical as an art form was the songs, plot and dance routines becoming more integrated. The book musical made a conscious attempt to develop plot, dialogue and characterisation through each of the art forms, and to make them work together to move the action along. This meant that the songs and dance routines in each work were an integral feature of the drama and that the work aspired to be a coherent whole.

→ Fingerprints of the book musical

- ☑ The book musical developed in the 1920s, culminating in the production of *Show Boat* (1927). It contrasts with earlier loose collections of songs brought together in the style of a revue.

- ☑ Book musicals were produced by teams of practitioners who worked together. Some of the most famous partnerships were Rodgers and Kern/Hammerstein, Lerner and Loewe, Kander and Ebb. Other practitioners such as Bernstein, Sondheim and Loesser worked with a variety of partners.

- ☑ The musical reached its peak in the 1950s, a decade that has been referred to as the golden age of the American musical.

- ☑ The musicals of the mid twentieth century were in many cases produced by practitioners who were first- or second-generation immigrants to the USA and who wanted to take part fully in the American Dream. This is most obvious in the pieces produced between 1927 and 1957 although a few isolated works outside these dates also have elements of the Dream.

- ☑ After *West Side Story* the musical became more stark, gritty and critical of the American Dream and the place of America in the world. This led to the development of the art musical in the hands of Stephen Sondheim. This took the art form in a different direction.

→ Sample American musicals

The following book musicals are studied in this unit to demonstrate how particular dance numbers, songs or dramatic passages contribute to that ideal. They are presented in the order in which they were written to help build up a picture of how the genre developed during the century. Although musicals were produced by teams, the list is designed to enable you to study three practitioners from each of dance, drama and music. There is obviously some overlap between practitioners and works, however.

1927 Jerome Kern – *Show Boat*	**1959** Richard Rodgers – *The Sound of Music*
1943 Agnes de Mille – *Oklahoma!*	**1970** Stephen Sondheim – *Company*
1956 Oscar Hammerstein II – *The King and I*	**1972** Bob Fosse – *Liza with a Z*
1956 Alan Jay Lerner – *My Fair Lady*	**1975** John Kander – *Chicago*
1957 Jerome Robbins – *West Side Story*	

→ *Show Boat* (1927)
Focus on Jerome Kern

Music Jerome Kern   **Lyrics** Oscar Hammerstein II
Book Oscar Hammerstein II   **Choreography** Sammy Lee

Producer Florenz Ziegfeld, who had made a reputation for his extravagant revues, known as the Ziegfeld Follies, which ran on Broadway from 1907 to 1931
Productions Broadway 1927, most recently revived 1994
Films There have been three films of *Show Boat* – 1929, 1936 and 1951.

Show Boat is generally considered to be the first fully fledged book musical. It is often referred to as a musical play, in order to distinguish it from the musical comedies of the previous decades. In comparison with them, the drama is credible and the characters three-dimensional. Both the book and the lyrics to the songs were written by Oscar Hammerstein II and this meant that he was able to reflect the dramatic action in the songs. The music is by Jerome Kern and *Show Boat* is the only real success that the Hammerstein and Kern partnership produced, although after Kern's death in 1945, Hammerstein went on to produce several very successful musicals with Richard Rodgers (1902–1979).

Show Boat is bold in its treatment of dramatic subjects that were taboo in 1927, although some of the language used now appears dated and has been adapted in more recent performances. The show tackles issues of violence, gambling, racism, interracial marriage and the first performance was racially integrated, itself a major step forward at the time.

■ Synopsis

Show Boat is based on Edna Ferber's 1926 novel of the same name. The action spans almost 50 years, but starts on a show boat called the *Cotton Blossom*. Gaylord Ravenal meets Magnolia Hawks (the daughter of the boat's owner,

Scene from *Show Boat*

Cap'n Andy Hawkes) on board. Gaylord is a striking man, but also a compulsive gambler. Magnolia quickly falls in love with him and they soon marry.

Several years pass, and the couple and their daughter Kim are living in Chicago, very poorly off financially as a result of Gaylord's gambling debts. Magnolia still loves him in spite of this, but soon Gaylord abandons her and Kim. Magnolia obtains work as a singer at the Trocadero, where she is very popular with the audience. The plot takes an unexpected turn as Cap'n Andy pays a surprise visit to the Trocadero to take her and Kim back to the show boat, where Gaylord is waiting for them, repentant of his misdemeanours. The couple are reunited as the chorus sings a final version of *Ol' Man River*.

■ Jerome Kern's music

Jerome Kern was a well established songwriter by the time he composed the songs for *Show Boat*. He had a natural gift for melody and harmony and had been successful in getting his songs included in musical shows on Broadway. However, he wanted to write songs that were integral to the plot of a musical, rather than following the tradition of producing songs that were simply appendages to the drama. In *Show Boat*, Kern achieved this aim, as the mood and style of the music help to reveal the thoughts and feelings of the characters singing the songs. He was fortunate in finding in Hammerstein a lyricist who shared the same vision and there are several examples of his songs developing the theme of the drama.

Two of the most famous musical numbers in *Show Boat* are also among the best known of Kern's songs: *Ol' Man River* and *Can't Help Lovin' Dat Man*. Both appear in the first half of Act 1 (although both have a reprise in Act 2).

Ol' Man River is a slow, contemplative song. It is sung by the stevedore Joe (played originally by the virtuoso bass singer Paul Robeson), who has been asked for his advice about Gaylord by Magnolia. Magnolia is excited about the prospect of falling in love with Gaylord although Joe tells her that there are plenty of Gaylord's type around. That being the case, he suggests asking the river for advice. The melody of the song fits this perfectly. It starts low, and rises with each

Melody of refrain of
Ol' Man River

phrase until it gets to the word 'nothin'', at which point the melody falls in pitch, reflecting the way the river rolls on in spite of difficult human questions.

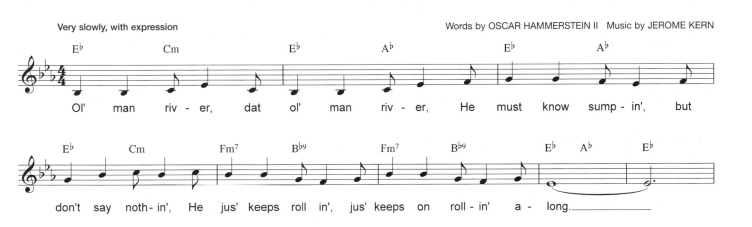

Half an hour later, Magnolia is telling Julie (the star of the show boat) that she has fallen in love with Gaylord. This seems very sudden to Julie. She responds by giving Magnolia sound advice about taking care when falling in love, since love can be fickle and she must ensure that her lover is worthy of her love. Magnolia responds by singing *Can't Help Lovin' Dat Man of Mine*. The shape of the melody

Melody of refrain of
*Can't Help Lovin' Dat
Man of Mine*

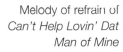

complements the style of *Ol' Man River* but, sung by a female voice, has a much higher register and expresses the excitement of new love and none of the fatalism of the river's inability to answer.

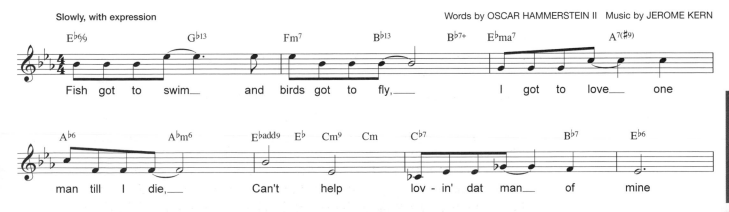

→ *Oklahoma!* (1943)
Focus on Agnes de Mille

Music Richard Rodgers	**Lyrics** Oscar Hammerstein II
Book Oscar Hammerstein II	**Choreography** Agnes de Mille

Productions Broadway 1943, most recently revived 2002
Films The film version dates from 1955.

Oklahoma! has the same broad historical setting as *Show Boat* although it was not produced until 16 years later. The book and lyrics are again by Oscar Hammerstein II, although he had had no significant success with a show since *Show Boat*. The music is by Richard Rodgers, who had already enjoyed considerable success in his collaboration with Lorenz Hart (1895–1943) although this was strained to breaking point by Hart's descent into alcoholism. The new partnership of Rodgers and Hammerstein gave the American musical its best known and most enduring collaboration and built on the successes of *Show Boat*. In contrast to Lorenz Hart's crisp, witty lyrics, Hammerstein's crafting of the words in *Oklahoma!* is tasteful and supports the narrative. In turn, Rodgers began to write ballad melodies more akin to those turned out by Jerome Kern.

Oklahoma! took the book musical to a new level of innovation and rejected many of the accepted conventions of the Broadway musical, although the importance of dance was heightened rather than diminished. In particular, there were no leg-kicking dance routines, contrived plots or elaborate choruses – the aspects of the style most derived from vaudeville. Instead, the intention was to depict the lives of ordinary people, but in a sophisticated artistic style. The opening scene typifies everything that comes after: a single cowboy singing offstage *Oh What a Beautiful Morning*. One critic of the 1943 premiere is quoted as saying 'no legs, no jokes, no chance'. *Oklahoma!* proved this view wrong by breaking box-office records both on Broadway and in London's West End.

In this National Theatre Production from 1998, Maureen Lipman played Aunt Eller and Hugh Jackman was Curly.

■ Synopsis

Oklahoma! is based on Lynn Rigg's 1931 play *Green Grow the Lilacs* but set in the early 1900s at the time the Indian Territory was becoming the state of Oklahoma. The removal of the audience from the action by means of historical distance was something that typified Rodgers and Hammerstein's approach.

The plot explores the pettiness and fragilities of human relationships through a cowboy, Curly McLain, and a farm girl, Laurey Williams, who both refuse stubbornly to show their love. At the start of the show, the two rag each other as Aunt Eller watches. Jud Fry emerges as a sinister rival for Laurey's love and invites her to the box social; to annoy Curly, Laurey accepts. This confuses Laurey and she is torn between her feelings for Curly and Jud. This takes a twist in the *Dream* ballet when she cannot escape from Jud. Will Parker returns from a trip to Kansas City, but also becomes embroiled in the politics of romance when Ado Annie, his girlfriend, flirts for the attention of other men, in particular Ali Hakim, a pedlar. The relationship between Will Parker and Ado Annie forms a subplot to *Oklahoma!*

Act 2 takes place at the box social, where the bidding in the auction becomes a metaphor for the bidding of Curly and Jud for Laurey's love. When later confronted by Jud, though, Laurey tells him that she feels nothing for him and a conflict ensues, at which point Curly appears to rescue her. Curly and Laurey marry but the morning after their wedding Jud turns up drunk and, in a fight with Curly, falls on his knife and dies. This leads to a celebration of the marriage of Curly and Laurey, and a happy ending for the musical.

■ Agnes de Mille's choreography

Agnes de Mille (1905–1993) was a key figure in the development of dance in the American musical. Trained in classical ballet, she studied with Marie Rambert and in 1940 became a founder member of Ballet Theatre. In 1943, following the success of *Rodeo*, a ballet to music by the American composer Aaron Copland, Agnes de Mille was approached by Rodgers and Hammerstein to create the choreography for *Oklahoma!* This began a successful collaboration with the partnership, and she produced the choreography for *Brigadoon* and *Carousel* as well working with another Broadway partnership, Lerner and Loewe, on *Paint Your Wagon*. Her main contribution to the development of the American musical was to introduce into it techniques normally associated with ballet.

Whereas song-and-dance routines had been used in the musical comedies of the 1920s as a diversion from the story, *Oklahoma!* integrates dance and song into the dramatic plot and comment on character development. There are a number of significant dance numbers in *Oklahoma!* that do precisely that. These include *Kansas City* and *The Farmer and the Cowman*, but in order to understand the importance of de Mille's work, we will focus on the *Dream* ballet at the end of Act 1. In the 1955 film version, the sequence starts at around 1 hour and 5 minutes. The ballet sequence lasts for around 15 minutes and is an excellent example of how Agnes de Mille's choreography interprets the increasingly nightmarish scenario where Laurey is confronted by Jud, culminating in Jud killing Curly.

The sequence makes use of a number of melodies from the show, and begins with Laurey singing *Out of My Dreams*. In contrast to the vaudeville-inspired show numbers of the early twentieth century, de Mille's choreography shows how ballet techniques can be used in a popular art form. It is used here to interpret Laurey's emotionally confused state, culminating in the end of the act where the real Jud arrives to take her to the box social.

→ ## *The King and I* (1956)
Focus on Oscar Hammerstein II

Music Richard Rodgers   **Lyrics** Oscar Hammerstein II
Book Oscar Hammerstein II   **Choreography** Jerome Robbins
Productions Broadway 1951, most recently revived 2000 in London's West End
Films The film version dates from 1956.

Deborah Kerr as Anna with Yul Brynner as the King in the 1956 film version of *The King and I*

The King and I was Rodgers and Hammerstein's fourth musical collaboration. After *Oklahoma!* there followed *Carousel* (1945) and *South Pacific* (1949). Both of these demonstrated their ability to establish the musical as a genre that brought together music, drama and dance in a way that supported the development of a complex plot with believable characters. In *The King and I* the choreography was produced by Jerome Robbins, and the film version reproduces that devised for the Broadway stage. Robbins was a significant collaborator whose choreography spanned a significant part of the twentieth century and who worked with a number of composers and lyricists.

■ Synopsis

The King and I is based on Margaret Landon's 1944 book *Anna and the King of Siam*, which is itself based on a true story. The action is set in 1862 in Siam (now known as Thailand). Anna Leonowens is a young widow from England who has been invited by the King of Siam to teach his 106 children. The King's desire to bring western culture to Siam is historically accurate and Hammerstein's libretto is sensitive in recognising the importance of education in achieving this.

The plot explores the comic potential for misunderstanding where there is a clash of cultures. As Anna teaches the King's children, a number of misconceptions emerge but there is a darker subplot as well: the secret relationship between Tuptim, a slave girl in the King's court who has been given as a 'gift' by the King of Burma (Myanmar), and Lun Tha, also from Burma. The King is desperate that he should be seen as civilised by the outside world, but his behaviour towards Tuptim in front of the British ambassador undermines this. The musical ends with the King's death but also an indication that he achieved some state of enlightenment through the action of the musical.

■ Oscar Hammerstein II as a dramatist

It is difficult to envisage the development of the American musical in the twentieth century without Oscar Hammerstein II. His collaborations with Jerome Kern and then Richard Rodgers produced some of the most significant examples of the genre, and he influenced the next generation since he was Stephen Sondheim's teacher. He was much more than a mere lyricist, and in most cases wrote the book as well. This enabled him to take an overview of the drama and ensure that the songs enabled the action to move forward, and that the words and music were equal partners.

Although Hammerstein's plots can seem dated from a twenty-first-century perspective, in their time they were innovative and challenging and dealt with a number of social, cultural and historical issues in depth. Many writers have seen the American musical of the 1950s as reflecting the American Dream – the idea of a meritocracy in which hard work is rewarded by achievement. Although Hammerstein's plots are generally set at some historical distance from the date of writing, his view of progress is reflected in them, together with the theme of other countries' place in the modern world order (and by implication America's place in the modern world).

Just after halfway through Act 2 of *The King and I*, the King entertains the British ambassador's party to a 'surprise' performance that has been put together for the occasion. In the 1956 film, this section starts at around 1 hour 32 minutes and is of a similar length to the *Dream* ballet in *Oklahoma!* (although later in the show). It is a retelling of Harriet Beecher Stowe's *Uncle Tom's Cabin* by the slave girl Tuptim (the 'present' from the King of Burma). Tuptim has borrowed the book from Mrs Anna and recast it as a Siamese ballet called *Small House of Uncle Thomas*. The ballet acts as a parallel story to Tuptim's life: a slave girl who is subject to the whims of an evil king tries to escape. The stylised movement is authentic and the whole episode is used by Hammerstein as a commentary on the main drama; Robbins' choreography reinforces this. The attempted escape of Tuptim after the performance leads to the King attempting to beat her for her insubordination.

→ *My Fair Lady* (1956)
Focus on Alan Jay Lerner

Music Frederick Loewe	**Lyrics** Alan Jay Lerner
Book Alan Jay Lerner	**Choreography** Hermes Pan

Productions Broadway 1956, revived 2001 in London's West End
Films The film version dates from 1964.

My Fair Lady is the most significant musical to come from the partnership of lyricist Alan Jay Lerner (1918–86) and composer Frederick Loewe (1901–1988). Although they worked together less regularly than Rodgers and Hammerstein, their work was highly successful and includes *Brigadoon* (1947), *Paint Your Wagon* (1951), *Gigi* (1958) and *Camelot* (1960). Their musicals were produced during the 'golden age' of the 1950s, and are an excellent example of how the genre had established itself in that decade.

The two men had worked with classical-ballet choreographer Agnes de Mille in *Brigadoon* but in *My Fair Lady* the choreography was produced by Hermes Pan (1909–1990). Pan was experienced in producing dance for the Broadway stage and was the choreographer for *Kiss Me Kate* (1953), in which Bob Fosse performed. He was better known, however, for his collaborations with Fred Astaire. He was involved in 17 of Astaire's films and had a strong feel for how dance could be used effectively in musical entertainment.

My Fair Lady is in the tradition of American musicals that were derived from, or based on, existing books or plays. Unlike *Kiss Me Kate* or *West Side Story*, which were inspired by the plots of Shakespeare plays, *My Fair Lady* is an adaptation of George Bernard Shaw's 1913 play *Pygmalion*, itself based on a classical Latin tale by Ovid.

Rex Harrison and Audrey Hepburn in the 1956 film of *My Fair Lady*

■ Synopsis

My Fair Lady centres on the improbable relationship between a linguistics professor and a flower girl. Professor Henry Higgins has a wager with Colonel Pickering that he can transform Eliza Doolittle from being a common flower girl into a society lady by training her how to speak and behave. The action of the musical follows the various shenanigans that result from this as Higgins makes Eliza his project, with the intention of presenting her at an embassy ball. There are comic episodes to the story from Eliza's father, Alfred P. Doolittle, who is a drunken dustman but unexpectedly comes into money, as well as romantic infatuation with Eliza by the upper-class Freddy Eynsford-Hill. Despite Eliza's transformation, the tensions between her and Higgins are all too apparent. Lerner adapted the ending of the play to have the main characters fall in love with each other, as a concession to the essential nature of the musical genre.

■ Alan Jay Lerner's approach to libretto

Alan Jay Lerner did not have an easy task on his hands in adapting *Pygmalion* into a musical. The dialogue of the original play is quite dense and difficult to inject songs into. It is also much more elevated than the language of most musicals, with the comedy growing naturally from the exchange of extended conversation. The setting is completely removed from America, as are several of Lerner and Loewe's musicals.

Lerner's final libretto is a highly sensitive adaptation of Shaw's play, with the same characters but cut-down dialogue, the same sequence of events and an innovative approach to producing songs that capture the spirit of the characterisation. The opening scene of the musical introduces the three main characters: Henry Higgins, Eliza Doolittle and Colonel Pickering. Higgins adopts a patronising and supercilious tone to Eliza and claims that her cockney accent will ensure that she remains a flower girl all her life. This leads into the song *Why Can't the English Teach Their Children How to Speak* with its dense lines mirroring Higgins' intricate and pedantic dialogue. The song is in the tradition of the patter songs of Gilbert and Sullivan's operettas but with two significant differences. The lines are of irregular length and are more akin to the style of the American poet Ogden Nash. Secondly, their melodic shape lends itself to a type of *Sprechgesang* (spoken song), which is what Rex Harrison adopts in the film version. The lyrics also betray an imperialist attitude to the rest of the world, with all other countries damned with faint praise!

Why can't the English teach their children how to speak?
This verbal class distinction by now should be antique.
If you spoke as she does, sir, instead of the way you do,
Why, you might be selling flowers, too.
An Englishman's way of speaking absolutely classifies him,
The moment he talks he makes some other
Englishman despise him.
One common language I'm afraid we'll never get.
Oh, why can't the English learn to set
A good example to people whose
English is painful to your ears?
The Scotch and the Irish leave you close to tears.
There even are places where English completely disappears.
In America, they haven't used it for years!
Why can't the English teach their children how to speak?
Norwegians learn Norwegian; the Greeks have taught their
Greek. In France every Frenchman knows
his language from 'A' to 'Zed'
The French never care what they do, actually,
as long as they pronounce in properly.
Arabians learn Arabian with the speed of summer lightning.
And Hebrews learn it backwards,
which is absolutely frightening.
But use proper English you're regarded as a freak.
Why can't the English,
Why can't the English learn to speak?

➜ *West Side Story* (1957)
Focus on Jerome Robbins

Music Leonard Bernstein	**Lyrics** Stephen Sondheim
Book Arthur Laurents	**Choreography** Jerome Robbins

Productions Broadway 1957, revived 1980
Films The film version dates from 1961.

A scene from the London revival of *West Side Story* at the Prince Edward Theatre in 1998

West Side Story is regarded by many as the greatest of all musicals, showing the genre at its maturity in the late 1950s and bringing together the art forms in a powerful and complementary manner. It is one of the best examples of the book musical, being loosely based on Shakespeare's *Romeo and Juliet* retold in the context of 1950s Manhattan. *West Side Story* also marks the beginning of a new realism in the musical. The gang warfare, disaffected youth and racial tensions were aspects not associated with the achievement of the American Dream but reflected the reality of life in East Coast urban America.

The work was Stephen Sondheim's Broadway debut and paved the way for his later art musicals with their less optimistic view of human nature. Sondheim, however, was the lyricist responsible for interpreting through the songs the drama of Arthur Laurents' book. Unlike his teacher, Oscar Hammerstein II, Sondheim did not write the book for *West Side Story* or his later musicals.

The team that came together to write *West Side Story* represented a high level of artistic mastery and each member also worked (before or after) in other collaborations. One of the most significant features of the team was the central partnership between the music and dance: Bernstein's orchestral music and Robbins' choreography perfectly reflect the angular, spiky nature of the drama. Bernstein had the added advantage of being a classical musician who did not need to rely on employing a professional orchestrator (unlike, for example, Richard Rodgers, Jerome Kern, Cole Porter and Irving Berlin).

■ Synopsis

West Side Story is a tragic romance set in Manhattan's Lower West Side, played out through the rivalry of two gangs: the all-American Jets and the Sharks, a gang of Puerto Rican immigrants to America. Tony, the former leader of the Jets, falls in love with Maria, the younger sister of Bernado, leader of the Sharks. Maria has been in New York for one month and is full of excitement at the prospects of living in America.

From the start of the show, a 'rumble' between the two gangs is hatched and this gang conflict becomes the focal point of the drama as Maria and Tony's relationship develops. The balcony scene where they sing the love duet *Tonight* parallels the balcony scene in *Romeo and Juliet* and portrays the tragic lovers against the conflicts of two warring factions.

The rumble takes place under the highway. Tony attempts to stop the fight but exacerbates things by his presence. As events move rapidly, Maria's brother, Bernado, kills Riff (the current leader of the Jets) but is then stabbed by Tony and dies. In the end, Tony is also killed by one of the Sharks and the show concludes with Maria grieving for him.

■ Jerome Robbins' choreography

Jerome Robbins (1919–98) was both the choreographer and the director of the original production of *West Side Story*, which meant that the direction had a distinctive dance orientation. It made the point that these were to some extent the same job. Robbins' approach built on Agnes de Mille's approach in *Oklahoma!* in bringing together ballet and Broadway and expanded it across the whole piece.

As well as *West Side Story*, Robbins' output includes *On the Town*, *The Pajama Game*, *The King and I* and *Fiddler on the Roof*. Both Robbins and de Mille were members of the Ballet Theatre (later the American Ballet Theatre), and staged many works for the company. Robbins' approach combined a high level of ballet technique with the showmanship and razzmatazz of Broadway, an approach ideally suited to the subject matter of *West Side Story*.

There are a number of carefully choreographed sequences, and the rivalry between the two gangs allowed Robbins to capitalise on the element of conflict inherent in the story. The opening sequence is particularly impressive in setting the scene for the rumble that will take place later in the show. As an example of Robbins' energetic and witty choreography, look at the dance sequence that accompanies the extended song *America*. In the film this starts at around 45 minutes.

Hal Prince, the producer of 'West Side Story', said: 'The marriage of dance movement and story-telling was new to the theatre.'

PERFORMANCE CONTEXTS 2

UNIT 3

159

By contrast with Agnes de Mille's choreography in *Oklahoma!*, there is a purposeful attempt to respond to the nature of the music and words, rather than just the theme of the episode. Bernstein's music perfectly captures the natural rhythms of Sondheim's lyrics and has a frequently changing pulse, moving naturally between the time signatures of 3/4 and 6/8 to reflect the rhythmic shape of the phrases. Robbins' choreography complements the rhythmic diversity of the music, and he is able to use individual dancers and subgroups within the ensemble to represent the latent tension within the Sharks as they debate their role as outsiders in American culture.

→ ## *The Sound of Music* (1959)
Focus on Richard Rodgers

Music Richard Rodgers **Lyrics** Oscar Hammerstein II
Book Howard Lindsay, Russel Crouse, Maria Augusta Trapp
Choreography Joe Layton

Productions Broadway 1959, revived 2006
Films The film version dates from 1965.

The Sound of Music was Rodgers and Hammerstein's last major collaboration and its completion marked the end of their work in the golden age of American musicals, the 1950s. It is probably the best known of their works, and thanks to the sentimental nature of the plot, probably the most popular.

Unusually, the book was not by Hammerstein and this presented him with the challenge of producing independent lyrics that captured the spirit of the book and still moved the action of the show along. Hammerstein was one of the few lyricists who generally wrote the book for his musical collaborations: lyricists were normally tasked with bringing out the drama inherent in a book written by someone else.

The choreography for the Broadway show was by Joe Layton (1931–94) and was his first major work of musical theatre. A number of further Broadway commissions followed the success of *The Sound of Music*.

■ ## Synopsis
The Sound of Music starts shortly before the start of the Second World War, and is set in Austria. Maria is a nun who appears unsuited to life in a convent; as a result, the Mother Superior asks her to leave. She becomes governess to the children of Captain Georg Ritter von Trapp, an Austrian who is strongly opposed to the Nazi regime. The children are unruly at first but warm to Maria when they realise she is sympathetic to their desire for more liberal parenting. Maria and the Captain seem attracted to one another but Maria's departure is engineered by the jealous Baroness Elsa Schrader. In due course, however, Maria leaves the convent a second time and marries the Captain. Their happiness is short lived: on arriving back from their honeymoon, the Captain is called up for service in the Third Reich. The show finishes with the family fleeing from the Nazis.

■ Richard Rodgers' music

Richard Rodgers (1902–1979) was one of the most prolific and successful composers who wrote for the American musical. His career spanned 40 years and overlapped with Gershwin in the 1920s and Sondheim in the 1960s. As a result his style changed and matured over the years, particularly as he moved from collaboration with Lorenz Hart to collaboration with Oscar Hammerstein II. Whilst Rodgers' natural ability to craft and shape a melody stayed with him, the style of his melodies moved from jaunty show numbers to mature songs that reflected the action of the drama. In this sense, his output follows the development of the genre itself.

The Lonely Goatherd from the film version of *The Sound of Music* with Julie Andrews

The ability to produce songs with regular melodic phrases and a well defined structure has been one of the hallmarks of a successful Broadway songwriter. *The Sound of Music* is full of well crafted songs, many of which can stand on their own as well as working well within the plot of the musical. Given the centrality of the von Trapp children to the plot, it is no surprise that many of the songs have a childlike quality to the melodies.

My Favourite Things and *Do-Re-Mi* occur close to each other, starting around 47 minutes into the film. Both have simple strophic structures with memorable phrases, *Do-Re-Mi* being specifically designed to enable the children to sing using tonic sol-fa. The song itself is based on a series of simple scale passages and is therefore a musical device to teach singing, which also has dramatic purpose in preparing the children to sing later in the show. The subtext here is that the Captain does not like or encourage his children to sing. The learning of the song is therefore, in spite of its apparent simplicity, an act of defiance.

The Lonely Goatherd and *Edelweiss* similarly follow each other fairly closely, starting at 1 hour 15 minutes in the film version. Both also utilise simple strophic structures, although the influence of yodelling in *The Lonely Goatherd* means that the melody has some complex leaps that challenge the singer. By contrast, *Edelweiss* is a patriotic song that follows in the next scene sung unexpectedly by the Captain. It is a simple but effective song with a waltz-like rhythm and uncomplicated harmonic progressions.

Although these songs do not resemble the glitzy show numbers of Rodgers' earlier career, they demonstrate his contribution to mature songwriting in the genre, aimed at reflecting and interpreting plot and characterisation through music.

→ *Company* (1970)
Focus on Stephen Sondheim

Music Stephen Sondheim	**Lyrics** Stephen Sondheim
Book George Furth	**Choreography** Michael Bennett
Director Hal Prince	

Production Broadway 1970, revived Broadway 2006
Films Not yet adapted for screen

'"Company" does deal with upper-middle class people, with upper-middle class problems. Broadway theatre has been for many years supported by those people. They really want to escape and here we're bringing it right back in their faces. What they came to a Musical to avoid, they suddenly find facing them on the stage.'

Stephen Sondheim

By 1970, Stephen Sondheim had collaborated on six shows, including the highly successful *Gypsy*. He made the decision to write both music and lyrics for this and also for *A Funny Thing Happened on the Way to the Forum*. *Company* is a quite different type of musical and represents a significant change in direction in the history of the genre in the 1970s. It has been described as a 'concept musical' because the way in which the piece is constructed is as significant as its content.

Company does not follow the standard pattern of the book musical. Instead, it consists of five separate stories, adapted by George Furth from a set of short plays he had written. It provides a view of modern marriage that is far from ideal or sentimentalised. It tackles head on the boredom and trivialities of married life, the attempts of couples to 'make a go of it' in spite of quarrels, violence and drink and drug abuse. Yet in spite of this raw examination of marital relations, the message of the musical is that marriage is better than being alone, the subject of Robert's final song and the conclusion of *Company*.

Boris Aronson's *Jungle Jim* set is non-representational and divorces the action of the musical from a specific context. It includes a working lift to move characters between different levels of the urban framework.

■ Synopsis

There is no plot as such and this was a challenge to preconceived ideas of how musicals should be constructed. To some extent, the influences of postmodernism are evident in the nonlinear structure of a series of episodes set at a birthday party. It is not clear whether the guests know each other.

The setting is the 35th birthday party of the central character, Robert (Bobby), held in New York City. Robert is frightened by the commitment of marriage, but marriage is the subject of each of the five stories. The musical is unified by the interaction of and influences on Robert, his married friends and three girlfriends.

■ Stephen Sondheim's words and music

The most important contribution of Oscar Hammerstein in the first half of the twentieth century was the principle that the songs in a book musical should grow organically from the action of the plot. In *Company*, the songs function as a commentary on the action and therefore stand outside what is directly happening. Sondheim has described the songs as having been 'inserted like nuts into a fruit cake'. This is a technique that was developed by Sondheim in his later musicals.

→ *Liza with a Z* (1972)
Focus on Bob Fosse

Music and lyrics Various	Choreography Bob Fosse
Director Bob Fosse	Filmed for television 1972

Liza Minnelli in *Liza with a Z*

Bob Fosse (1926–87) was a very significant choreographer for the American musical. Born in Chicago, his background was in popular dance styles, and he was a performer in vaudeville and burlesque. His style was strongly influenced by jazz dance techniques, combined with strongly suggestive movement content. Female dancers were often required, for example, to thrust their hips forward, put their hands on their hips, adopt a squeezed-in back and a pouting expression; at other times this would be replaced with locked ankles and a backward lean. Although much of Fosse's later work allowed the showcasing of the talents of his third wife, Gwen Verdon, his output spanned a highly creative career from the 1954 show *The Pajama Game* to *Chicago* (1975).

■ Synopsis

Liza with a Z is not a book musical. It was conceived in 1972 as a one-hour TV special, directed by Bob Fosse. Described as a 'concert for television', it went on to win four Emmy Awards. It is very much in the tradition of the song-and-dance shows of the early part of the twentieth century, stylistically updated for the 1970s. There is no story as such, and the inspiration for the show was the title song, *Liza with a Z*, which itself was determined by the show's central character, Liza Minnelli (born 1946), daughter of the renowned singer and actress Judy Garland. The original recording from May 1972 was re-released in 2006 on DVD, and Minnelli has since claimed that the piece was the first broadcast concert on network television.

'I have found for a long time people still have been calling me "Lisa". Wrong! My name is Liza. It has a "z" in it. For example, someone might come up to me and say, "Hello, Lisa, how are you?". And I'd say, "Fine, but my name is Liza". Or someone would come up and say, "Oh, Lisa, what a nice hat you have on." And I'd say, "Thank you very much, but my name is Liza, and that's my hair." '

Liza Minnelli

■ Songs in *Liza with a Z*

The show is essentially a collection of 12 musical numbers, each of them used as a vehicle for Fosse's choreography. The songs are from a variety of sources, with the largest number by John Kander and Fred Ebb:

1   *Yes*
2   *God Bless the Child*
3   *Say Liza*
4   *It Was a Good Time*
5   *I Gottcha*
6   *Son of a Preacher Man*
7   *Ring Them Bells*

8   *Bye Bye Blackbird*
9   *You've Let Yourself Go*
10 *My Mammy*
11 *Cabaret* medley of five songs:
    Wilkommen, Married, Money,
    Maybe This Time, Cabaret
12 Curtain calls and titles.

Fosse's choreography was risqué for its time. Rehearsals were undertaken in secret so as to avoid attention from the censor on the show's scantily clad dance routines. In principle, however, these were no different to the glitzy and raunchy show numbers staged at the start of the century by Florenz Ziegfeld; both were of their time. Fosse's deliberate celebration of overtly sexy, slinky dance styles shines through each of the show's numbers.

Fosse's dance style itself is particularly distinctive, and can be seen very clearly in the eighth number, *Bye Bye Blackbird*. This is also performed by Ben Vereen on the 2001 DVD *Fosse: A Celebration of the Choreography of Bob Fosse*. The number reflects the blackbird motif implicit in the lyrics, and contains other characteristic features of Fosse's style, particularly the use of bowler hats, generally worn at a particular angle. Fosse claimed that he started to wear hats because he was losing his hair rather than because of a particular artistic concern. He also claimed that the use of inward knees was because he was unable to perfect the technique of turning out, and that even the rounded shoulders associated with his technique were something he could do naturally. All of these features are fully present in *Bye Bye Blackbird*.

Although the songs in *Liza with a Z* do not form part of a book musical, Fosse nevertheless took them individually and used his choreographic style to interpret the nature of the song in an engaging and entertaining manner.

→ *Chicago* (1975)
Focus on John Kander

Music John Kander   **Lyrics** Fred Ebb
Book Fred Ebb and Bob Fosse
Director and choreography Bob Fosse

Productions 1975 Broadway, revived 2006 in UK tour
Films A film version was released in 2002.

■ John Kander's music

John Kander (born 1927) is best known for his work with lyricist Fred Ebb (1933–2004). The duo were introduced to each other in 1963 having shared the same music publisher, Tommy Valando. The greatest hits for the partnership were *Cabaret* (1966), *Chicago* (1975), *Kiss of the Spider Woman* (1992) and *Fosse* (1999). Their work was strongly associated with Liza Minnelli, who memorably performed their theme song from the 1977 film *New York, New York,* although it is more famous in the version sung by Frank Sinatra. They also wrote songs for a number of famous American singers, including Barbra Streisand, Frank Sinatra and Gwen Verdon.

Kander's early work as a rehearsal pianist for the stage version of *West Side Story* in 1957 brought him into contact with Stephen Sondheim, and he later took the same role for the musical *Gypsy* (lyrics also by Sondheim), for which Jerome Robbins invited him to write dance music. His musical style complemented Ebb's lyrics effectively, and the duo are best known for their work as songwriters. In this sense, they stand in contrast to the two other major partnerships of Rodgers and Hammerstein, and Lerner and Loewe, where the lyricist also took charge of writing the book. Whilst working within the traditions of the book musical, Kander and Ebb were successful primarily for writing witty, entertaining songs, and for the way their music inspired the performances of Liza Minnelli and, most important, the choreography of Bob Fosse. In particular, Fosse produced the choreography for *Cabaret* and *Chicago*.

■ Songs in *Chicago*

Two of the most famous songs in *Chicago* are *And All That Jazz* and *Razzle Dazzle*. Both capture the decadence of the era in which the show is set, in the sordid vaudeville theatres of the 1920s and 1930s, complemented by Fosse's lithe, sexy dance numbers. Both also work perfectly well as stand-alone songs, however.

And All That Jazz has a simple melody, based firmly in C major. It is introduced by an equally simply series of C major chords, with an intermittent swing figure.

Opening of *And All That Jazz*

Words by FRED EBB   Music by JOHN KANDER

The first two verses have the same music, although verse 2 moves up a semitone from C to Db major, and has a ragtime piano accompaniment, also evocative of the era in which the show is set. This leads into a third verse in which the emotional tension of the music builds through modulation to D major and a lengthening of the start of each line. Next comes a duet in the original key of C

Opening of duet section of
And All That Jazz

major in which the elongated version is sung against the original version of the melody. The song finishes with an extended ragtime piano solo.

Words by FRED EBB   Music by JOHN KANDER

Find a flask,_ we're play-ing fast and loose   And all that jazz!_

Oh,_____ you're gon-na see your She-ba shim-my shake,   And all that jazz!_

Razzle Dazzle uses a similar structural approach, with verses using similar music but periodically modulating to a new key. The opening establishes the rhythmic figure on which the whole song is based, the finger snaps between bars 1 and 2 providing the perfect inspiration for Fosse's jazz-inspired choreography.

Opening of *Razzle Dazzle*

Words by FRED EBB   Music by JOHN KANDER

This rhythm is picked up by the vocal melody, which in turn mirrors exactly the natural inflections of Ebb's words. His witty rhyme schemes are reminiscent of those of Ira Gershwin in such pairs of lines as 'Give 'em an act with lots of flash in it/and the reaction will be passionate' (verse 1) and 'Give 'em a show that's so splendiferous/row after row will grow vociferous' (verse 2).

The first two verses are both in the home key of F major, but the key changes to Ab major for the third verse. This is maintained for the fourth verse, which culminates in the snappy couplet 'Long as you keep 'em way off balance/How can they spot you got no talents'. Unlike *And All That Jazz*, there is no instrumental finale.

Approaches to Performance in the **Far East**

In this topic you study three countries rather than nine examples. For each country, you must study how the art forms work together in the traditions of that country.

→ What sort of influence has the Far East had on European practitioners?

There were the trade routes from Europe to the Far East for many centuries. These brought travellers' tales to the West but these countries remained a mystery to Europeans, with their different religions, beliefs, social, cultural and political systems. In the last century, however, the arts of the West embraced oriental influence in all spheres. For example, the influence of the gamelan on modern Western music is easily seen in the works of Béla Bartók, Philip Glass and Lou Harrison. In theatre, the ideas of Antonin Artaud were transformed after witnessing the Balinese Theatre at the Paris Colonial Exposition in August 1931. Bertolt Brecht drew inspiration from Chinese poetry, stories and the opera tradition, which can be seen in *The Good Woman of Setzuan*. Post-modern dance has developed the abstraction of everyday gestural movements, the pedestrian, which has been the mainstay of classical dance in the Far East for centuries.

→ Studying three countries

Unlike the other topics in this unit, the option 'Performance in the Far East' requires you to study dance, drama and music in **three** countries. There are a total of 14 countries from which you can choose the three you wish to study: Borneo, Brunei, Burma (Myanmar), Cambodia, China (embracing Hong Kong and Taiwan), Indonesia, Japan, Korea, Laos, Malaysia, Singapore, Thailand, the Philippines, Vietnam. Your study could include elements of Kabuki, Noh plays, Javanese puppet theatre, or the drama of specific countries such as Japan, Singapore, Malaysia and India.

In the Far East, the art forms as we might consider them are naturally integrated in a way that defies traditional Western arts classification. Much is transmitted from memory by word of mouth and training within family and company traditions. Specific works in different art forms are not so easy to identify or analyse as in the other topics. Here we must attempt to explain style, technique, common approaches and refer to what is accessible, available and of particular interest. There is not space here to deal in detail with every distinctive nuance of difference found in the performance elements of the entire Far East. Thus you should choose three countries relevant to you and use the examples that follow in this unit as a model upon which to base your own research and interest.

You will encounter both similarities and differences in your study. Some art forms are highly disciplined and text based; others exist primarily through detailed performance conventions or oral tradition. Each is culturally distinct, yet shares a common geographic provenance. In the examination, you will have to demonstrate a thorough understanding of how the art forms work in each country you have studied and identify points of similarity and contrast between them. Your examples of works must be drawn equally from across the three countries. Remember also that the works from each country should cover all of the performing arts.

The Performing Arts in China: Beijing Opera (Peking Opera)

In February 2008, schoolchildren in 200 Chinese schools across the nation returned from their New Year holiday to find a new subject on their music curriculum. Jingju, Beijing opera, was introduced to begin to restore the status of a traditional performing art form entirely banned only 40 years earlier. There was an immediate reaction to this move, not just from young people who had very little experience of this quaint form, but also from purists who claimed that, as there were as many different forms of opera as there were dialects in China, it was not appropriate to impose only one style. This was not unlike the debate over the inclusion of Shakespeare on the National Curriculum for schools in the UK.

It is worth remembering that in the West, Beijing opera is generally referred to as Peking opera, 'Peking' being an older Western name for 'Beijing'.

→ Origins

Despite its name, the origins of Beijing opera go back to the founding of the Pear Garden troupe by Emperor Xuanjong (AD 712–55) during the Tang dynasty. As is often the case, a stable economy and government went hand in hand with patronage of the arts. Performers of Beijing opera are still known as Followers of the Pear Garden.

During the Yuan dynasty (1279–1368), the four roles were established and vernacular Chinese became the dominant language on the stage. Beijing operatic style is thought to have begun in 1790 when four opera troupes from Anhui performed in Beijing. Some 30 years later, a troupe from Hubei jointly performed with the Anhui players and the respective musical forms of xi pi and er huang gave Beijing opera its distinctive melodies. Mixing with the local indigenous forms of kunqu, yiyang, hanju and luantan over the next 20 years, it developed into one of the major cultural expressions of Chinese society. The form reached its culmination during the time of Emperor Guangxu (1871–1908), a keen performer in the opera, and his aunt the Empress Dowager Cixi (1835–1908), an enthusiastic patron who built the three-storey theatre in the Summer Palace.

A student performs in Beijing Opera's *Fortified Village Muke* at a college in North-East China.

→ Style

Beijing opera is a mixture of acting, mime, dance, voice and acrobatics. Like Zeami's sense of flower in Japanese Noh theatre, there is an underlying sense of beauty sought by both the performer and the audience in the way in which the tales are told. How stories are told is one of the features that unites performance approaches in South-East Asia.

Meaning is transmitted through the four key skills that every performer must develop: speech, song, dance-acting and stylised combative movement with weapons of all types. The acting is deliberately stylised and gestural, acknowledging and often addressing the audience. Dialogue is generally interspersed with arias, although duets and ensemble choral sections appear. Often these are one-line observations, almost like an aside to the audience, rather than full set-piece songs. Actions are taken from daily life, such as drinking tea, or welcoming a guest, but stylised, abstracted, not attempting to imitate real life as is more familiar in European drama. Such mannered gestures are also part of performance traditions across South-East Asia.

Beijing opera was originally an all-male form of particularly low status, until its blossoming in the middle of the nineteenth century. By the 1870s, female performers and troupes were becoming common, and today there are mixed and single-sex professional and amateur companies all over China.

→ Hangdang – Roles in Beijing opera

Besides the four key skills, the four roles of Sheng, Dan, Jing and Chou are central to understanding Chinese opera.

■ Sheng

This can be a military or civilian male role and has a variety of subcategories. Thus Lao Sheng, the familiar elderly man with a long beard, is refined and sedate in his bearing, as befits a man of experience and wisdom.

Xiao Sheng, a 'man without a beard', is a young man who must be able to sing and speak at a very piercing level, but also suddenly lower his tone, to indicate the variance of the breaking voice. Wu Sheng is an acrobatic male role, often linked to the military, which involves less singing than the other male roles, but exceptional skill in the stylised acrobatic fighting that takes place regularly on stage. The Official's attendant in *Honest Official Yu Chenglong* is one example of the Wu Sheng role. The Monkey King is one of the most famous and popular Wu Sheng characters.

■ Dan

The Dan characters are female roles with parallel character types to the males. Thus Lao Dan is an old woman, Wu Dan a female acrobat. As in *commedia dell'arte*, there is a quiet, modest young woman, Qing Yi Dan, and a flirty lower-class girl, Hua Dan, who has a lot to say, and a very active face with eyes everywhere. Hua Dan uses her hands to express herself as well, which would have been considered improper for a woman of standing. The Gui Men Dan, a newly married girl, and the Dao Ma Dan, a stronger, mature female general, make up the rest of the six main female roles.

■ Jing

The Jing is an instantly recognisable male painted-face role, a commanding presence in any scene in which he appears. Often a military general, with a low gruff voice, there is something of the *miles gloriosus* about his swaggering across the stage.

■ Chou

The Chou role is the 'nice but dim' clown. He can play the traditional villainous

The Hua Dan role in *Silang Visits His Mother*, with the characteristic hand gesture and the red handkerchief to wave coquettishly

servant as well as a gormless prince. The Wu Chou is an acrobatic version of the role.

Besides the complicated singing in the style, the performers have to speak in two voices, jing bai, the actor's natural voice, and yun bai, a forced poetic one.

→ Music

Traditionally, the orchestra for Beijing opera was quite small and led by the drummer. In the modern style, the orchestra has become larger with bigger violin sections added. The traditional string instruments that give Chinese opera its distinctive sound are

- the jinghu, a small two-stringed, very high pitched, bowed 'fiddle', based on the traditional Chinese erhu
- the yueqin, a four-stringed lute-type plucked instrument
- the sanxian, a three-stringed plucked instrument.

Various percussive drums, gongs and cymbals are also used.

There are two melodic styles, xi pi and er huang, both with two beats to the bar. In xi pi (literally, 'western skin puppet show') the melodies are high, loud and brash. Xi pi invariably accompanies lively happy stories and has the jinghu tuned to A and D. In er huang the jinghu is in C and G, to reflect the lower, more sombre style used for lyrical stories. The two melodic styles each share six different tempi used across the common forms of arias, which are performed by the characters with movement, gesture and vocal line following the music. Fixed-tune melodies are used for characters' entrances, to work as underscore and to make musical statements juxtaposed with the vocal statements of the actors. Percussive patterns are used for effects such as conjuring up a storm or chase.

→ Production

Staging of Beijing opera is characteristically sparse. Essentially, there is a platform with audience on three sides, musicians in front, and a painted or embroidered cloth which delineates a backstage area. The audience is always seated in the South, so North has the same potency as upstage centre. Characters enter from stage right, (East) and exit stage left (West). Props are equally limited. A table, chairs and a mat may be used to represent different objects, such as a bed or garden wall. Other props may hint at something larger – for example, a riding crop may suggest a horse, as in *The Seizing of Wei Hu Shan*.

Costume, however, can be quite colourful and elaborate. Colour coding indicates levels of officialdom and rank in terms of position or worth. Embroidered panels, sashes and belts all indicate different status. The mang is a robe worn by a high-level person, whilst the chezi is a basic gown with long sleeves which also have a dramatic function. At moments of high emotional tension, performers use the sleeves both suddenly and smoothly to represent the storm raging inside them.

→ Repertoire

There are some 1400 works in Beijing opera, based on folklore, myths and legends, Chinese history and modern life. During the establishment of the People's Republic, from 1949, Beijing opera was considered increasingly decadent, unless the plays had Communist ideals at their heart. By the time of the Cultural Revolution (1966–76), with the exception of five operas, the majority of the repertoire had been banned.

Of the Eight Model Plays approved by Jiang Qing (the wife of Mao Zedong) and the Gang of Four, five were Beijing operas concerned with moral topics, the triumph of class war and the Communist struggle against the Nationalists in the Civil War. For example, *The Legend of the Red Lantern* is about a railway worker who sacrifices himself to the struggle and how his daughter is inspired to emulate him in carrying through the revolution. *Sha Jia Bang* is set at the time of the Japanese invasion, when Communists and Nationalists agreed to work together to fight the common foe. The Eight Model Plays were all made into films and are still very popular, being regularly played in the repertoire. The Chinese government has been at pains to revive the traditional art form and more new pieces are being written.

The Performing Arts in Indonesia: Balinese Wayang Kulit

Across South-East Asia, one of the most ancient and still popular performance traditions is called wayang from the Javanese word meaning 'shadow' or 'ghost'. Wayang orang is performed by living actors, wayang golek by three-dimensional puppets, particularly in Western Java. The most familiar is wayang kulit, literally 'shadow of leather', which uses two-dimensional puppets made from buffalo hide, played behind a translucent screen lit by an oil lamp.

Wayang kulit shadow puppets

→ The road to Bali

Indonesia, made up of thousands of islands, lies between the Indian and Pacific oceans, and has been at the centre of trade for thousands of years. Formerly known as the East Indies, these islands are the Spice Islands, and it is not surprising that their culture has influenced and has been influenced by a range of adjacent civilisations, Chinese from the East and principally Indian from the West. The island of Bali, now a popular tourist resort, is separated from its nearest neighbour, Java, by only a few miles of straits, and it is significant in the Indonesian archipelago because it is still predominantly Hindu, whilst Islamic culture is now predominant in many of the surrounding bigger islands.

→ Origins of wayang kulit

The first references to wayang in Indonesia occurred 1100 years ago, but it is thought that wayang began with the arrival of Hinduism in the first century AD. Like the Japanese bunraku, wayang kulit originated as a popular folk tradition, but there is less snobbishness about the puppet form in Indonesian society. Wayang kulit flourished for 1000 years in the royal courts of Java and Bali, in private houses, temple courtyards, public theatres and village squares. Performances would often be held for community or family celebrations, as wayang kulit acted as the vehicle for the social, religious and moral cohesion of the community. As the twentieth century progressed, with less extended families staying together and the lure of work in urban centres, fewer of these communal events took place.

The ancient tradition shows signs of adapting to modern times. One puppeteer in Jakarta in Java employs condoms not only structurally for almost transparent effect, but as part of the racy sections of romantic stories to 'bring them up to date' and also to fulfil the traditional role of moral guidance within the stories enacted. There are even some internet references to 'Wayang Teletubbies'!

More than just entertainment, wayang kulit is a mixture of morality play, spiritual experience, myth and topical satire. It is thought that the form has survived largely because of the satire. Comical characters make pointed comments on local and national politics and on wider social and moral issues. For example, for a celebration of local government officers, the story may involve aspects of anti-corruption and altruistic service to the community. For an audience of young people, the same tale may emphasise responsibilities of growing to adulthood and warn against indulgent behaviour. The purpose of wayang kulit is to educate as well as entertain, by using the simplest of all storylines – how good triumphs over evil, even though in Hindu thinking both are necessary in order to create the natural balance.

→ Roles in wayang kulit

A wayang kulit performance is organised, managed, led, conducted and performed by the dhalang, the storyteller and master puppeteer. This is one of the most demanding roles in all the performance styles across the world. The dhalang has to know by heart some 200 lakon (wayang episodes) and the symbolic meaning of over 100 characters. The dhalang also has to

- choose and conduct the music from the gamelan
- compose and sing songs
- act as the official for the religious ceremonies and rituals, like a priest
- act all the characters in the story using appropriate vocal flexibility and differentiation in the dialogue so that the audience can understand that conversation is taking place
- interact with the audience, encouraging their participation at times
- include local gossip and political references alongside philosophy in epic stories of gods and heroes
- tell jokes
- improvise new parts of the well known stories and conflicts
- give moral guidance on correct behaviour
- advise on all areas of society
- transmit the history and culture from memory
- make and operate the puppets against the screen in appropriate stances and relationships.

And all this whilst sitting cross-legged for several hours at a time!

Behind the linen screen: a dhalang operates his puppets in front of a traditional oil lamp.

The dhalang is expected to have absolute control of all aspects of the performance. Dhalangs are hence venerated as teachers, craftsmen, historians, artists, journalists, philosophers and stand-up comedians. This focus on the individual is very different from the collective approach to a Noh performance (see page 184).

The pengrawit are musicians in the gamelan and the pesindhen or swarawati are singers sometimes supporting the dhalang's narrative or providing individual songs related to the narrative being told. Members of the same extended family will take many of these roles. Assistants to the dhalang learn the role whilst passing the puppets in the right order for the story. Traditionally, if not already family members, they may marry the dhalang's daughter, who will already be proficient in the gamelan.

→ Staging the show

The players of the wayang kulit all sit behind a stretched linen screen (the kelir) with the dhalang in the centre just below the light source, traditionally an oil lamp burning in a coconut husk, a blencong. Although some performances use naked bulbs, the flickering flame of the traditional lamp gives an impression of movement to the animations of the figures, especially during chases, battles and fights, which are frequent. Beneath the screen is a 'stage' made up of the trunk of a banana tree, representing the Earth. Its soft flesh also functions as a 'parking place' for puppets that are in use but not active.

The dhalang keeps the puppets in a wooden chest called a kotak, which also plays a part in the performance. The dhalang taps it three times before the start of the performance, to wake the puppets, before they are removed. During the performance, the keprak or kekrek, which are metal or wooden plates attached to the chest, are played with the dhalang's right foot as sound effects to enhance battle scenes or imitate the growl of an ogre, for example. The dhalang also uses a tabuh keprak, a small wooden hammer against the inside the chest, to keep time for the gamelan.

The audience can watch the show from either side of the screen. Performances last overnight, so they will also have food and drink and move about whilst the show is in progress. The stories are very well known, often word for word, so the dhalang's individual diversions and expansions on the tales are welcomed, and being there is as much part of the event as watching the whole of it. Many of the children will sleep during the philosophical debating around the moral correctness of a character's action. Around midnight the clowns will appear, which is the signal for wild revels, bawdy humour, joke telling at the expense of characters in the story, like the Kyogen interludes in Noh. The clowns' antics are enjoyed by all, and many tourist guides recommend joining a performance especially for this element.

Particularly popular are the satirical caricatures of local people who have embarrassed themselves in some recent episode according to the gossip of the village or organisation sponsoring the performance. In order to acquire this local knowledge, a meal at which the dhalang officiates in a religious capacity is held in his honour prior to the endurance test of the performance. During the meal, members of the host group will feed him titbits about others in the hope that they do not become a target. Thus they have the same licence to criticise and comment on those who might act arrogantly or pretentiously as did the jesters of medieval European courts.

In Bali, the performances are usually shorter, at 4–6 hours, but start later than Javanese wayang, which can last for 9 hours. Perhaps because they come from older Hindu traditions, the Balinese wayang kulit performances are suffused with religious rite, ceremony and spiritual intention and are still used regularly for temple ceremonies. Whilst performances for family events no longer take place as frequently, in Bali there are still religious performances at family funerals. These take place in daylight without a lamp, the screen being represented in mime by the drawing of an imaginary curtain.

→ Stories and characters

Puppets of the sage, Begawan Bisma, and a maidservant

The stories and characters are drawn primarily from the major epics from South India, the Mahabharatha and the Ramayana, which had reached Java by at least the first century AD and probably earlier. It may even be that in the development of these huge narratives, influences moved back and forth much like the trade, before specific versions were established.

The successful establishment of the Indonesian versions of these stories was through the patronage of King Airlangga (AD 991–1049), raja of the kingdom of

Kahuripan, which he established on Java but expanded across his home island of Bali and beyond. He brought peace to the islands and thus more trade and wealth. He promoted religious tolerance between Hindus and Buddhists and he promoted the arts. Around 1035, one of his court poets, Mpu Kanwa, wrote the literary classic *Arjunavivaha* (meaning 'marriage of Arjuna'), based on the story of Arjuna from the Mahabharata. It is in fact a poetic compliment to Airlangga, much like the complimentary verse masques honouring the Queen in Elizabethan times in England. Arjuna is portrayed in the story as a reincarnation of the Hindu god Vishnu and that may be how Airlangga was seen, or wanted to be seen, by his people.

Arjuna is one of the five Pandawas, main protagonists in the Mahabharatha, who are set against their hundred Kurawas cousins. It is Arjuna's great grandson, Janamejaya, who is being told the story of the Bharatha dynasty by a sage. In the Indonesian versions of the stories from the Mahabharatha, there is greater expansion of the minor characters than in the Indian version. This may well have come about through the embellishments of the dhalangs over the centuries being passed on from generation to generation. Thus Arjuna is attended by the loyal Pandawa servants, called panakawan.

The panakawan are popular with all audiences. They are crude and basic in their humour, but deliberately counteract the high-flown ideals of some of the lead characters. They are used structurally to undercut moments of high pathos, especially in the goro-goro section, an hour-long scene combining the turning point of the play with chase, counsel, toilet humour, wisdom and absurdity. Sadness and intense feelings must always be counterbalanced with humour to maintain the equilibrium of the soul, just as the wayang kulit offers a balance of dark and light in the silhouettes of the puppets against the flaming light of the lamp.

→ Puppets

For every performance, the puppets are 'brought to life' by ritual ceremonies performed by the dhalang, by whom they were made in the first place. For many, they take on a spiritual presence, just as the dhalang may be perceived to be in a trance-like meditative state during the lengthy performance.

The development of the puppets is also ritualistic. The soft hide of a four-year-old female buffalo is cured for up to ten years to stiffen it and avoid splitting as the filigree of holes and lines are cut and punched. The profile of the body, shape of mouth, slant of eyes, position of head, nose length, all have significance to the characters represented, so carving is precise and highly skilled. Balinese puppets are different in that they have articulated mouthparts operated by a string by the dhalang. They can appear from the side of the stage or in front of the lamp, giving them a ghostly appearance as they drift to sharper focus closer to the screen.

Some of the puppets are large scale like Rampogan, an army puppet featuring several soldiers on the move, and most important of all, Gunungan or Kayon, from *gunung* (mountain) and *kayon* (forest).

→ Music of gamelan

The name 'gamelan' comes from the Javanese word *gamel*, meaning 'hammer'. The gamelan is predominantly a percussive orchestra, using a variety of soft and hard hammers on the differing forms of instrument.

The main constituents of a gamelan orchestra are metallophones (usually tuned brass bars suspended over a wooden resonating box or individual bamboo resonators), two-handed barrel-shaped drums and gongs, both suspended and cradled. There may also be a flute and stringed instruments, particularly in Javanese style. There are as many variations as there are groups. In fact, gamelans are each completely individual as they are tuned to themselves. The intervals in the two laras or tuning scales – pelog, which has seven tones per octave, and slendro, which has five – remain the same, but there is no standard frequency tuning as in Western music. The instruments of a gamelan are made, tuned and must stay together; each works to perfect a unified sound.

A full Javanese gamelan comprises two sets of instruments, one tuned to each lara. The music is created through patterns of repeating ostinati, a modal polyphony rather than traditional harmony. This was a particular inspiration for the Minimalist composer Steve Reich (please see examples in the section 'Post-Modern Approaches to the Performing Arts', page 104).

When the Majapahit dynasty began to collapse in the fourteenth century and Islam moved East from the cities of Western Java, the Hindus of Java fled East to Bali and took with them the music of the Javanese gamelan. A further impact was the Dutch insurgence at the beginning of the twentieth century, which almost destroyed the traditional music forms. They survived in the villages and traditions

A Balinese gamelan orchestra

of the ordinary people and most Balinese gamelans are still non-professional. One large village may have several family gamelan groups. Thus, despite its proximity to the parent island, Bali has a developed gamelan style of its own. So much so that there are several features which distinguish it from the traditional Javanese style.

■ Balinese gamelan

In Balinese gamelan, the distinctive shimmering sound of the metallophones is created by instruments played in pairs, but with one de-tuned to play slightly flat against the other. This exploits an acoustic phenomenon called interference beating, where the slight variance in sonic vibrations causes an internal rhythm of its own. This helps to represent the magical and sacred presence of the gods and inspires a transcendental contemplation. This effect is further enhanced by the use of thicker bronze keys, which give a brighter sound, the use of more metallophones than gongs in the ensemble and the frequent inclusion of cymbals that add a rattling sound complementing the acoustic variance of the kotekan.

Balinese gamelan is faster, livelier and noisier than the softer, lyrical, contemplative Javanese style. It has distinctive sudden changes in tempo and dynamics, and is characterised by the kotekan style of playing, involving interlocking kotek. This is the sharing of a musical line by trading pitches between players – more or less, playing in each other's rests. The pattern can be divided into two, three or more sections, which then interlock, allowing, in turn, much faster performance tempi.

The other major characteristic distinguishing Balinese gamelan from its Javanese cousin is that it is strictly composed and rehearsed rather than improvised. The distinctive complex style is refined by players memorising the patterns through rehearsal from a score in the same way that the dhalang memorises huge lengths of narrative. Balinese gamelan therefore attracts composers and the repertoire over the twentieth century has grown and developed, building on what in fact was the pre-Islamic Javanese style.

When it is played with wayang kulit, the gamelan is known as gender wayang. Gender players are held in awe by their gamelan-playing counterparts, as this is considered the most complicated of all the Balinese styles. The gender wayang is a smaller ensemble made up of four ten-key slendro-tuned genders, two tuned in the medium register and two an octave higher. Each musician has two mallets to play kotekan with the right hand and a supporting melody with the left. The combinations possible across the four instruments provide the rich and varied music to support the variations of the wayang.

→ More from Indonesia and Bali

Wayang topeng – Balinese masked dancing, a composite of dance, drama, music, spoken word, opera and song behind wooden masks, playing out ritual and courtly legends – is just one of a number of other wayang styles on Bali alone. There are further variations on Java and the other Indonesian islands as well as in Malaysia.

The Performing Arts in Japan

→ Gods and spirits

The roots of performance traditions are often found in myth and traditions of the ancients. One Japanese tale tells of Amaterasu, sun goddess of fertility and light, a direct ancestor of the Emperor of Japan, who is frightened by the jealous fury of her storm-god brother into a cave from which she refuses to return to the sky. The land remains dark and withers, until the enterprising and entertaining Uzume, goddess of humour, dance and the art of drumming, hits on a plan to lure Ameratsu from the cave. She dances bawdily on a barrel outside the cave mouth. Clothes are shed to the insistent rhythmic beat of her footwork, much to the delight of the assembled gods, whose laughter draws the curious Ameratsu from the cave and back to the sky.

In this story, we can see the possibilities for combined performance in bringing the art forms together. It has a spiritual message of healing through entertainment, laughter, dance and music, and it is this tradition that is at the heart of much performance in the Far East, and none more so than in Japan.

Those same gods are the basis of Shinto, the native religion of Japan and until the end of the Second World War the state religion, with the emperor himself worshipped as a living deity. Although having its major gods, Shinto is primarily a religion of spirit worship that recognises the inner spirituality of all living things. This can be traced back to the epics of Kojiki and Nihonshoki of the Nara period (AD 710–94), which offer many folklore tales in which the spirits of the natural world are strong, and men and women are portrayed as manifestations of their own inner spirits and the ghosts of those gone before. This spiritual concept of human strength through connection with an inner spirit is familiar in the West through the popularity of martial arts, but is also central to the performing arts we will consider in this rest of this unit.

→ Influences

During the Nara period (AD 710–94), the culture of Japan, an island state, was influenced by its nearest neighbour, China. Whilst Europe was in the period known as the Dark Ages, Japanese culture was rich and diverse, actively importing two distinct musical styles from its Chinese neighbours: gagaku and sangaku.

Gagaku (elegant music) is a slow and solemn music and dance (bugaku) form used for ceremonies at the imperial and aristocratic courts. Played by string, wind and percussion instruments, it uses the same yo pentatonic scale as Buddhist chants with intervals of two, three, two and two semitones between the five scale tones. In the late 1950s and early 1960s Western composers Britten, Messiaen, Young and Cowell were influenced by Japanese gagaku. The following are examples in Western notation.

In the Heian period (794–1192), the Chinese art form known as sangaku became established in Japan as sarugaku (monkey music). This involved a riotous mix of clowning, dance, acrobatics, magic, mime, drumming, juggling, pantomime, comic sketches and dialogues. It was popular for over 300 years, between the eleventh and fourteenth centuries, and performed for the ordinary public, outside shrines and temples.

Kagura (god-entertainment) is the name given to early Shinto shrine dances and accompanying music, which are still in existence today in a range of diverse court and folk forms, particularly associated with the agricultural calendar.

Many kagura dances use ritual props, masks and costumes.

They were mixed with the indigenous dengaku (field music), which involved rice planting and harvesting rituals with dance and music, and made fashionable in the city courts of the fourteenth century. This provided a rich background for the establishment of one of the three major Japanese performance art forms, nogaku, or more commonly Noh, and its comic counterpart Kyogen.

→ Noh theatre

During the Muromachi period (1333–1573), Noh and Kyogen developed together and were supported by the imperial court and aristocracy, showing how the performing arts flourish with patronage and government approval. Kan'ami Kiyotsugu (1333–84), a Noh actor, author and musician, established a sarugaku troupe, which incorporated dengaku, in the city of Yamato and formed the Yuzaki Theatre, which would eventually become the school of Noh theatre. He also was the first to build in the kusemai (unconventional dance) song and dance style popular around Kyoto, which emphasised an irregular stamping beat at the expense of melody. It was a performance in Kyoto that brought him to the attention and subsequent patronage of the Shogun Ashikaga Yoshimitsu. Whilst many of Kan'ami's plays are still performed today, it was his son Zeami Motokiyo (1363–c.1443) who created Noh as we know it.

Noh players. Use of particular masks is a feature of Noh theatre. Here, in a scene from *The Lady Aoi*, the mask of a young woman is being worn (see page 187 for further discussion). This is a popular choice in other Noh plays, such as *Izutsu*.

■ Zeami and *Izutsu*

A close acquaintance of the Shogun, Zeami was trained at the highest level in all the arts. He performed with his father until Kan'ami died and Zeami, aged 20, took over the company. He was also known as Kanze, and the Noh Theatre school his father founded still bears that name and works in the style he initiated.

Zeami refined his father's plays and wrote many of his own, *Izutsu* (*The Well Head*) being one of the most famous. Taken from a tenth-century tale, the play relates how a wandering monk stops to pray at a shrine. He is approached by an old lady who tells him the love story of Narihira (the ancient poet to whom the shrine is dedicated) and his wife, Lady Izutsu, who from an early age measured their heights against the well head. The old lady disappears, but the monk looks for some confirmation of the story from a passer-by.

In the second half of the play, as the monk sleeps during the night, the woman returns in his dream. She is dressed as the man Narihira and performs a dance that shows her love for him, even looking at his 'reflection' in the well. At dawn, the ghost of Izutsu disappears and the monk awakens.

■ Players of the Noh

In Noh there are four types of roles, or players, called 'kata'. This is a key word in Noh as the stylistic gesture patterns are also called 'kata' (see section 'Movement' on page 188). This indicates the lack of any separation between the doers and the thing done. The gesture patterns are just as important as the music patterns, vocal patterns and role patterns. There are no stars in Noh.

The shite-kata play the shite, the major protagonist in the play, often an old man or woman, a madwoman, a ghost of a samurai warrior or a spirit of a lover. The role played in the first half of the play is called the mae-shite and the role in the second half, the nochi-shite. Although these roles may be connected, they will be played entirely differently. Thus, in *Izutsu*, the shite is expected to play first the mae-shite role of the village woman and then, as the nochi-shite, the same person as a young woman dressed as her husband.

Shite-kata also play the jiutai, a chorus group led by the jigashira, who provide the vocal music (utai) for the dance, describe action and the scene in which the drama takes place, and explain emotional aspects of the story when the shite is unable to do so. The tsure (assistants to the lead shite in the story), the kokata (any child roles) and even the koken (the stage assistant who arranges the shite's costume and hands the shite any props) are all played by shite-kata players.

The waki-kata play the waki role, often an itinerant Shinto priest, Buddhist monk or wandering samurai. The waki is always a real person and therefore does not wear a mask. Waki-kata also take the waki-tsure roles, which may be fellow travellers, monks or local people.

The kyogen-kata are Kyogen actors who play the comic interlude in Noh but also have a form of their own (see page 190). The interlude is often an extended retelling of the story involving parody and sometimes exposing social and political inference. According to tradition, the kyogen also advises the waki on what to do next.

The hayashi-kata (music players) are split into four formal roles: fue-kata are flute players, kotsuzumi-kata play small shoulder drums, otsuzumi-kata play small hip drums and taiko-kata large stick drums.

■ Forms and structure of Noh

Essentially, there are two types of Noh: Genzai Noh, which deals with the realistic, telling a story in the here and now, and Mugen Noh, which moves between the real world, the narrative and a dream world. Zeami's play *Izutsu* is one of the best examples of this. Although often more complicated to follow than Genzai Noh, Mugen Noh does have a formalised structure, which plays out the story in three different ways. The first half of the play, called the maeba, is introduced by the waki. The waki is then joined by the shite, who tells the historic story, usually involving a local reference, through a process of questioning from the waki and narration from the jiutai. The following example is from *Izutsu*.

The story told by the village woman

The village woman (the shite) tells the love story of Ariwara no Narihira and the daughter of Ki no Aritsune, in reply to the request of the monk (the waki).

Monk Would you tell me more about Narihira?
Reciters Once upon a time, Ariwara no Narihira gracefully lived in this old village of Isonokami, admiring the beautiful transitions of seasons with flowers in spring and the moon in autumn.
Woman He eventually married a daughter of Ki no Aritsune and they loved each other deeply. However, Narihiri had another woman in the village of Takayasu in Kawachi. He secretly visited her. Then the wife made a poem, When the wild winds rise, white waves rise in the sea, the pass of Tatsuta mountain (lying between our village and Kawachi).
Reciters I worried about you crossing the dangerous pass at night alone. Narihira understands the sincere heart of his wife and stopped the relationship with another woman.

■ Music

There is no fixed scale in the vocal music (utai). The shite and the jigashira determine the tuning and tempo of this very flexible music. The jigashira also has the job of integrating the various voices of the jiutai, who do not aim to create harmony, but sing, albeit in a higher pitch, with their own voices. Three styles of vocal delivery are used to represent the mood of the musical recitation: tsuyo-gin is strong, deep and forceful with no clear pitch relationship, yowa-gin is a more sentimental, lyrical and melodic tone with noticeable scale relationships between pitches, and kotoba is stylised speech, rather like poetic intonation.

The instrumentalists (hayashi) have a complete independence from the utai and the dance. The purpose of the music is to drive the drama and build the tension, often taking the audience almost to the climax but then deliberately pulling back to further increase the tension. It is highly structured with instrumental sections for entrances, exits and dances, sections where chant and musicians work together, although not necessarily in any pitch relationship, and sections which are just chant. Specific patterns, melodic for the flute and chanters, rhythmic for the drums, are unique to the literary and dramatic structure. The timing of the instrumentation is controlled by meaningless shouts from the drummers that add to the auditory experience of Noh.

The flute (fue or nohkan) is the only melodic instrument in the four-piece ensemble but is hardly ever used melodically. Flutes have three octaves and are built to different lengths with seven holes, but not necessarily in the same place, so each has its own pitch and tonal scale. They are deliberately constructed so that the pitch intervals are different in the overblown octaves than in the fundamental. They also have an internal secondary tube for the high note that traditionally starts and ends the play. The fue-kata role in Noh is to create specific atmosphere, to complement, but not necessarily melodically, the utai, and to attempt to reflect musically the emotion of the shite.

■ Staging, costume and masks

The Noh stage is a formal thrust space with four pillars holding up a shrine-like roof, which reflects the time when these plays were performed outdoors. Whilst the roof is now traditional decoration, the pillars still have a very important function. They serve to orientate the shite, whose mask allows limited vision. Each performer has their specific 'home' place on the stage, with the musicians in the rear beneath a pine tree symbolic of the spiritual presence.

The hashigakari, a gangway bridge, leading on/off stage on stage right is one of the many important elements of the Noh stage. More than just an extended entrance or exit, it has three pine trees along its length, at which the actors may stop and speak/sing as they enter or leave. It is very much the bridge between the world of the audience and performers and the spiritual world of the Noh performance. In Kabuki, another of Japan's leading performance art forms, which came after Noh, the hashigakari becomes the hanamichi, or 'flower path', which also has significant spacing and traditions for the performer.

Staging is sparse with scenery created in skeletal form from bamboo. The 'inner room' in the play *Adachigahara*, for example, is a cupboard-sized frame, with, of course, nothing in it to represent the stinking human remains of previous visitors. Similarly, there are few props. The fan the most important as it is used to represent everything from drinking cups to swords, letters or walking sticks.

The costumes of the shite are elaborate and colourful but thick and bulky with a strong flat line intended to neutralise any natural body shape of the performer. In the same way, the mask, literally, masks the performer's expression. By comparison, the waki is dressed conservatively in a more realistic period costume of, for example, a priest, samurai or monk. The jiutai are dressed alike in kimonos, usually dark, and the hayashi-kata, similarly, have their own kimono uniform to distinguish them.

There are around 60 different types of mask, or omote (literally, 'face'), in Noh performance, grouped in categories such as deities, vengeful demons, elders, man and woman masks. The photograph on page 183 shows a ko-omote mask representing an attractive young woman. The plumpness of the face is an indication of youthful beauty, together with the artificial eyebrows expressing naiveté. The mouth, with its fashionable blackened teeth, can create both sadness and mirth depending on the performer's skill and gesture. Note also the hair at the sides of the mask, here thick and dark. For older characters, the hair on the

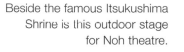

Beside the famous Itsukushima Shrine is this outdoor stage for Noh theatre.

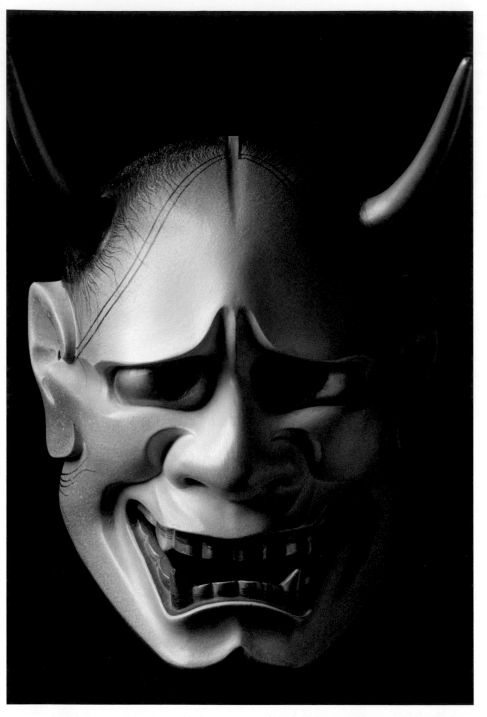

The hannya mask

mask becomes greyer and thinner. It is the shite who decides which mask is most appropriate for the role.

Probably the most famous of the Noh masks, and certainly the most popular in the tourist shops of Japan, the hannya mask is a distorted combination of female grief, jealousy, sadness and revenge. With its devil-like horns, extended wailing mouth, frowning brows and stretched cheekbones it captures precisely the spirit that possesses the post-divorce suit-shredders in contemporary idiom.

■ Movement in Noh

Noh is often referred to as 'the art of walking' because its distinctive shuffling gait, which preserves stillness and equilibrium in all other parts of the body, is a practised art in itself. It is a deliberately minimalist expression of the potential energy the performer keeps unseen within mask and costume. Walking is one of the kata or patterns of stylised movement, of which there are some 250, known by audience and performers alike, much like some of the Elizabethan theatrical tradition.

Every kata has meaning and the performer's duty is to move effortlessly between the patterns, often working with the music to represent the mood of the role. Given that the key performer is usually masked, there are no facial gestures, but the mask is animated. Sharp turns of the head indicate anger whereas a half-lowered head and a slow hand gesture across the body from eye to chest indicate sadness and tears. There is a kata for dancing without movement, like the still flat surface of a moving river, and others based on wielding a sword, riding a horse or weeping. One kata involves stamping, reminiscent of Uzume's dance on the barrel (see page 181). In Noh this is accentuated by large jars placed under the stage that create both amplification and reverberation of the stamping on the cedar-wood stage floor.

In Japanese there are two words for 'dance', stemming from ancient traditions: 'odori' and 'mai'. It is the latter that is predominant in Noh. Kamigata-mai is a dance form drawn directly from the Noh form, and is quieter, more introspective than odori, which involves lively and energetic arms and legs, jumps and leaps. The intensity of mai generates tension in the performance. Movement is reduced to a minimum with every movement symbolic.

The basic stance in Noh is with the body tense and tilted forward. The knees are bent and the arms extended forward, all providing a lengthening in the back, but in a very grounded position. Unlike the stretching-upward aspiration of European ballet, this basic stance reflects Noh's relation with the Earth and, some have argued, its agricultural origins in rice planting. Similarly, Japanese gods traditionally descended to Earth, as opposed to Western deities, who generally remain up in the skies or heavens.

■ Performance conventions

Noh is made up of many conventions intended to achieve the highest level of performance and a spiritual engagement by the audience, but three are of particular interest.

Ichi-go ichi-e is a convention developed from the sense of 'moment' of the tea ceremony. It means 'for once only' or 'never again'. Linked with Zen Buddhism and concepts of transience or impermanence, it is a particularly important idea for performance, as each performance becomes deliberately unique. Thus, the tradition of Noh is that actors, musicians, choral chanter(s) rehearse separately, refining their movements, songs and dances under the direction of a Noh master. The pace of the final performance is a dynamic improvisation not set by any one performer or group, but with all performers working their rehearsed pieces sympathetically together to achieve an aesthetic whole. The immediacy and freshness of the performance is preserved, both for the performers and for the audience.

In martial arts, 'ichi-go, ichi-e' is often shouted by the teacher as a sharp reminder that moves and techniques, even if incorrect, should always be carried through rather than stopped halfway. Similarly, the director of a school/college production may exhort the players to 'keep going!' in rehearsal in order to establish sense and flow.

Hana and yu-gen are both what is intended in the performance, but also the way in which it is created. Hana is the apparent beauty, what Zeami equated to 'flower'. This is a multisensory experience of beauty made up of the movement from bud to open flower and then fading without any of the change being noticed. Like ichi-go ichi-e, the flower is also related to the concept of transience, particularly in the way in which it can be easily damaged and destroyed, especially by human touch that does not respect nature. Similarly, the performers in Noh are attempting to achieve that 'accidental' beauty in nature created by an apparently haphazard arrangement of flowers that evokes an overwhelming emotional response.

Yu-gen, on the other hand, is inner beauty. 'Yu' implies 'quiet, depth, being somewhere else' whilst 'gen' means 'subtle, profound and dark', key concepts in

Zeami's analysis of Noh theatre. Hence, there is little that is sudden in Noh, unless for deliberate effect – for example, the Kyogen interlude may well offer less subtlety of movement in its reflection of the story. Many of the 250 or so extant Noh plays are concerned with sadness, loss, grief, retribution and consequently there has to be some means by which the audience can engage with them. The aesthetic combination provided by the inner and outer sense of beauty – hana and yu-gen – produces the critical tension that communicates with the audience.

➜ More from Japan

Kyogen, the comic parallel to Noh, is more dialogue based. Whilst the stylistic forms and the spiritual intention of Kyogen mirror the formal Noh theatre, the outcome is different and provides a fine complement in its interlude form.

There are also later performance forms from Japan which offer the same richness of tradition, potential and interest for studies in performance contexts. The puppet theatre of bunraku is a fascinating art form for which leading playwrights chose to write. It involves the close imitation of human form, still using the stylised gesture and movement combined with music we have seen in Noh. However, because it was seen as provincial, it is treated as a 'country cousin' to Noh and Kabuki.

Kabuki is another later, and highly popular, form of theatre. It developed in the early seventeenth century partly from Noh, but is a lot livelier. It involves elaborate staging with secret entrances and a fast paced and colourful playing style. Butoh, first performed in Japan in 1959, combines performance art, theatre, musical and dance elements from Noh and Kabuki.

Examination Practice:
Sample Questions

In the written examination, you will need to bring together all of the work you have studied to answer a single question, for which you will have 2 hours. Here are some samples that you may find it useful to work through with your tutors.

Post-modern approaches to the performing arts since 1960
'The only way to go on is to go back.' Discuss this view of post-modern approaches to the creation of performance work.

Politics and performance since 1914
Discuss the view that political performance challenges both individuals and societies to come to terms with their own identity.

The twentieth-century American musical
'The history of the genre is bound up with the creation of the book musical, but not limited by it.' Discuss the most significant aspects of the pre-book musical, and assess how effectively these roots were used in later works.

Approaches to performance in the Far East
'The cultures of the Far East may be very different, but it is possible to identify approaches that unite them.' What might these unifying approaches be?

Ten Tips for the
Written Examination

The following ten tips have been published by examiners to help you prepare for the examination. Read them and use them as a mental checklist for the examination.

1. Have you written the titles of the works you have studied in the table on the front of the paper? Don't irritate the examiner from the outset by expecting them to search for the extracts you have studied in your answer.

2. Do you answer the question? Don't just mention it at the beginning and end, but try to work in references to it throughout the answer.

3. Do you offer a clear overview of the topic, which shows a confident knowledge and understanding of the generic area being discussed?

4. Do you give, where appropriate, traceable influences upon the area under discussion without indulging in unqualified historical background merely for the sake of it?

5. Do you make use, where appropriate, of wider social, cultural and historical context from which the genre arose and in which it was nurtured?

6. Is there evidence that you have studied nine examples from a range of practitioners? For example, if you only ever mention two works in your answer, or all your references are music and drama without any dance, you will be throwing marks away!

7. Do you make points by using examples and cross-referencing across the works you have studied, as opposed to bold glossy statements with no evidence?

8. Can the examiner give extra credit for further reference beyond the nine works that amplifies the point you are making and indicates wider understanding of the context?

9. Do you use appropriate vocabulary, terminology and possibly reference to other practitioners?

10. Is your writing legible, fluent (e.g. linking between paragraphs so one thought leads to the next) with some sense of structure (plan it quickly beforehand so you know where you're going and how much time you can spend), expressing and explaining ideas clearly, with correct spelling, punctuation and grammar?

Unit 4
Performance Project

Everyone loves a good performance, and the reason you have chosen Performance Studies is probably because you enjoy performing. In your AS studies, you will have learned skills and techniques in devising and performing dance, drama and music. You will need to build on these in your work for your A-level performance project.

In this unit, you will need to work on **two** performances: a performance of a piece of repertoire (performance realisation) and a performance of an original piece (student-devised performance). The number of students in each performance is left for your tutors to decide. In the case of the repertoire performance, it could be anything between one and six performers. For the devised piece, a group performance is required and this group will consist of between three and six performers. In both pieces, the length of the performance is related to how many performers there are in it. For the student-devised performance, 5 minutes per student is the rule, with a maximum total of 30 minutes. For the performance realisation, each candidate is allowed 3 minutes, with a maximum of 18 minutes for the piece as a whole.

Performance Realisation

The piece of repertoire chosen can be taken from anything studied in Unit 2 or Unit 3.

During the course of studying for your Performance Studies written examination papers, you will have come across a number of pieces of repertoire. In *Unit 2: Performance Contexts 1*, you will have studied at least two pieces of repertoire, each in a different art form. An extract from one of those might be ideal for you to perform now, especially if there is a particular piece that you enjoyed working on, and that went well when you performed it. On the other hand, those pieces may be a distant memory by now and you might find it more interesting to perform something from one of the nine pieces you are studying for *Unit 3: Performance Contexts 2*. This is also acceptable, and offers a wide choice of potential extracts, although a decision needs to be taken early on as to whether the style of a piece you are studying is something you would be happy to perform.

There are no easy answers, and the best way is probably to work on two or three pieces during the year, and make a final choice by February of the year of the A2 practical examination. Important advice from examiners is not to leave it too late to choose: rehearsal is a vital part of the performance process and certainly not something to be left too close to the date of the examination.

The images in this Unit are stills from an actual A2 exam submission DVD.

→ Performance skills

Irrespective of which art form your performance is in, there are a number of performance skills that you will need to master. Each art form has its own set of unique performance skills, and we will discuss these later. When audiences watch performances, they tend not to analyse the specific details. They are more interested in the generic aspects of performance. For example, was it fluent? Was it well projected? Was the pace contrasting? Examiners too are more concerned with these when they first watch a performance, so we shall concentrate on these initially.

Checklist of essential performance skills
- Fluency, pace, energy
- Use of space
- Use of body, eyes, voice
- Demeanour, posture
- Movement
- Interaction with the group
- Contribution to the group dynamic

■ Fluency

Everyone remembers a performance that breaks down! If there is one aspect of a performance that must take precedence over all others, it is the ability to keep going. There is nothing funny about forgetting a line, getting the wrong note, stumbling over a prop: if these things are intended, they have to be rehearsed. Comedy does not happen simply by things going wrong.

■ Use of space

The space in which the performance is given is vital to how the piece communicates with its audience. Performances that work well often do so because of the relationship between the performer and the performance space. A monologue delivered on a large stage can appear lost; a piece of physical performance delivered in a confined space can look constrained. A cluttered performance space is likely to turn the audience's focus away from the performer. It is important that, when rehearsing a piece, it 'fits' the space in terms of how you want to use the set.

■ Use of body, eyes, voice, demeanour, posture and movement

The human body is absolutely central to live performance. If you intend to record on CD or on radio, it may be less important, but for a performance in

Individual performances come into their own when they contribute to the larger group dynamic.

this unit, the way you look is as important as the way you sound. This means thinking about how you stand (even if you're singing a song), not slouching, focusing on the audience and occupying the space with confidence. It also means projecting your voice to fill the space that you are performing in. One of the biggest criticisms that audiences have of performers is that they cannot hear what is being said, or that the song was not projected. Often these problems are caused by poor breath control, and poor breath control is often related to poor posture.

■ Interaction with the group and contribution to the group dynamic

If you are performing with other members of the group, it is important that the piece looks as if the performance is a strong ensemble. A piece that looks like a competition between prima donnas will either be unintentionally comical, or will simply irritate the audience as each member of the group tries to outdo the others. Unlike a film performance, where there are lead roles and famous names, the purpose of doing this performance is to create a strong sense of ensemble. Everyone is of the same importance in an examination performance: a vital word to remember in performance is 'generosity', wanting everyone in the group to perform to the best of their ability.

→ Selecting repertoire

As the performance realisation consists of only one performance, it is essential that this piece is the very best that you can produce: think of it as a kind of party piece that you will use to showcase your performance abilities. In the AS course you will have studied two pieces of repertoire, and in A2 you will have studied extracts from nine pieces of repertoire. You therefore have a total of eleven pieces from which to choose your final performance extract. Here are some criteria you might use in deciding which one is most suitable.

- Enjoyment of the piece – this must come across during the performance
- Knowledge of the piece to the extent that it becomes second nature to you – if you have to think about it, you do not know the piece well enough to perform it
- Understanding of the nature of the piece – its style, performance conventions
- Commitment to the piece – you need to be able to demonstrate an absolute identification with your role.

→ Performance values

'Performance values' refers to the overall quality of the performance 'event': aspects such as costumes, lighting, make-up, set design. These do not form part of the assessment, but they are essential in enabling you to give of your very best. For example, the songs of George Gershwin are often associated with the glitz and glamour of Broadway. So performing them in jeans, slogan-emblazoned tee-shirt and dirty trainers is likely to undermine the performance, even if you know the song well.

In extracts from plays, a decision needs to be taken early in the rehearsal process as to how the performance is to be handled: full costume or theatre blacks, or perhaps representational costume. Performing in everyday clothes is not likely to bring out the nature of a piece such as Caryl Churchill's *Top Girls*, where the drama centres on the differentiation between the characters. In dance pieces, costume is likely to be less representational but it still needs to be appropriate to the performance. Costumes should fit well, and there should be no possibility of having to fiddle with them during the performance; the same applies to hair – keep it tied back. Performances are not fashion statements, so if you have any piercings, remove them before you start the performance, especially tongue piercings, which are likely to seriously affect your ability to speak or sing. Make-up is not essential to the performance, although it may be a helpful addition to particular roles.

> Lighting and sound are quite likely to be an important feature of your piece and will require a full technical rehearsal before the day of the performance. They will need to be handled by someone with a good grasp of the technical apparatus available in your school or college. It is best if this is a qualified technician, or your tutor. There is too much at stake in an examination performance to rely on other candidates.

Technical tips

- Cut the music expertly – it needs to fit the exact length of the scene or episode. Do not rely on playing CDs and trying to find the correct place to start and stop. Make a master CD with separate tracks, or create a playlist in iTunes.
- Adjust sound levels so that they are appropriate to the energy of the performance. If your performance lacks energy, simply turning up the volume will not improve things.
- Plan the lighting effectively so that each part of the performance is well lit. In simple terms, this means standing in the light, or refocusing the lights for the needs of the performance. Do not rely on the use of blackouts for dramatic effect.
- Gloomy lighting is unlikely to be effective. What can appear atmospheric on television, or in a film, is likely just to appear dim or dismal on stage.
- If you decide to build a set, keep it simple and effective. You will not need full scenery – something representational will be sufficient.

→ Programme notes

Audiences like to be informed about what they are watching, and an examination performance is no different. A simple programme note should be produced, along the following lines.

Summertime
by George Gershwin

Performed by Melanie Williams
Accompanied by Mrs Arbethnal (Piano)

George Gershwin (1898–1937) was one of the greatest songwriters of the early twentieth century. Having worked as a song plugger on Tin Pan Alley at the start of his career, he went on to write numerous hits for Broadway, and later for Hollywood.

Most of his songs were composed in collaboration with his brother Ira, who supplied the lyrics. The majority of these songs were written for shows on Broadway, although Summertime was written with DuBose Heyward as part of the folk opera Porgy and Bess.

In this performance, I shall attempt to capture the emotional nature of the lullaby as the mother sings to her baby. I have transposed the song down a tone to suit my natural singing voice.

→ Getting an audience

Performing to only an examiner and a couple of teachers can be a nerve-wracking experience, and is one that should not be undertaken lightly! A supportive audience with a cross-section of friends, teachers, parents, relatives and the general public is much more appropriate and will be much more likely to give you the confidence you need to perform. If at all possible, avoid performing *only* to other members of your group, but if this is the only way you are able to get an audience, it is essential that they watch quietly and clap politely at the end.

You will almost certainly find that the performance will zoom by and that it is over as quickly as it has begun. There is a minimum length of 3 minutes for a solo piece, and a maximum of 18 minutes for a group of six. You should aim to have 3 minutes' worth of exposure for each student in a group, although if the performance has everyone on stage for the whole time this may overlap. Four students performing three songs, for example, might take only 9 minutes, but would probably give enough exposure for each person.

Student-Devised Performance

As well as performing an existing piece of repertoire, you will be expected to take part in a group performance of an original piece that you have devised in a group consisting of three, four, five or six students (including yourself). Your group will have to choose a commission from a list of ten, and devise a piece lasting between 15 and 30 minutes based on this commission. There will be five different types of commission, with a choice for each type. You will be able to choose only one of these. The types of commission will vary from year to year, but the categories might include

- Performance inspired by an image
- Performance inspired by a historical event
- Performance inspired by poetry
- Performance inspired by a story
- Performance inspired by other performers.

Your group will need to decide which type of commission you will be most likely to work best with. The vital thing is that your piece interprets the commission in an original way, but sticks closely enough to it so that everyone can see the link with the commission.

■ Research

Everyone reacts differently to devising from a commission. It is a disciplined activity and your group needs to be prepared to craft your creativity to fit the commission you have chosen. This means having a detailed knowledge and understanding of the commission type, and being familiar with the various intricacies of it. You need to research it as fully as you can, but there is no point in simply finding out facts. Research is useful only if it enables you to produce effective and original performance work.

→ How should different types of commission be approached?

The challenges of different types of commission vary greatly. In this section we list the most important points you should consider for each of the five examples of commissions given above.

■ Images

Look carefully at the image, taking in as many different aspects as you can. Make notes on what you see, then consider the following questions, in order to prepare you to work through the process of improvising–rehearsing performing.

- What is the structure of the image – what is the eye drawn to most? Is that the centre of the image? What is the context?
- Are there recurring themes in the image? If so, could these be used as a structural device in your piece? What is the balance between things that appear only once and things that are duplicated in the image?
- How are light and shadow, black and white, variety of colours used in the image? Do these give any clues as to how your piece could be structured? For example, darkness could be equated with intensity and light with relaxation.
- What levels are used in the image? Could these be translated into scenes or episodes?
- Is there any physical movement implied in the image that could become a motif to structure your piece?
- Is there an implied story to the image? If not, there is no need to invent one but you might use the context of the image if it has a naturalistic dimension.
- What possibilities are there to work within all three art forms?

Here are some examples of images that you could use for practice.
- **Hieronymous Bosch –** *The Ship of Fools*
- **Pieter Bruegel –** *The Tower of Babel*
- **Salvador Dalí –** *The Persistence of Memory*
- **L. S. Lowry –** *Market Scene, Northern Town*
- **Pablo Picasso –** *Guernica*
- **Paula Rego –** *The Dance*

■ Historical events

Find out as much as you can about the historical event. Make sure that you have an accurate understanding of the history of the time, as your piece will be expected to have historical authenticity. Make notes on what you find out, then consider the following questions, in order to prepare you to work through the process of improvising–rehearsing–performing.

- What period of time is covered by the event?
- Is it possible to cover this effectively in a naturalistic manner or would it be better to avoid simply telling the story to ensure that the art forms are fully integrated?

- Is it possible to take episodes in the order they occurred or is there scope for adapting the historical timeline? For example, you could start at the end, jump to the beginning and work back.

- How many characters are involved in the event? This may have to be adapted to the group size (minimum three, maximum six). Do characters need to be omitted – or introduced? Can multi-role playing cover the event effectively?

- Is there anything controversial about the event? This could be embedded in the structure of your piece as a good structure takes the audience where the performers want them to go. You could create some intrigue or mystery by the way you structure the piece. For example, in the commission *Did They Really Land on the Moon?* it would be possible to convince the audience either that the whole thing was a hoax or that there was no room for doubt, simply by the way in which the episodes were organised.

- What possibilities are there to work within all three art forms?

Here are some examples of historical events that you could use for practice.

- **The signing of Magna Charta**
- **Bloody Sunday**
- **The assassination of John F. Kennedy**
- **The potato famine in Ireland**
- **Abraham Lincoln's campaign against slavery**
- **Lech Walesa and the Polish Trade Union movement in the 1980s**

■ Poetry

Read the poem through several times, sometimes out loud, sometimes silently to yourself. Try reading it dramatically in a group, perhaps making some lines into choral speech, others into dialogue. Listen for the metre of the poem. Make notes on what you hear, then consider the following questions, in order to prepare you to work through the process of improvising–rehearsing–performing.

- How is the poem organised? Are there sections that could be turned into performance episodes?

- Are there repeated lines that could be used as a structural or thematic device in your piece?

- Is there a rhythmic structure to any of the lines that could be used to create some music?

- Could any of the words be set to music? You are not allowed to use large chunks of the poem but it might be effective to take a line and repeat it as a choral motif, or as a short musical motif that could be passed around the ensemble. Or you could use a repeated single line to indicate a change of episode.

- Is the poem telling a story? If so, you need to decide whether your piece will also have narrative elements. You shouldn't just animate the poem, though – be creative in how you handle aspects of story.

- What possibilities are there to work within all three art forms?

Here are some examples of poems that you could use for practice.
- Maya Angelou – *Still I Rise*
- Wendy Cope – *Lonely Hearts*
- William Henry Davies – *Leisure*
- Grace Nichols – *Wherever I Hang*
- William Shakespeare – *My Mistress' Eyes are Nothing Like the Sun*
- Stevie Smith – *Not Waving but Drowning*

■ Stories

Read the story through several times, making a note of the main characters, events, settings and locations. Try reading it through dramatically as a group, looking out particularly for ways in which you might start with dance or music, rather than relying on a simple animation of the story. Consider the following questions, in order to prepare you to work through the process of improvising–rehearsing–performing.

- What is the structure of the story?
- What are the key moments in the story? Can these be turned into transition points in the performance?
- How many episodes do there need to be?
- How much potential is there for dance and music in this story?
- What characters are there? How could these be covered in your piece? Is it possible to use a 'parallel story' approach where a contemporary version is interspersed with the original?
- Is it possible to change the setting of the story to a different period or time? Could this be done through dance or music?
- What possibilities are there to work within all three art forms?

Here are some examples of stories that you could use for practice.
- Arthur and the Court of Camelot
- The Blinding of Oedipus
- Hansel and Gretel (*Grimm's Fairy Tales*)
- The Parable of the Good Samaritan (Luke 10:25–37)
- St George and the Dragon
- The Emperor's New Clothes

■ Performers

Find out as much as you can about the life of the performer. You will need to know the main events, as well as some of the details that may not be commonly known. Try to avoid simply creating a drama of the person's life. Focus instead on the potential for using dance and music as significant components in your piece. Consider the following questions, in order to prepare you to work through the process of improvising–rehearsing–performing.

- What is this person's best-known contribution to the world of performing arts?

● How will you incorporate these skills into your piece?

● What aspects of the person's career or life will you focus on?

● What is the time span of these aspects within the person's life?

● Are there key moments that can be used as separate episodes?

● Will your piece be essentially a documentary about the person's life?

● Is it possible to take an angle that will give your piece some originality – perhaps by juxtaposing scenes from contemporary events?

● What possibilities are there to work within all three art forms?

Here are some examples of people that you could use for practice.

● **Marlene Dietrich**

● **Isadora Duncan**

● **Billie Holiday**

● **Jacqueline du Pré**

● **Paul Robeson**

● **Florenz Ziegfeld**

→ Improvising–rehearsing–performing

This unit is intended to be synoptic. That means that it brings together what you have studied during the different parts of this course, and helps you to show what you have learned not just in this unit, but also across the course as a whole. When you are devising your piece, you must make sure you take account of

● The way of working that you learned in *Unit 1: Creating Performance*, particularly the process of improvising, rehearsing, performing (see pages 21–31)

● Your evaluation of the community piece in *Unit 1: Creating Performance* (see pages 31–32)

● Influences from the practitioners you have studied for *Unit 2: Performance Contexts 1* (see pages 33–97) and *Unit 3: Performance Contexts 2* (see pages 99–166).

Improvising

In the improvising phase of the work, you need to structure your ideas to make a powerful impact on your audience. To be able to create a strong performance image, you will need to negotiate with your group to agree on the performance image or message that you want to convey to the audience. This should be inspired entirely by the commission, and build on your experience of creating the community piece in Unit 1.

Rehearsing

You may find that the process of creating the piece is exciting and absorbing, and that you are tempted to carry on creating more and more ideas as you go on. You must work with your tutors to create a rehearsal schedule, so that there is enough time to rehearse the finished piece several times. You must include a technical rehearsal and a dress rehearsal, and ensure that the risk, health and safety aspects of the performance are fully considered. The rehearsal process may well identify some aspects of the piece that need to be adapted. This is perfectly acceptable, as long as they are adaptations, and not an attempt at a different piece!

Performing

Finally, perform the piece straight through several times before the actual performance for the examination. If possible, try to arrange for an audience to be present for at least one of these performances, in order to ensure that you get some feedback as to whether your intentions have been realised.

→ Case study: *Little Red Riding Hood*

This case study is based on an actual examination piece submitted by four students who were taught at a school in the Midlands. They chose to devise and perform a piece based on the commission *Little Red Riding Hood* – a performance inspired by that story.

■ Initial performance decisions

The group had four members: Vickie, Lorna, Isabel and Jack. They aimed to produce a piece that lasted for about 20 minutes, as the A-level specification required 5 minutes' performance from each of them. They decided that the piece would have four sections, and that each member of the group would take the lead in one section. Having decided this, however, they also ruled out the option of each person having a solo in each section. They had worked well as an ensemble in their AS work and had produced a very effective community piece for their *Creating Performance* unit. So they decided that an ensemble approach, where everyone played a broadly equal part, was best for them. They had the advantage that the group did not have any prima donnas who were concerned only with themselves and their own results! That made it easier to come to performance decisions that were best for the group as a whole.

■ Using the commission

The next decision was how to use the commission. The story of Little Red Riding Hood was well known, but how closely were they expected to stick to it? In any, case, what were the key elements of the story? In other words, what aspects were essential, without which the story would cease to be recognisable? Was the wolf essential? The grandmother? They started to list the elements: Little Red Riding Hood, the grandmother, the wolf, the woods, the grandmother being eaten, the wolf being slain.

They decided to keep all of these elements, although there were some lively debates because some members of the group thought it would work to keep all the same sorts of characters but in a modern setting. So they tried devising modern parallels: the young girl walking in the woods, stalked by a stalker – a wolf-type figure. But it there was something about it that did not quite seem to work. When the tutor saw it, he was complimentary about the work the group had done, but made the point that someone watching might never think of the story of Little Red Riding Hood.

So they went back to the story and re-examined its elements. This meant they were able to get the heart of the story: a young girl sets off through the woods to see her grandmother, the grandmother has been eaten by a wolf, the wolf gets slain, the grandmother pops out of the wolf's belly, all live happily ever after.

■ Not just a drama piece!

This song was the result of the group work in research and writing as well as performance.

The group wanted to use all three art forms, so they started to think about how the story could be told in a way that meant it was not just a piece of drama.

They were influenced by the techniques of musical theatre and did some research into the musicals of Stephen Sondheim. They had studied the twentieth-century American musical as their topic for *Performance Contexts 2*, and they were familiar with some of Sondheim's techniques for integrating music and drama. In particular they looked at *Into the Woods*, since this was also based on the story of Little Red Riding Hood. Having listened carefully to the songs in *Into the Woods*, the group set about creating a song that used techniques similar to those of Sondheim. These included: creating a melody that perfectly reflects the rhythm of the words, composing a song that moves the action along whilst still commenting on what is taking place, using harmonic and melodic structures that have interesting shapes. They also tried to create a patter song in the style of Sondheim – a useful tool for cramming a lot of words into a song. All four members of the group worked on the music as an ensemble, each taking an individual responsibility for melody, lyrics, harmonies and instrumental timbres.

The group had produced a considerable amount of dance throughout their course and were very keen to ensure that all four of them were able to show their dance skills in the performance. They decided to do this in two ways. First, they decided to use three established dance forms – tango, waltz and ballet – and to create a short dance in each of these styles. They also decided that they would try to incorporate some more general movement content inspired by two practitioners they had studied: Lea Anderson, with her heavy emphasis on everyday gestures; Christopher Bruce, because of the influence of ballet on his style. The dances were used within scenes to interpret the action, and comment on it, often in a comic manner.

■ Creating a structure

The group wanted to surprise their audience with their interpretation of the story of Little Red Riding Hood, and worked on creating a structure that would help them communicate this interpretation to the audience. As there were four students in the group, they decided that the piece would have four sections, each consisting of a different version of the tale, and that each person would change role in each tale.

The four roles were

● the narrator
● the young girl
● the grandmother
● the wolf.

Most important, it was decided that the reason why the version of the story would be slightly different in each section would be because the Little Red Riding Hood character had a different personality. The purpose of the piece was to explore how these personalities affected the story. The group felt that the fairy tale had deep undertones and a strong moral message. In each of the four sections, Grandma has contacted Little Red/Pink/Yellow/Blue Riding Hood with a different reason for coming to see her. In spite of this, the group wanted a message of unity to come across as the four Riding Hoods are re-united to help Grandma at the end of the piece.

The four Riding Hoods

The scenario is that four grandchildren have fallen out with each other. Grandma has different reasons for getting each of them to come to her house to try to reunite them. As a result of each of them saving her from the wolf, this brings them together. In each scene, there is a different Riding Hood.

Tale 1: Vicky plays Little Red Riding Hood. She speaks in rhyme to show that she is a fairy-tale character.

Tale 2: Jack plays Little Pink Riding Hood. There is a play on colours here, as Jack seeks to assert his masculinity through the role.

Tale 3: Lorna plays Little Yellow Riding Hood. She is absent minded and forgetful and the role maximises this to comic effect.

Tale 4: Isabel plays Little Blue Riding Hood. She is an angry teenager.

There is a prologue at the start of the piece, and an epilogue at the end. The transitions between the four stories are very obvious, reinforced by the changing of costumes on stage.

→ Evaluating the piece

It is impossible not to have a viewpoint about a performance, but this can vary considerably between different members of the audience. That is why examination boards devise marking criteria that ensure all examiners will take the same view of your performance. There are three things that examiners are looking for:

● How the piece interprets the commission
● The role that each person has created for himself or herself
● The level of each person's performance skills.

Let's consider how *Little Red Riding Hood* would fare on these criteria.

■ Commission

The group stuck to the commission well. Their interpretation has some originality but this does not get in the way of the audience understanding what the commission was. However, in the final performance, the piece lasted for 25 minutes and this was a little longer than the group intended. When they watched the DVD recording afterwards, they could see that there were some aspects of the story that were a little laboured. For example, there was some overlap between scenes in the dialogue, but instead of providing a link between the four stories, it had the effect of slowing down the action and making the piece look less original. The group could have made the piece 5 minutes shorter if they had reduced the overlap between dialogue. There was a good attempt at originality, although the structure became rather tedious (and formulaic) by the time the audience had seen it four times. The group clearly thought that this was a clever piece of comedy whereas in reality it was merely amusing.

■ Roles

This was a strong ensemble piece, which means that everyone was fully involved in all aspects of creating it, and that in performance, everyone was on stage all the time with an equal amount to do. The decision to have each performer play each of the four roles across the four scenes ensured that all students received a similar mark. However, in a weaker piece, this might have meant that they all received the same low mark. The decision to compose the music as an ensemble reinforced this, as did the dance work across the piece. The roles were fairly well crafted, although with the tale being a children's story, the group had tended to create characters that were one-dimensional. This meant that the music was often more complex than the drama or the dance of the piece.

■ Performance skills

Each of the four performers in the piece was fluent, but the pacing was not always as varied as the group intended. Their teacher thought that the piece would have been 5 minutes shorter if the pacing had been quicker. Nevertheless, the piece was fluent, and everyone remembered their part. The singing was tuneful and well delivered; the dance work was well crafted; the drama was competent and showed that each student had mastered their part well. Everyone performed in all three art forms and this meant that the piece was a genuine example of an integrated performing arts piece.

Glossary

Action	A physical movement and/or an intention, e.g. a kick.
Afro-fusion	A hybrid of African rhythms and Western contemporary music.
Allegory/Allegorical	Use of an apparent meaning to symbolise deeper moral and/or spiritual understanding.
Allusion	A figure of speech such as a passing reference to a well known person, place, event, work of art or piece of literature.
Ambient music	Music that places more significance on the sound than the notes, which can conjure up an atmosphere, e.g. Brian Eno's music.
American Dream	A metaphor for the freedom of Americans to attain any goal set. Often used to depict Broadway hopes and ambitions.
Aria	An Italian term, usually referring to opera, for a self-contained piece for a solo singer with accompaniment.
Arpeggio	A musical device that involves breaking up a chord into I-III-V-I (do-mi-so-do).
Atmospheric reverb	Delayed sound, often feedback from samples or hooks, often found in progressive rock music such as Pink Floyd's.
Atonal	Term for a piece of music in which there is no defined key.
Audience address	A technique where the audience is directly addressed by the performers on stage.
Ballet	A classical style of dance that involves an upright torso, long, extended lines and graceful movements. There are five principal positions for the legs and arms.
Beijing opera	Traditional Chinese theatre involving music, vocals, mime, dance and acrobatics.
Bharata natyam	South Indian dance that is often sacred and involves dramatic and/or mime techniques.
Black comedy	Comedy that satirises serious topics such as death or violence, e.g. *The League of Gentlemen*.
Blue notes	The notes from the major scale that are often lowered by a semitone in order to enhance the expressive features of a piece of music.
Blues	A style of music that surfaced in America amongst African-Americans. It uses blue notes and comes from Negro spirituals and work songs of the time. It has been said to influence jazz, R 'n' B, hip hop and rock and roll.
Body language	Physical and bodily form of communication.
Book musical	A form of musical theatre that places particular emphasis on the plot and characters.
Bourgeoisie	The middle classes, often capitalists, manufacturers, bankers and other employers, who are regarded as exploiting the working classes.

Brechtian	Term for techniques inspired by the playwright Bertolt Brecht.
Burlesque	Bawdy comedy show of late nineteenth and early twentieth centuries, often satirical in flavour. The striptease became one of its more characteristic elements.
Cabaret	A form of light entertainment (usually singing and/or dancing) that takes place in a nightclub or restaurant.
Cadence	A musical 'full stop' at the end of a phrase.
Canon	A technique involving a line or phrase being imitated by one or more other parts in turn.
Centre stage	The space in the centre of the stage.
Chamber music	Music performed by a small group of instrumentalists, or chamber ensemble.
Chance method	A technique developed by Merce Cunningham that involves choosing movements or developing ideas by chance, e.g. throwing a dice.
Choral speaking	A technique when all the performers speak in unison.
Choreography	The composition of dance steps. A choreographer is the person who creates the movement content for a work.
Chromatic	Neighbouring notes a semitone apart. Flattening/sharpening notes to create pitches not in the key of the music.
Collaboration	When two or more artists work together on a joint project.
Commedia dell'arte	A style of theatre originating from Italy that involves slapstick humour, improvisation round a basic plot and stock characters.
Commission	A task committed (given) to a group or individual to perform.
Community play	Theatre that is aimed at the community in which it is based and often depicts experiences and interests of the people within that community.
Consonant	Term for a harmonic chord that is pleasing to the ear.
Contact improvisation	A form of dance whereby the movements are governed by the momentum, friction and gravity of dancing with others.
Contemporary dance	A form of dance that is free from the restrictions of ballet.
Counterpoint	A musical technique where different forms of a melody or tune can be combined with freedom but which maintains the harmonic progression.
Cross rhythm	Opposing rhythmic patterns that are performed within the same metre.
Cunningham	See Graham and Cunningham.
Dialogue	In drama this is a conversation between two or more people on stage.
Dissonant	Term for a harmonic chord that is displeasing to the ear, e.g. the interval of a second.
Divertissement	In ballet this refers to a variety of dances with no particular plot. In music it means an arrangement of familiar tunes.
Double time	In dance or music this refers to moving or playing at a speed twice as fast as the original speed.
Downstage	The part of the stage closest to the audience.
Dynamic	In music this refers to how loud or soft a piece of music is. In dance it refers to the sharpness or fluidity of the movement.
Dystopian	Term for an imaginary place where things are often as bad as they can be.
Eclectic	Using a mixture of a variety of styles, ideas, methods, etc.
Elevation	A movement that is raised from the floor or in a raised area.
Ensemble	A group of two or more performers.

Episodic	Term for a play, dance or piece of music consisting of short extracts, self-contained sections or episodes.
Expressionism	A genre in which artists express their emotions through their art. It is often characterised by use of symbolism, exaggeration and distortion.
Fanfare	A ceremonial short tune, often for trumpets.
Femme fatale	French term for a woman whose seductive prowess often leads men to fall in love with her to their own distress.
Film noir	1940s term, literally meaning 'black film', that usually refers to a film where a happy ending is not provided.
Fingerprint	Term for an overview of someone's style.
Flashback	In drama/dance this means a transition to an earlier scene and/or event.
Floor work	Movement involving contact with the floor and low levels.
Folk	Term for something established within a community that is traditional to the common people of the country.
Fragmentation	Breaking down into the elements that make up the whole.
Freeze image	A still image, tableau or position.
Funk	A fusion of jazz, soul and R 'n' B that originated in the USA in the late 1960s.
Fusion	A hybrid of different styles that are blended together. *See also* Afro-fusion.
Gamelan	Indonesian musical ensemble where the instruments are tuned together and work together as one. Instruments often include metallophones, xylophones, drums, gongs, bamboo flutes, bowed and plucked strings, sometimes with vocalists.
Genre	A style or category.
Gesture	Non-verbal communication technique using one part of the body.
Glissando	A musical technique (plural: glissandi) used to produce an uninterrupted scale, often by playing a note and sliding up or down the instrument.
Gospel	Term for music that gives praise, worship and/or thanks to God. It expresses a communal or personal belief in Christian life.
Graham and Cunningham	Two contemporary dance practitioners who pioneered movements in dance history, e.g. contraction and release (Graham) and independence of movement from other aspects (Cunningham).
Harmony/Harmonic	The effect when two or more notes are played at the same time – a simultaneous combination of sounds.
High/Low art	Terms meaning sophisticated and less sophisticated. The works of the composer Mozart are often considered high art with those of the Spice Girls being low art.
Hitch kick	A movement in dance involving leaping from one leg to another and kicking at the same time.
Hyperreality	Inability to distinguish reality from fantasy. This term is often used in a post-modernist context when trying to distinguish what is real in a media-induced society.
Impresario	Someone who organises and/or funds concerts, tours and other events.
Intertextuality/Intertextual reference	Use of references to things outside the art form or artefact itself.
Jazz	Syncopated and polyphonic music that is often improvised. Developed in the USA at the beginning of the twentieth century.

GLOSSARY

Kathak	A style of dance popular in North India with a strong narrative aspect.
Labanotation	A system for writing down dance steps. Dance notation.
Legato	A musical term meaning 'smooth'.
Loop	A repeated sample or motif in an electronic musical composition.
Melodrama	A drama piece that uses music to enhance stereotypical characterisation.
Melody/Melodic	A succession of sounds that form a tune.
Metaphor	Description of a subject as something to which it is seemingly unrelated.
Metre	Rhythm of poetry or speech represented by a regular beat.
Metronome	A device used to keep the tempo or speed of the music.
Miles gloriosis	Latin term used for a boastful soldier, a stock character often found in comedic drama.
Mind map	A device to help discussion of ideas.
Minimalism	A movement after the Second World War defined by stripping down to the fundamental basics, often avoiding embellishment, e.g. the music of Minimalist composer Philip Glass.
Minstrel show	A form of entertainment in the USA that parodied black men by white men painting their faces, e.g. Al Jolson.
Mirroring	Copying someone's movements as if looking in a mirror.
Modulation	A movement from one key to another in music.
Monologue	A speech for one person.
Montage	A collage that combines or puts together different aspects of a piece to form a whole.
Motif	A recurring element within a dance or music piece. A characteristic feature that forms the basis and is then developed.
Multimedia	A style of theatre involving more that one media form.
Multi-role	Technique when one performer takes on more that one role.
Multi-track recording	Using a device that enables recording of several tracks at the same time.
Music hall	A form of entertainment similar to vaudeville but British. It involves comedy, speciality acts and rousing songs.
Musical comedy	A form of musical theatre with a simplified plot and comedy aspects.
Musical theatre	A form of theatre involving song, dance and the spoken word. *See also* Book musical.
Mystery play	This medieval form of theatre was popular in the fifteenth century and focuses on enacting Bible stories with song.
Naturalistic	Term for a style that focuses on the environmental, scientific or philosophical.
Nonlinear time/structure	A technique used in theatre where a narrative is told out of chronological order.
Operetta	Popular in Europe, this is a play with extensive musical content. It is often light hearted. Gilbert and Sullivan are a famous partnership who wrote for this genre.
Orchestration	The scoring of a composition for a full orchestra.
Ostinato	A repeated rhythmic/melodic phrase. Plural: ostinati.
Pacing	The pace of a piece of theatre.
Pageant	A ceremonial procession that can follow a particular festival.
Pantomime	Originating from *commedia dell'arte*, pantomime has similar aspects and is often performed around Christmas or the New Year. It involves slapstick humour as well as songs and familiar stock narratives/characters.

Parody	A work of art or literature that mocks, makes fun of or comments on an original work, subject or author in a satirical manner. Also used as a verb: to parody.
Pas de deux	A duet for two dancers.
Passive unity	A unity that is formed by outside sources.
Pastiche	A work of art or literature that imitates or satirises another's style.
Patter song	A song, often comic in flavour, that relies on many syllables being delivered to quick music.
Pedestrian movement	Term used to describe an everyday movement such as brushing your teeth.
Peking opera	Another (older) name for Beijing opera.
Pentatonic	Term for a five-note scale, popular in China. The black notes on a piano form a pentatonic scale.
Percussion	Musical instruments that can be hit or shaken.
Percussive moment	A moment in a musical piece that places particular emphasis on the percussion section of the orchestra or band.
Persona	This refers to a 'mask'. It is usually a not literal mask but a social mask that a person 'puts on' in order to hide their real character or self.
Phrase	Term for a musical 'sentence'. Phrasing shows the length of the musical sentences and usually indicates where to take a breath in singing.
Physical theatre	A form of theatre involving intense physical movement, e.g. the work of the dance company DV8.
Physicality	Using the physical form to demonstrate movement.
Pirouette	A 360 degree turn usually associated with ballet.
Plainsong	Medieval church music. Sung in unison without harmony or defined rhythms.
Plié	Term used in ballet meaning to bend the knees.
Political performance	A performance that places significant focus on a political theme. For example, *Billy Elliott* has a focus on the miners' strikes of the 1980s.
Polyphony	Term meaning 'highly textured' used for music combining two or more parts each with an individual melody.
Post-modern	Mixing old styles with new in a value-free manner.
Practitioner	A person who writes about or devises pieces in a particular art form, e.g. Brecht.
Propaganda	Messages that aim to influence the opinions, beliefs and behaviour of others.
Proscenium (arch)	Term for a traditional type of stage with entrances and exits at the sides in the form of wings.
Proxemics	Term used to describe space and character relationships on stage.
Pulse	In music this refers to the beat. It should remain regular, like a heartbeat.
Punk	A genre popular in the 1960s and 1970s with bands like the Sex Pistols and the Clash. Often anti-establishment, anti-authoritarian and highly political in flavour.
R 'n' B	Rhythm and Blues music. *See also* Blues.
Ragtime	Syncopated dance music of African-American origin. Scott Joplin was a famous ragtime composer.
Register	A range of pitches that a singer can reach.
Relationships	This refers to the relationships between actors/dancers/ musicians on the stage and their relationships with the audience.

Repertoire	A selection of pieces that can be performed by an actor, singer, dancer or company.
Revue	A showcase of excerpts from a play, dance, song and/or theatre piece.
Rhetorical	Term for questions asked by someone who already knows the answer.
Rhythm	A pattern of notes that make up the skeleton of a piece of music.
Riff	In music this refers to an ostinato figure, usually a short repeated melody, chord progression, pattern or refrain.
Rock and roll	A style of dance/music popular in the late 1940s and 1950s. Instruments included bass, drums and electric guitars (rhythm and lead).
Romantic	Term for a period in music from about 1810 to 1900. Composers such as Tchaikovsky and Rachmaninov dominated this era.
Rubato	Italian word meaning 'robbed'. Used as a term for distorting, varying or not keeping strictly to the beat for expressive effect.
Satire	Vice, folly, abuse or evil being held up to scorn, e.g. *Have I Got News for You*.
Scale	A sequence of pitches that establish the key to a piece of music. A scale is determined by its starting note or tonic and may be major or minor in tonality.
Scenario	Description of events and/or series of actions used in theatre.
Score	The presentation of a dance or music composition.
Sequence	Term for a melody that transposes to a different key sequentially.
Serialism	A later form of the 12-tone theory (post 1950) that takes a set of 12 notes and manipulates that set for compositional effect.
Social dance	A form of dance where the primary focus is on the social aspect, e.g. ballroom dancing.
Soliloquy	A monologue (solo speech) that often depicts the state of mind and/or inner thoughts of that character.
Song plugger	Someone who 'sells' a song to a customer by allowing them to try out its key and melody.
Soul	Music that fuses R 'n' B with Gospel and is characterised by funk influences. Sometimes referred to as the Philadelphia sound, or philly soul, and said to influence contemporary jazz.
Soundscape	A sound or combination of sounds that comes from the natural environment, e.g. wind blowing.
Space	The area in which an actor, singer or dancer performs.
Stasis	In political theatre this is a set of symptoms that indicate calm and stability.
Stereotype	A typical example of a character type, e.g. Vicky Pollard from *Little Britain* might be described as a stereotypical teenage mother.
Stock phrase	Typical and frequent saying of a person or group.
Stock type	*See* Stereotype.
Stream of consciousness	A term that often refers to someone's thought processes.
Street theatre	An outdoor theatrical performance without a specific paying audience, e.g. buskers.
Strophic	In music, when each verse is set to the same music.
Subtext	A level of meaning which lies beneath and may be different from the meaning in the words that characters explicitly use.

Swing	A form of jazz music involving a distinctive swing rhythm that developed in 1930s America.
Syncopated	A musical term meaning 'off beat'. The emphasis is on a beat that would normally be unaccented.
Systems music	A type of Minimalist music that uses experimental sound.
Tango	A South American style of dance in slow 2/4 metre that is quite passionate in flavour and dynamically strong.
Tempo	The speed of the piece of music. Plural: tempi.
Tension	A heightened moment in theatre performance.
Ternary form	In music this refers to a composition where the first and third sections are similar, giving it an ABA structure.
Texture	The layers to a piece of music, dance or drama. The density of composition.
Theatricality	Suitability for dramatic performance.
Thrust space	A stage with an audience on three sides (like a catwalk).
Timbre	The tone quality or colour of the sound, e.g. dull or shrill.
Time signature	In music, a pair of numbers that indicate how many beats there are in a bar. This is given at the beginning of a piece.
Tin Pan Alley	The nickname given to a district in New York because of the 'tinny' sound of all the pianos in the music publishing establishments there.
Tonal	Term for a piece of music with a defined key. See also Scale.
Tonal centre	The central key of a piece of music.
Tonic sol-fa	The scale in singing (do-re-mi-fa-so-la-ti-do). A method for teaching music which aids the learning of intervals between notes.
Total theatre	Theatre that suggests a complete and compelling live performance experience.
Totalitarianism	A one-party state where every aspect of a civilian's public and private life is regulated.
Transition	A passage connecting two scenes/sections of dance or music.
Tremolo	A musical technique that using very quick 'trembling' movements. Rapidly pulsating on one note.
Triad	Three notes making a chord (usually I-III-V). There are four types – major, minor, diminished and augmented.
Tutti	An instruction in music meaning 'all together'.
Unison	All performers doing the same thing at the same time. In music this means that there is no harmony.
Unity of place/time/action	A performance that is set in one single place, about one single action or takes place in a single time, e.g. Bouncers. See also Passive unity.
Upstage	The space on stage that is furthest away from the audience.
Variety	Term for a show using different acts to entertain the audience. This could include magicians, musicians, acrobats, comedians, etc.
Vaudeville	Light musical stage entertainment popular in America at the beginning of the twentieth century.
Verfremdungseffekt	Coined by playwright Bertolt Brecht, this is a German term that means distancing yourself from the audience.
Waltz	A style of ballroom/folk music and dance that has three beats in a bar.
Wayang	Indonesian/Malaysian word meaning theatre or shadow puppetry.
Wayang topeng	Traditional Javanese type of theatre with masks involving dance and drama.
World Music	Term that generally refers to music originating from places other than Europe or North America.

Acknowledgements

The Publishers would like to thank the following for permission to reproduce copyright material:

Photography
p. 14: OCR/Impington Village College; pp. 29 & 31: OCR/Brockenhurst College; p. 34 (top): Hugo Glendinning; pp. 34 (bottom), 38, 39 & 41: New Adventures/Bill Cooper; pp. 42 & 44: Shobana Jeyasingh Dance Company; p. 43: Corbis; p. 47: DV8 Physical Theatre/Eleni Leoussi; p. 49: DV8 Physical Theatre/Peter Jay; p. 52: DV8 Physical Theatre; p. 53: DV8 Physical Theatre/Matt Nettheim; p. 54: Getty Images/Gemma Levine/ Hulton Archive; p. 60: Donald Cooper/Photostage; p. 61: Corbis/Hulton; p. 62: Donald Cooper/ Photostage; pp. 67 & 73: Adrian Gatie; p. 74: Getty Images/Carlo Allegri; p. 76: Getty Images/AFP; p. 82: Corbis/Bettmann; p. 83: Getty Images/Michael Ochs Archives; p. 90: Corbis/Bettmann; p. 91: Alamy/ Pictorial Press Ltd.; p. 100: Imagno/Hulton Archive/Getty Images; p. 102: Simon Annand; p. 103: Wonge Bergmann for Ensemble Modern; p. 105 (top): Topfoto/Chris Davies/ArenaPAL; p. 105 (bottom): Donald Cooper/Photostage; p. 107: Getty Images/Jamie McCarthy/WireImage; p. 109: Rex Features/David McHugh; p. 111: Rex Features; p. 113: Roger Morton Photography/Steven Berkoff & East productions; p. 114 (top): Andrew Fox; p. 114 (bottom): Pau Ros; p. 116: Rex Features/Paul Cooper; p. 118: Rex Features; p. 120: Frantic Assembly/ Manuel Harlan; p. 123: Motionhouse Dance Company/Chris Nash; p. 124: Rex Features/Everett Collection; p. 126: Popperfoto/Getty Images; p. 127: Corbis/Bettmann; p. 128: BBC; p. 131: Rex Features/Alastair Muir; p. 135: Getty Images/Michael Ochs Archives; p. 137: Rex Features/Peter Carrette; p. 138: Rex Features/AGF s.r.l.; p. 140: Rex Features/John Rahim; p. 142: Courtesy Houston Ballet; p. 146: ACE Dance & Music/Brian Slater; p. 150: Corbis/Underwood & Underwood; p. 152: Topfoto/Ben Chrostopher/ArenaPAL; p. 154: Rex Features/Sipa Press; p. 156: Corbis/Bettmann; p. 158: Topfoto/Ben Chrostopher/ArenaPAL; p. 161: Rex Features/20th Century Fox/Everett; p. 163: Rex Features/Everett Collection; pp. 169 & 171: Getty Images/China Photos; p. 173: Getty Images/Paul Chesley; p. 175: Corbis/Luca Tettoni; p. 177: British Museum, London, UK/The Bridgeman Art Library; p. 179: Getty Images/Sylvain Grandadam; p. 182: Getty Images/Gallo Images; p. 183: Getty Images/ Manan Vatsyayana/AFP; p. 187: Alamy/Malcolm Fairman; p. 188: Getty Images/Japan Images; pp. 195 & 204–207: UCLES/St Benedict Roman Catholic School, Derby

Other material
Shaker Loops: music by John Adams © 1982 Associated Music Publishers Inc. (BMI), all rights reserved, international copyright secured; *A Short Ride in a Fast Machine*: music by John Adams © 1986 Hendon Music Inc., reproduced by permission of Boosey & Hawkes Music Publishers Ltd.; *She's Leaving Home*: words & music by John Lennon & Paul McCartney © 1967 Sony/ATV Music Publishing (UK) Ltd, used by permission of Music Sales Ltd, all rights reserved, international copyright secured; *When I'm Sixty Four*, words & music by John Lennon & Paul McCartney © 1967 Sony/ATV Music Publishing (UK) Ltd, used by permission of Music Sales Ltd, all rights reserved, international copyright secured; *Piano Phase*: music by Steve Reich © 1980 Universal Edition (London) Ltd., all rights reserved; *Symphony No 7 in C, Op. 60*: Dmitri Shostakovich © Boosey & Hawkes Music Publishers Ltd., reproduced by permission of Boosey & Hawkes Music Publishers Ltd.; *Hurricane*: lyrics by Bob Dylan/Jacques Levy © Ram's Horn Music/Jackelope Publishing Co. Inc., administered by Sony/ATV Music Publishing, all rights reserved; *The Times They Are A Changin'* & *Like a Rolling Stone*: lyrics by Bob Dylan © Special Rider Music, administered by Sony/ATV Music Publishing, all rights reserved; *Why Can't the English*: words by Alan Jay Lerner & music by Frederick Lowe © 1956 Chappell & Co. Inc., all rights administered by Warner/Chappell Music Ltd., London W6 8BS

Every effort has been made to trace all copyright holders, but if any have been inadvertently overlooked the Publishers will be pleased to make the necessary arrangements at the first opportunity.